OXFORD CLASSICAL MONOGRAPHS

*Published under the supervision of a Committee of the
Faculty of Literae Humaniores in the University of Oxford*

The aim of the Oxford Classical Monographs series (which replaces the Oxford Classical and Philosophical Monographs) is to publish books based on the best theses on Greek and Latin literature, ancient history, and ancient philosophy examined by the Faculty Board of Literae Humaniores

Cicero, Rhetoric, and Empire

C. E. W. STEEL

OXFORD
UNIVERSITY PRESS

OXFORD
UNIVERSITY PRESS

Great Clarendon Street, Oxford, OX2 6DP
Oxford University Press is a department of the University of Oxford.
It furthers the University's objective of excellence in research, scholarship,
and education by publishing worldwide in
Oxford New York
Athens Auckland Bangkok Bogotá Buenos Aires Cape Town
Chennai Dar es Salaam Delhi Florence Hong Kong Istanbul Karachi
Kolkata Kuala Lumpur Madrid Melbourne Mexico City Mumbai Nairobi
Paris São Paulo Shanghai Singapore Taipei Tokyo Toronto Warsaw
and associated companies in Berlin Ibadan

Oxford is a registered trade mark of Oxford University Press
in the UK and certain other countries

Published in the United States
by Oxford University Press Inc., New York

British Library Cataloguing in Publication Data
Data available

Library of Congress Cataloging in Publication Data
Data applied for

ISBN 0-19-924847-8

1 3 5 7 9 10 8 6 4 2

Typeset in Imprint
by Regent Typesetting, London
Printed in Great Britain
on acid-free paper by
T. J. International Ltd.,
Padstow, Cornwall

To
Ailsa Bertram
Rachel Moriarty
Louise Pavey

ACKNOWLEDGEMENTS

THIS book began life as a D.Phil. thesis, written between 1995 and 1998 at Corpus Christi College Oxford, and funded by a three-year studentship from the Humanities Research Board of the British Academy: my thanks to both institutions. Michael Winterbottom was a tactful and generous supervisor; my gratitude also to Andrew Lintott, who supervised my work for a term, and to Chris Pelling and Robin Osborne, who read and commented on almost all of it at various stages. My examiners, Doreen Innes and John Richardson, offered much useful guidance and advice; the latter has also played a key part in the process of turning the thesis into a book, and, insofar as it is an improvement on what went before, this is very much due to his meticulous criticism. For advice on specific points I'm grateful to Anton Bitel, Katherine Clarke, Lynn Fotheringham, Miriam Griffin, Edith Hall, Stephen Harrison, Kathrin Lüddecke, Gideon Nisbet, Robin Nisbet, Ian Ruffell, Greg Woolf, and Katherine Woolfitt.

I have undertaken the process of rewriting since taking up a post at the University of Glasgow, and I must thank my colleagues in the Department of Classics here for their genial welcome and support. Finally, the dedication records my debt to three superb classics teachers whom I was lucky enough to encounter while a pupil at South Hampstead High School.

CONTENTS

ABBREVIATIONS

Abbreviations of journal titles follow *L'Année Philologique*. Other abbreviations used are:

BEFAR   *Bibliothèque des écoles françaises d'Athènes et de Rome*

CAH   *Cambridge Ancient History* (Cambridge: Cambridge University Press, 1924–)

ILLRP   *Inscriptiones Latinae Liberae Rei Publicae* (Florence: La Nuova Italia, 1957–63)

ILS   *Inscriptiones Latinae Selectae* (Berlin: Weidmann, 1892–1906)

LIMC   *Lexicon iconographicum mythologiae classicae* (Zurich: Artemis, 1981–97)

MRR   T. S. R. Broughton, *The Magistrates of the Roman Republic* (New York: American Philological Association, 1951–86; 3 vols.)

OLD   *Oxford Latin Dictionary* (Oxford: Oxford University Press, 1968–92)

ORF   *Oratorum Romanorum fragmenta liberae rei publicae*, 3rd edn. (Turin: G. B. Paravia, 1967–79)

SIG   *Sylloge Inscriptionum Graecarum*, 3rd edn. (Leipzig: S. Hirzel, 1915–24)

SVF   *Stoicorum veterum fragmenta* (Leipzig: Teubner, 1903–24)

TLL   *Thesaurus Linguae Latinae* (Leipzig/Stuttgart/Munich: Teubner/K. G. Saur, 1900–)

Quotations of Cicero are taken from the Oxford Classical Text and are cited by small paragraph number.

Introduction

At the time I thought that people in Rome did nothing except talk about my quaestorship. I had dispatched a large quantity of corn at a time of great shortages; I'd been friendly to the businessmen, fair to the traders, generous to the tax-farmers, not predatory in relation to our allies, and had appeared to everyone extremely careful in fulfilling all obligations; various novel honours had been devised for me by the Sicilians. And so I'd left the province in the hope that the Roman people would, unasked, give me everything I desired. But, on coming to Puteoli, in order to continue my journey to land, which as it happened I did just when it was full of fashionable people, I almost collapsed, gentlemen of the jury, when someone asked me what day I'd left Rome and what the news there was. I told him I'd come from my province: he said, 'Of course, yes, Africa I believe.' And I, now getting angry, said disdainfully, 'No, Sicily', someone else, acting as though well informed, added, 'Didn't you know that our friend here was quaestor at Syracuse?' Well, what more can I say? I stopped being angry and pretended I was there to take the waters. But I rather think, gentlemen of the jury, that the episode did me much more good than if everyone had congratulated me. After I'd realized that the Roman people were a bit deaf, but had very sharp and keen eyesight, I stopped worrying about what men would hear concerning me and made sure that they would see me every day: I lived in the public eye, I frequented the Forum, I didn't allow either sleep or my doorkeeper to keep anyone from my presence . . . and so whatever reputation I might have has been won in Rome and acquired in the Forum, and public events too have justified my private plans, with the result that the vital interests of the state needed me as their agent in Rome, and the city needed me to save it by action in the city.[1]

[1] *pro Plancio* 64–6: sic tum enim existimabam, nihil homines aliud Romae nisi de quaestura mea loqui. frumenti in summa caritate maximum numerum miseram; negotiatoribus comis, mercatoribus iustus, mancipibus liberalis, sociis abstinens, omnibus eram uisus in omni officio diligentis-simus; excogitati quidam erant a Siculis honores in me inauditi. itaque hac spe decedebam ut mihi populum Romanum ultro omnia delaturum putarem. at ego cum casu diebus eis itineris faciendi causa decedens e

CICERO uses this self-deprecating anecdote about his quaestorship at Lilybaeum to illustrate his argument that his client Plancius could and did defeat his more impressive rival Laterensis in the contest for the aedileship without resorting to bribery: Laterensis may have done splendid things in Cyrene, but it is actions at Rome that really count with the electorate. But the story is also a suggestive approach to the connections between Cicero and Rome's empire. The patent falsehood of Cicero's analysis is striking: the Roman people might have no interest in the actions abroad of a quaestor, but they were certainly impressed by overseas conquests, and Cicero's problem at Puteoli was not the location of his public activity but his lack of seniority. Even more significant is his justification of his own, urban, career. Cicero was highly unusual among Roman politicians in choosing not to spend time outside Italy: he chose not to take provincial commands after his praetorship and consulship, and apart from the time in Sicily and his earlier trip to Rhodes his absences were forced upon him: exile, the province of Cilicia, and the vain pursuit of Pompeius during the civil war. And this geographical concentration on the city of Rome is closely entwined with his activity as an orator: oratory is an urban phenomenon, and for Cicero Rome was the only urban context that counted. His surviving speeches were all delivered in the city of Rome, and absences from Rome meant silence in a public arena: it is in these periods, his year of exile in 58–57 and his time as a provincial

prouincia Puteolos forte uenissem, cum plurimi et lautissimi in eis locis solent esse, concidi paene, iudices, cum ex me quidam quaesisset quo die Roma exissem et num quidnam esset noui. cui cum respondissem me e prouincia decedere: 'etiam me hercule,' inquit, 'ut opinor, ex Africa.' huic ego iam stomachans fastidiose: 'immo ex Sicilia,' inquam. tum quidam, quasi qui omnia sciret: 'quid? tu nescis,' inquit, 'hunc quaestorem Syracusis fuisse?' quid multa? destiti stomachari et me unum ex eis feci qui ad aquas uenissent. sed ea res, iudices, haud scio an plus mihi profuerit quam si mihi tum essent omnes gratulati. nam postea quam sensi populi Romani auris hebetiores, oculos autem esse acris atque acutos, destiti quid de me audituri essent homines cogitare; feci ut postea cotidie praesentem me uiderent, habitaui in oculis, pressi forum; neminem a congressu meo neque ianitor meus neque somnus absterruit . . . itaque si quam habeo laudem, quae quanta sit nescio, parta Romae est, quaesita in foro; meaque priuata consilia publici quoque casus comprobauerunt, ut etiam summa res publica mihi domi fuerit gerenda et urbs in urbe seruanda.

governor in 51–50, that Cicero the orator is replaced by Cicero
the letter-writer. Moreover, a cursory survey of the corpus of
speeches might seem to confirm the domestic bias in Cicero's
political career; many of the forensic speeches deal with
electoral malpractice of one sort or another, and violence in
domestic politics, and among his deliberative speeches the Catilinarians concern an internal threat to the state and the speeches
on the agrarian law relate ultimately to the grievances of the
urban *plebs*. Many of Cicero's biographers use his apparent
preoccupation with home affairs to draw a distinction between
a blinkered Cicero, fatally enmeshed in the minutiae of Roman
politics, and the bold and clear-sighted adventurers, above all
Pompeius and Caesar, who were redrawing the boundaries of
the empire and destroying the Republic along the way.

And yet a large number of Cicero's speeches *do* deal directly
with issues arising from Rome's possession of an empire. There
are numerous occasions, throughout his career, in which he
grapples with foreign, or imperial, affairs: when prosecuting or
defending provincial governors accused of extortion, when
speaking in cases concerning the claims to citizenship by men
not born Roman, and when he contributes to debates before the
people or in the Senate concerning the choice of commanders
for particular military campaigns. The relevant speeches are
the *Verrines*, the *pro Flacco*, *pro Fonteio*, and *pro Scauro* as
speeches in *repetundae* trials; the two speeches from citizenship
trials, the *pro Archia* and the *pro Balbo*; and the speeches *de
imperio Cn. Pompei* and *de prouinciis consularibus*. This book
addresses this oddly neglected group of works, which are the
chief contemporary sources for the imperialism of the late
Republic. Moreover, they offer the spectacle of a key figure in
the political life of the late Roman republic grappling with the
issues and problems which lie at the heart of the transformation
of that political system into a monarchy; and, through the
conundrum of a speaker on imperial issues who had extraordinarily little exposure on a practical level to the empire, or to
the military activity which was its essential underpinning, these
speeches also provide an opportunity to explore the means by
which Cicero seeks to present himself as an authoritative
speaker and, by extension, as an authoritative public figure.

The aim of this book is to examine Cicero's analyses of

imperial problems. I argue that he is operating, in the speeches, with a concept of empire which depends not on territory, but on the power wielded by individuals, and that this in turn means that the problems which arise in the running of empire can be presented as the result of personal failings rather than endemic to the structures of government: questions of morality rather than administration. Cicero's lack of experience in the field might, it could be suggested, point him in this direction; and it seems, too, to have been the mindset of most of his contemporaries, Pompeius being the most convincing exception. But a moralizing view of empire which concentrates on the failings of individuals is not simply, I contend, the result of incomprehension. Comparison with Cicero's letters and philosophical work suggests that the presentation of empire in the speeches is the result of a conscious simplification to enable Cicero to avoid having to make public choices about the exploitation of imperial resources which could alienate many of his supporters. The terms of his contribution to the imperial debate are formed by his weaknesses as a politician as much as by his strengths: and insofar as he was active in shaping the views of his contemporaries on imperial issues one can trace a paradoxical connection between Cicero's attempts to maintain his position as a politician who did not have direct access to the spoils of empire and the ultimate collapse of the republican system of government, which gave Cicero access to public life, under the attacks of war-lords fuelled by imperial conquest.

I.1. ROMAN IMPERIALISM AND THE FALL OF THE REPUBLIC

Roman imperialism is a subject of perennial scholarly interest. Much of the interest has been on the process of expansion, seeking to answer Polybius' opening question in his *Histories*, how it was that the Romans could have conquered almost the whole of the known world.[2] In particular, there has been

---

[2] See e.g. E. S. Gruen, *The Hellenistic World and the Coming of Rome* (Berkeley: Univ. of California Press, 1984); A. N. Sherwin-White, *Roman Foreign Policy in the East, 168 B.C. to A.D. 1* (London: Duckworth, 1984); J. S. Richardson, *Hispaniae: Spain and the Development of Roman Imperialism* (Cambridge: Cambridge Univ. Press, 1986); J.-L. Ferrary, *Philhellénisme et impérialisme* (Rome: *BEFAR* 271, 1988); R. M. Kallet-Marx, *Hegemony to*

vigorous debate about the Romans' motives in expansion, centring on the validity of the 'defensive imperialism' thesis as an explanation for their increasing involvement in the Greek world during the middle Republic.[3] Other work has looked at the economic consequences of empire, and in particular at the opportunities which the empire afforded for the enrichment of individual Romans.[4] When imperialism in the late, as opposed to the middle, Republic is considered, there is a broad scholarly consensus that the empire was one of the key factors in the collapse of the republican system of government: the administrative structures of a small city state were no longer capable of running an extensive and largely overseas empire, and the ad hoc solutions to this problem led to the phenomenon of the warlord.[5] Struggles between rival warlords—Marius and Sulla, and then Pompeius and Caesar—led to civil war; Sulla attempted to restore oligarchic government, but Caesar did not, and even his assassination failed to halt the concentration of power in one man.

It is not only modern scholars who treat empire as a factor in the fall of the Republic. Already Polybius sees the expansion of Rome and the wealth to which the ruling classes now have access as sources of political instability and change.[6] There is a strong tendency also among Roman writers to explain historical change by moral decline, which in turn is a result of foreign riches. Once the republican system of government has come to an end, Sallust and Livy both connect the change of

Empire: The Development of the Roman Imperium in the East from 148 to 62 B.C. (Berkeley: Univ. of California Press, 1995). Polybius states his question, more pungently than my paraphrase, at 1. 1. 5.

[3] The 'defensive imperialism' thesis challenged by W. V. Harris, *War and Imperialism in Republican Rome* (Oxford: Oxford Univ. Press, 1979); cf. the discussions of J. A. North, 'The Development of Roman Imperialism', *JRS* 71 (1981), 1–9; J. W. Rich, 'Fear, Greed and Glory: The Causes of Roman War-Making in the Middle Republic', in J. W. Rich and G. Shipley (eds.), *War and Society in the Roman World* (London: Routledge, 1993).

[4] E. Badian, *Publicans and Sinners* (Oxford: Blackwell, 1972); I. Shatzman, *Senatorial Wealth and Roman Politics* (Brussels: Latomus, 1975).

[5] C. Meier, *Res publica amissa*, 2nd edn. (Frankfurt: Suhrkamp, 1980); P. A. Brunt, 'The Fall of the Roman Republic', in *The Fall of the Roman Republic and Related Essays* (Oxford: Oxford Univ. Press, 1988); contra E. S. Gruen, *The Last Generation of the Roman Republic* (Berkeley: Univ. of California Press, 1974). [6] 6. 57; 18. 35; 31. 25. 2–8; 39. 1. 10–12.

government to the results of degeneration due to empire.[7] But although Cicero appeals to the virtues of an idealized past in his treatises, his *speeches* on empire show us a politician attempting to be persuasive when dealing with the issues without the benefit of hindsight. They are thus a valuable corrective to the mournful schematization of a Livy or a Sallust.

The inflation in the system of special commands was the crucial area where the possession of empire contributed to the end of the Republic, and two of Cicero's speeches, *de imperio Cn. Pompei* and *de prouinciis consularibus*, directly address issues arising from this development. In the former, delivered in 66, Cicero argues in support of a law giving Pompeius exceptionally wide-ranging powers, which in the event enabled him to bring large tracts of land under Roman control and establish a formidable personal power base, and in the latter, some ten years later, Cicero supports Caesar's desire to be allowed to retain the command which was giving him the opportunity to emulate in Gaul Pompeius' eastern successes.

The other speeches which I examine deal with issues, provincial misgovernment and access to citizenship, which are not on the surface so crucial to the transition from Republic to Empire, but which were matters for considerable concern and debate about the running of the empire at the time when Cicero spoke. The *repetundae* trials are ultimately concerned with the duties of the holder of *imperium*, and with the mechanisms by which the Roman state can control such individuals. This is precisely the same issue, albeit on a smaller scale and relating to more obscure people, as the one raised by the exceptional commands held by Pompeius and Caesar. How to control the behaviour of governors was a considerable problem: we know of a large number of convictions on extortion charges and it would be overly cynical to deny that the Senate was concerned about the behaviour of its members.[8] Various attempts at legislation from 149 BC onward did not eliminate the problem, but it

[7] See esp. Sallust, *Catiline* 10–13, *Jugurtha* 41–2; Livy, *Preface*; A. W. Lintott, 'Imperial Expansion and Moral Decline in the Roman Republic', *Historia*, 21 (1972), 626–38; B. Levick, 'Morals, Politics, and the Fall of the Roman Republic', *G&R* 29 (1982), 53–62.

[8] On the development of *repetundae* legislation, see A. W. Lintott, 'The *Leges de Repetundis* and Associate Measures under the Republic', *ZRG* 98 (1981), 162–212.

is clear that the possibility of being prosecuted for corruption was a considerable anxiety even for governors who kept their hands clean. However, the autonomy of governors in the field meant that the only actual constraint on their behaviour was the threat of prosecution, and the legal system in Rome was sufficiently uncertain, and indeed corrupt, that it was if not an empty at least a far from compelling threat. Moreover, measures to control corruption were liable to subversion even when they were not ignored. A good example of this comes from the notorious case of Brutus' loan to the Salaminians: it was illegal to lend this money, and so Brutus covered himself by a special senatorial decree.[9]

Claims to the citizenship did not play any prominent part in the final round of civil war, but this had been, on most accounts, the grievance which had sparked the Social War, which in turn had contributed to the turbulence of the last fifty years of the Republic. The conclusion of the Social War had led to the extension of the franchise throughout Italy, but without any transformation in the structures of Roman government to accommodate a vast number of new citizens who were not resident in the city.[10] The logical next step was the granting of citizenship to those domiciled outside Italy, and in ad hoc ways this was beginning to happen. A law was passed to enable Pompeius Magnus to grant citizenship in Spain, and both Crassus and Caesar attempted to raise the peoples beyond the Po from the Latin status they had acquired in 89 to full Roman citizenship.[11] Yet there was in fact no further enfranchisement of significant numbers after the resolution of the Social War until Caesar's dictatorship. The citizenship cases in which Cicero appeared were thus not simply anomalies, but nor were

[9] See Sect. 5.1 below.

[10] On citizenship in general, see A. N. Sherwin-White, *The Roman Citizenship*, 2nd edn. (Oxford: Oxford Univ. Press, 1973); on the enfranchisement of Italy in particular, H. Mouritsen, *Italian Unification* (London: *BICS* suppl. 70, 1998).

[11] Crassus attempted to enrol the Transpadanes as citizens while he was censor in 65: that is the deduction from Dio 37. 9. 3. (Dio says merely that the censors disagreed about the issue, to the extent that they both resigned their office, and does not say which censor was proposing it. It seems much more probable, however, that Crassus was in favour and Catulus resisted, than vice versa.) For Caesar and the Transpadanes, see Sect. 5.2.2 below.

they standard and frequently encountered situations: rather, they touched on a potentially explosive area which was none the less ignored in the political debates of the post-Sullan period.

These speeches offer, therefore, a way into key political debates of the late Republic. Who should command the Republic's armies, and what controls, if any, could be imposed on the commanders? What was the appropriate remuneration for a provincial governor, and how should the state intervene to balance the wishes of its representatives and the welfare of its subjects? What were the criteria for being a Roman citizen?

This last question—who is a Roman?—relates to an area which is currently receiving a great deal of scholarly attention, namely the effects of Roman conquest and empire upon the cultural and ethnic identities of both the Romans and their new subjects.[12] This material, however, tends to be concerned either with the Hellenization of Rome in the second century BC or with the Romanization of the empire during the 'Empire', that is the period of monarchic government after 27 BC. There is a curious gap in between, part of a wider historiographical phenomenon which makes events at *Rome* the key to understanding the late Republic, and indeed which concentrates on the transformation of republican government into monarchy to the exclusion of other historical developments of the last century BC. And insofar as attention is directed outside Rome, it is to the military activity which can be invoked as an important factor in this historical process. Cicero's tactics in his citizenship and *repetundae* speeches suggest considerable anxiety about the nature of Roman identity: important evidence for the wider debate on culture and empire which has not hitherto been fully exploited.

---

[12] E. S. Gruen, *Culture and National Identity in Republican Rome* (Ithaca: Cornell Univ. Press, 1992); S. E. Alcock, *Graecia Capta: The Landscapes of Roman Greece* (Cambridge: Cambridge Univ. Press, 1993); E. Gabba, *Aspetti culturali dell'imperialismo Romano* (Florence: Sansoni, 1993); S. Swain, *Hellenism and Empire: Language, Classicism, and Power in the Greek World, AD 50–250* (Oxford: Oxford Univ. Press, 1996); D. J. Mattingly (ed.), *Dialogues in Roman Imperialism* (*JRA* suppl. ser. 23, 1997); R. Laurence and J. Berry (eds.), *Cultural Identity in the Roman Empire* (London: Routledge, 1998); G. Woolf, *Becoming Roman* (Cambridge: Cambridge Univ. Press, 1998). For a non-classical perspective, cf. E. Said, *Culture and Imperialism* (London: Chatto and Windus, 1993).

I.2. APPROACHES TO CICERO

Cicero's speeches would, then, provide valuable material for the study of late republican imperialism. But I should stress that this book is not intended as a direct contribution to the debate on Roman imperialism, nor even, primarily, is it about the conceptualization of empire at the end of the Republic; the focus of my inquiry is about the practice of oratory: the strategies through which Cicero makes oratory a politically effective tool.

To study Cicero's speeches as 'politically effective tools' is a question-begging exercise, and leads straight to the problem of how best to contextualize oratory: to provide readings of speeches which take account both of their generic conventions and of their aims. Another, cruder, way of expressing this is to ask how one can provide readings of the speeches which are both historical and literary.

The dominant mode of literary criticism of Cicero's oratory is, perhaps unsurprisingly, rhetorical. The focus of this kind of work is, ultimately, on the question of how Cicero constructs effective arguments, and the approach is often to apply the rules of the genre, the rhetorical theory which Cicero had absorbed during his training, in order to understand his mature practice. So Craig explores Cicero's use of one particular form of rhetorical argument, *dilemma*; Berger, the construction of narratives within speeches; May, his manipulation of *ethos*; Cerutti and Loutsch, the dynamics of a particular part of a speech.[13]

A purely rhetorical approach can be very illuminating in relation to a specific part of a speech, but has quite severe limits if one is attempting to make sense of an entire speech. As Vasaly points out, the precepts of rhetorical theory are a framework, which was not only used but also transcended by

---

[13] C. P. Craig, *Form as Argument in Cicero's Speeches: A Study of Dilemma* (Atlanta: Scholars Press, 1993); D. Berger, *Cicero als Erzähler: forensische und literarische Strategien in den Gerichtsreden* (Frankfurt am Main: Lang, 1976); J. May, *Trials of Character: The Eloquence of Ciceronian Ethos* (Chapel Hill: Univ. of North Carolina Press, 1988); S. M. Cerutti, *Cicero's Accretive Style: Rhetorical Strategies in the Exordia of the Judicial Speeches* (Lanham: Univ. Press of America, 1996); C. Loutsch, *L'Exorde dans les discours de Cicéron* (Brussels: Collection Latomus 224, 1994).

practising orators;[14] and one might hypothesize that Cicero's
pre-eminence as an orator implied that he did much more than
simply reproduce the rules which were openly available to all
his contemporaries. And indeed there has been work that has
acknowledged the need to look beyond rhetorical theory.
Stroh's brilliant book, for example, moves beyond rhetoric
alone to examine, through a number of case-studies, the ways
in which Cicero manipulates facts in his forensic speeches to
produce a persuasively distorted account of events; and Classen,
too, seeks to incorporate legal and political contexts into his
study of six discrete speeches.[15]

It is striking how prominent Cicero's forensic speeches are in
much of this work. Stroh, Berger, and Cerutti concentrate
exclusively on judicial oratory, and of the eight speeches to
which Craig devotes detailed discussions seven are forensic. A
similar bias is apparent among commentaries on the speeches:
of the eight commentaries which Berry picks out as 'substantial
[and] modern', seven are on forensic speeches (and Berry's own
commentary deals with a forensic speech).[16] These figures
should be set against the ratio between forensic and non-forensic in the corpus of speeches as a whole; disputes over what
counts as a speech rather than a fragment affect the figures
slightly, but of the sixty speeches which are printed separately
in the Oxford Classical Text, thirty are forensic and thirty are
not. Cicero the orator, as he emerges from much modern
scholarship, is a creature of the lawcourts to a misleading extent.

A number of reasons can be put forward to explain this
imbalance. Perhaps the most obvious is that some of the most
striking and enjoyable of the speeches are forensic: this alone
would explain the attraction of, for example, the *pro Caelio*, the
pro Cluentio, or the *pro Roscio Amerino*. Murder, in particular,
is a subject of enduring fascination.[17] And, from a pedagogical

---

[14] A. Vasaly, *Representations: Images of the World in Ciceronian Oratory*
(Berkeley: Univ. of California Press, 1993), 3–7.

[15] W. Stroh, *Taxis und Taktik: Die advokatische Dispositionskunst in Ciceros
Gerichtsreden* (Stuttgart: Teubner 1975); C. J. Classen, *Recht — Rhetorik —
Politik: Untersuchungen zu Ciceros rhetorischer Strategie* (Darmstadt: Wissen-
schaftliche Buchgesellschaft, 1985).

[16] D. C. Berry, *Cicero, Pro P. Sulla oratio* (Cambridge: Cambridge Univ.
Press, 1996), ix.

[17] One of the Penguin volumes of Cicero's speeches is entitled *Murder Trials*

point of view, the more straightforward of the forensic speeches are attractive to teach because it is not necessary to know a great deal about the historical background to understand them (whereas the non-forensic speeches often demand a breadth of historical knowledge which is beyond many students). But the bias is also due in large part to the sorts of approaches which Ciceronian scholars have been using. Stroh is explicitly interested in forensic tactics; and for those using the insights of rhetorical theory, the forensic speeches are the obvious quarry because ancient rhetorical theory was elaborated largely to deal with forensic cases. The complexity of *inuentio* in the hand-books relates directly to the challenges of presenting a legal case: how to deal with witnesses, with arguments from proba-bility, how to determine whether a case involves a question of fact or of law, and so on. *Inuentio* is only one of the five *partes orationis*, yet *inuentio* as it relates solely to judicial cases takes up half of the only surviving republican treatise on oratory, the *ad C. Herennium*, and was the only one of the five which Cicero covered in his uncompleted early work on rhetoric, the *de inuentione*. Rhetorical theory and oratorical practice relate to one another much more closely in judicial cases than in deliberative speeches, and so a rhetorical approach is much more enlightening and useful if one looks at forensic speeches: but this entrenches the neglect of the non-forensic speeches, and the failure to develop analytical tools to deal with them.

A more general potential weakness of a rhetorical approach is to accept the speech's own premises without analysis. In particular, it becomes easy not to ask why Cicero chose to speak at *this* trial or on *this* issue, when silence was an option; and why he then published his speech, when he did not always produce a written version; and why he chose a particular rhetorical strategy. It becomes too easy to regard the form which a speech takes as inevitable, and to explain it without regard for the *choices* which have shaped it.

Historical approaches to Cicero have been dominated by the biography;[18] unsurprisingly, perhaps, given how much we

(trans. M. Grant; Harmondsworth, 1973); one can cite too the series of detec-tive novels by Stephen Saylor, based largely on forensic cases in which Cicero was involved: see C. Steel, 'The Gordianus Knot', *Omnibus*, 38 (1999), 32–3.

[18] See e.g. D. L. Stockton, *Cicero: A Political Biography* (Oxford: Oxford

know about his life, and in particular given the survival of some of his correspondence, which features more prominently among the textual sources for biography than do either the speeches or the treatises. This is not perhaps a suitable place for an extended disquisition on the dangers of treating the letters as though they provided us with direct and unmediated access to Cicero's 'real' beliefs and character; but it can be remarked that biographers of Cicero are often more interested in the fact that Cicero gave a particular speech that in its content.

The other historical approach to the speeches is as sources for particular events or beliefs; for example, attitudes to empire. The information which Cicero's speeches provide is so extensive that their use is inescapable; but oratorical texts do not present a direct and straightforward representation of the world; they are the products of a highly sophisticated technical system, central to which is the need to subordinate facts to the argument which the speaker is propounding. It is dangerously naïve, therefore, to believe anything Cicero may say in a speech, without considering *why* he is saying it and who, in his audience, might be in a position to challenge the statement. This is fairly obvious, however often historians disregard it in practice. More difficult is the relationship between oratory, that is the text which has survived, and its success or failure: that is, whether the Senate, or assembly, or jury, voted in the way that the orator was advocating and if so, why. Cicero was rarely the only orator speaking in support of a case or issue, and of the speeches I deal with this is true only of the *Verrines*; not only need we take account of his opponents, but also the other speakers arguing for the same course of action or verdict as he is. Apart from the trial of Verres—which never, of course, came to a vote—the voting audience would have made up their minds on the basis of what a number of speakers had said, and none of this has survived apart from Cicero's contribution. But it is also clear that, in the late Republic, the effectiveness of an orator did

Univ. Press, 1971); Shackleton D. R. Bailey, *Cicero* (London: Duckworth, 1971); E. D. Rawson, *Cicero: A Portrait* (London: Allen Lane, 1975); W. K. Lacey, *Cicero and the End of the Roman Republic* (London: Hodder and Stoughton, 1978); T. N. Mitchell, *Cicero: The Ascending Years* (New Haven: Yale Univ. Press, 1979), and *Cicero: The Senior Statesman* (New Haven: Yale Univ. Press, 1991); M. Furhmann, *Cicero and the Roman Republic*, trans. W. E. Yuill (Oxford: Blackwell, 1992).

not depend solely on the quality of the oratory. *Auctoritas*, that elusive but vital mix of personal impressiveness and charisma with influence and connections, cannot be disregarded. An audience voted not just on the basis of what was said, but who said it, quite apart from its assessment of the issues which lay behind any one speech. It is only when we assess personal profile more generally that the oratorical success of, for example, Crassus, can be explained, since most accounts of his performances suggest that he was a dull and uninspired speaker.[19] Instead of concentrating exclusively on the brilliance of what was said, we need to envisage a range of ways of being an effective speaker, with oratorical fireworks at one end and overwhelming *auctoritas* at the other, and most orators of the period existing in the middle, bolstering their skill at speaking with the projection of a public persona derived from visible activities other than oratory.

The failure of either the biographical or the rhetorical approach to give fully convincing analyses of the speeches can be linked with a general unease about the role of oratory in late republican politics. Did it matter, and if so, how? If what Cicero says in a speech is not to be taken as an expression of his political beliefs, then the biographer need not pay close attention to it; and if the link between speech and speaker is weak, then there is little need to contextualize. And while it might seem self-evident that an activity into which so much energy was poured by so many politicians was important, the dominant trends in the study of the late Republic have indeed tended to focus the attention of historians away from oratory.[20] One of these is the concentration on factions as a way of explaining the results of elections and thus the distribution of power: if magistrates are chosen primarily on the basis of the identity of their friends and relatives, then what aspiring candidates *say* matters less, or not at all. And while the limitations of the prosopographical approach are being recognized, the perception that Roman politicians do not appeal to programmes when seeking election, but to personal popularity—dependent on a

---

[19] On Crassus' abilities as a speaker, see Cicero, *Brutus* 233; Plutarch, *Life of Crassus* 3.3–4.

[20] Though cf. G. Achard, *Pratique rhétorique et idéologie politique dans les discours 'optimates' de Cicéron* (Leiden: *Mnemosyne* suppl. 68, 1981).

range of factors—has the unfortunate effect of distracting attention away from the content of their public pronouncements.

One recent attempt to deal with the political aspect of deliberative rhetoric has been the article by Rose, which is also the only work of which I know to deal explicitly with Cicero's oratorical discussion of empire.[21] He considers the speeches *de imperio Cn. Pompei* and *de prouinciis consularibus*; his approach, firmly based in the Marxist tradition, is to use the theoretical insights of Macherey in order 'to explore the internal contradictions of the texts as pointers to the contradictions of late Republican society'.[22] He offers an analysis which looks past the focus on Rome in Cicero's career to the way that his actions were nevertheless implicated in the empire, and in particular he shows how Cicero's analysis of imperial expansion in the speech *de imperio Cn. Pompei* is riddled with contradictions. Moreover, the article throws open the question of what *sort* of account we want to give of the workings of political oratory. My reservations about *this* one arise because it does not give sufficient autonomy to Cicero, whose oratory, I would argue, can support more complex explanations. Rose himself seems unclear as to whether Cicero was conscious of the contradictions he reproduces in his oratory, and it is revealing that, while his discussion of the *de imperio Cn. Pompei* (in which Cicero conceals his own persona for much of the speech) is highly illuminating, the analysis of the *de prouinciis consularibus*, in which Cicero's advice is explicitly and inextricably linked with his own experiences and attitudes, is much less convincing.

A more widespread corrective to prevailing approaches has been the growing interest in the democratic element, and consequently on the figure of the speaker.[23] Public speech is

[21] P. W. Rose, 'Cicero and the Rhetoric of Imperialism: Putting the Politics back into Political Rhetoric', *Rhetorica*, 13 (1995), 359–99.

[22] Rose, 'Rhetoric of Imperialism', 359.

[23] See F. G. B. Millar, 'The Political Character of the Classical Roman Republic, 200–151 B.C.', *JRS* 74 (1984), 1–19, 'Politics, Persuasion and the People before the Social War (150–90 B.C.)', *JRS* 76 (1986), 1–11, and *The Crowd in Rome in the Late Republic* (Ann Arbor: University of Michigan Press, 1998); P. J. J. Vanderbroeck, *Popular Leadership and Collective Behaviour in the Late Roman Republic* (Amsterdam: Gieben, 1987); F. Pina Polo, *Contra Arma Verbis: der Redner vor dem Volk in der späten römischen Republik*, trans.

stressed as the means of communication between politician and
people, and it matters because if the people's voting choices,
whether electoral or legislative, are not irrevocably decided in
advance by the forces of patronage and bribery, then speech is
given the opportunity to be persuasive: it can affect the course
of events. It is interesting, however, that the surge of interest in
the crowd and the orator has not yet spread to close studies of
the means of communication themselves. In part this may be
precisely because our only complete surviving republican
speeches are those of Cicero, who was not sympathetic to the
democratic element in the republican constitution; one might
even suggest that the liberal sentiments which lead scholars to
search for democracy tend also to prejudice them against a man
who referred to the Roman people as scum.[24]

Moreover, the concept of the 'political' needs to be used with
extreme care. Riggsby has recently argued very persuasively
that Roman trials are *not* political in the sense that the verdicts
were decided by the political allegiances of the jurors: rather,
the Romans did believe their verdicts and a vote for guilty
meant that they believed the defendant had done what he was
charged with. Therefore, the aim of a forensic speech is to
prove that the defendant is innocent or guilty.[25] But, this still
allows room for Cicero's forensic speeches to be political in at
least two weaker senses: one being that they were a means of
showing where *his* political allegiances lay through the identity
of the men he chose to defend, and the other being that if
oratory is a form of political capital then every successful
oratorical outing—and, by and large, Cicero only published
his successes—is an opportunity for Cicero to increase his
stock.

That there is a political value, at least in a general sense, to
Cicero's oratory is a recurrent feature in this study, and is a
useful method of approaching the non-forensic speeches. They

E. Liess (Stuttgart: F. Steiner, 1996); G. Laser, *Populo et scaenae serviendum
est: Die Bedeutung der stadtischen Masse in der späten Römischen Republik*
(Trier: Wissenschaftlicher Verlag Trier, 1997); C. Döbler, *Politische Agitation
und Öffentlichkeit in der späten Republik* (Frankfurt am Main: Lang, 1999).

[24] *ad Quintum fratrem* 2. 5. 3; *in Pisonem* 9 (*faex*); *in Catilinam* 2. 7 (*sentina*)
(with *de lege agraria* 2. 70!).

[25] A. M. Riggsby, *Crime and Community in Ciceronian Rome* (Austin: Univ.
of Texas Press, 1999), 5–20.

are not the expression of a political 'programme', but manifestations of a constant need to maintain popularity. And, even
more than in forensic speeches, the content has political consequences: say the wrong thing, and you will lose supporters.
Cicero is a particularly interesting study here, quite apart from
being the only orator whose speeches survive entire, since,
unusually, his political position derived almost entirely from
his skill as a speaker. He did not have the ancestry and family
connections to make electoral success easy; he was not particularly wealthy; his military experience was exiguous. These are
all truisms of Cicero's biography, and one consequence is to
place great weight on his oratory, both to explain his successes
as a politician and to explain success in any particular oratorical
case: since he had few other resources to draw upon, his
speeches must have been exceptional. But the lack of alternative resources would also suggest that Cicero's opportunities to
take risks in his speeches was limited. If oratory was the
principal means by which he created and maintained his popularity, then he needed to pay particular attention to saying
things which were attractive to his audience.

To say this is not, however, to subscribe to the familiar
dichotomy between Cicero the brilliant orator of the literary
studies and Cicero the fairly ineffectual politician of the biographers and historians, overtaken by events and eventually
extinguished by them. The danger of this split is, once again,
that it removes oratory from consideration as a factor in
political events, albeit one whose effectiveness is not always
complete, while entrenching the tendency of literary studies to
emphasize Cicero's talent as an orator. If Cicero was as good an
orator as we want to believe, there is a problem in explaining
why his political career swerves so drastically between success
and failure: the triumph of 63 undone by his exile, his stance
independent of the first triumvirate turned into obedience in
the latter part of the 50s, the leader of the free state who ends
up pinned to the *rostra*. And yet, as I have discussed, to deny
all political importance to oratory cannot do justice to the complexity of political life. We cannot simply disregard oratory as a
factor in political life: the problem is rather to work out what
made some oratory successful, and some not. And this leads us
back to the question of the orator's persona. In effect, we run

into a brick wall: oratory matters, but does it work because of words or because of people? Studying Cicero's imperial oratory provides a way to peer over the brick wall, since this corpus of speeches can be set in a sufficiently wide context of actions and writings by other politicians of the period for it to become possible to determine where Cicero is arguing in line with contemporary assumptions and prejudices, and where he is taking an idiosyncratic view of a situation. We may still want to *explain* his idiosyncrasies in terms of narrow and personal aims, but the risks which he was taking and the chances of failure become easier to distinguish.

I return at the end of the book to the general question of the relationship between Cicero as orator and Cicero as politician. But the contextualization of the oratory is subsequent to the studies of individual speeches, since it is dangerously easy to find in a text what one is looking for. A recurrent theme of this book is that Cicero does *not* always argue as we might expect him to do on any crude and simplistic picture of his aims and methods as a public speaker, and that the unexpected twists and turns of his arguments spring from a much more complex and nuanced response to the problems which Rome faced as it extended as an imperial power than is often allowed. The first three chapters offer, therefore, readings of the imperial speeches which attempt to map their strategies of persuasion.

I look first at the speeches from extortion trials: in these the view of empire as an arena in which holders of *imperium* operate with considerable autonomy is most clearly articulated. Cicero's description of Verres' wickedness depends on the assumptions shared by speaker and jury about what constitutes a good holder of *imperium*. Cicero uses these in a variety of ways, prominent among which are the idea of a historical continuum of good Romans serving the state (which Verres has broken) and the sense that Verres has failed to maintain proper boundaries between himself and his officers: in both respects he diverges absolutely from due standards of behaviour. Similar tactics can be traced in the speech *de prouinciis consularibus*, which, although not a forensic speech, has as one of its aims to destroy the authority of Piso and Gabinius as governors. In the speech *pro Flacco*, too, Cicero attacks the prosecution because they have failed to behave as Romans should, but in this speech the emphasis is more on how they have taken on the characteristics of the Greeks whom Flaccus is supposed to have harmed, and thus have destroyed the credibility of the case they are arguing. The emphasis in these speeches upon individual behaviour is not surprising—that is precisely the concern of these cases—but it does enable Cicero to avoid making any statements about the theoretical basis of the *repetundae* legislation, or considering what are in fact the acceptable limits to exploiting provincials.

In the next chapter I consider the two cases in which Cicero defends the claim of his client to be a Roman citizen, in the speeches *pro Archia* and *pro Balbo*. Where we might expect a defence based on the successful integration of Archias or Balbus into Roman society, we in fact find strategies of persuasion which draw attention away from the personal qualities of the two men and portray them as valuable servants of the state, Archias through his poetic activities, Balbus because he is the valued assistant of Caesar. Cicero is here using well-established arguments for enfranchisement, with reminiscences, at least in the case of Archias, of Ennius, which allows him to draw attention away from the fundamental changes in the composition of the citizen body which followed the Social War, and the increasing demand for citizenship which could follow the Romanization of the provinces, and thus avoid radical questions about who should be a Roman citizen.

The third chapter looks at Cicero's treatment of Pompeius and Caesar in the two speeches in which he argues that they be given exceptional military commands, *de imperio Cn. Pompei* and *de prouinciis consularibus*. In both cases the exceptional command had been created by a highly controversial tribunician law, and was the focus of heated constitutional debate. Cicero sidesteps these issues, and presents both Pompeius and Caesar as dutiful servants of the Roman state, good holders of *imperium* of the sort familiar from Chapter 1. The implication of his argument is that constitutional worries are entirely misplaced: if Pompeius and Caesar are the sort of men that Cicero describes, then it is inconceivable that they should behave in ways detrimental to the state. The extent of special pleading in both speeches is clear from a comparison with Cicero's defence of Murena on charges of electoral corruption:

Murena was a relatively undistinguished soldier, and his career, presented as favourably as Cicero can manage, is laid out in terms of the men under whose command he fought or with whom he co-operated. He exists within a network of connections and a career structure which control his autonomy; both Pompeius and Caesar have escaped from this network, leaving them potentially uncontrollable. Cicero can deal with this only by presenting each man in a splendid isolation, which both emphasizes their superlative personal qualities whilst removing any rivals whose existence could provoke conflict.

At this point I broaden the scope of the inquiry, to ask, first, how Cicero deploys his persona to bolster his arguments, and conversely, how in some cases the speech functions in fact primarily as a vehicle to support a particular persona; and secondly, how Cicero's 'view of empire' (to put it crudely) relates to what his contemporaries were doing and saying. In Chapter 4 I continue to deal with *de imperio Cn. Pompei* and *de prouinciis consularibus*, but my focus shifts to the relation between oratory and Cicero's own career. I show how the various 'blind spots' in his arguments help his political position, and in the case of *de prouinciis consularibus* suggest that the way he argues for an extension of Caesar's command is specifically designed to bolster his position in the aftermath of the conference of Luca. Cicero cannot take centre stage in imperial debates as a military figure, but he does construct himself as someone uniquely qualified to advise military commanders and thus he attempts to claim, and to maintain, a prominent position within the state.

In the final chapter I set Cicero's presentation of empire in his speeches against that which we find in his letters and treatises, and that of his contemporaries. The prevailing mode of analysis is in terms of individuals; that is the basis of Cicero's analysis in the *de officiis*, and both Cato's attempts to control provincial governors and Caesar's *repetundae* legislation work on the basis that the problem is the individual. Pompeius does, however, seem to have a rather different approach; his settlement of the East seems to embody a distinct shift towards a territorial conception of empire, and his legislation in 52 imposing a five-year gap between magistracy and pro-magistracy breaks the key connection between election and *imperium*, on the one hand, and *imperium* and provincial government on the other. The outbreak of civil war in 49 makes it impossible to know what the long-term effects of this change might have been, but the similarities to the system which Augustus eventually put in place are striking.

Cicero's imperial oratory provides us with a superb opportunity to relate rhetorical technique to political debate and thereby illuminate not simply the techniques of Ciceronian oratory and the attitude to empire among the leading political figures of the late Republic, but also the ways in which oratory can interact with politics and with being a politician. Cicero's rhetoric of empire illustrates both his strengths and weaknesses as an orator; his capacity to be persuasive is breathtaking, but his lack of alternative political capital—military success, distinguished ancestry, exceptional wealth, unscrupulousness— places firm limits on what he can and cannot say. In the case of his imperial speeches, the result is that he colludes in a series of decisions which leave the Republic at the mercy of individuals who have exploited Rome's empire to acquire positions of great and autonomous power; but this, I argue, is due to the weakness of oratory rather than of the orator. The Cicero we are dealing with is neither the ineffectual politician of much Roman historiography, doomed to ultimate failure because he lacks sufficient insight and nous, nor is he the ineffectual Cicero of Rose, trapped by the society of his day; he is, rather, a Cicero trying not to rock the boat of the system whilst attempting to throw others overboard on his way to the *rostra*. The speeches under consideration show how Cicero used oratory in order to be a successful politician, while revealing the ways in which oratory could not guarantee the stability of that success.[26]

[26] The speeches with which I deal in this book were delivered between 70 and 56, and hence I do not consider the ways in which the uses of oratory were changed after the outbreak of civil war in 49, nor the importance of the *Philippics*, topics which would be central to a complete survey of the capacities of Ciceronian oratory. It is worth noting that the cut-off date matches the point at which Cicero withdrew largely from politics in the face of the renewed dominance of the first triumvirate, continuing as a speaker primarily in the courts.

I

Romans in the provinces: power, autonomy, and identity

CICERO'S *repetundae* speeches provide some of our best evidence for how the empire worked on a day-to-day basis during the Republic, with a mass of detail about the activities of provincial governors and their staff in dispensing justice, overseeing the taxation system, and defending Rome's possessions from external threats. Moreover, for this type of forensic case we are in the unusual position of having a prosecution by Cicero, that of Verres, as well as defence speeches.[1] From this material it is possible to explore the ways in which Cicero presents Romans as good or bad within provincial contexts. Here I shall concentrate particularly on men behaving badly: on Romans behaving in provincial contexts in ways that can be presented in order to rouse hostile feelings in Cicero's audiences. The judgements are based, of course, not solely on the actual behaviour of the men he talks about, but on the particular case that Cicero is arguing; but the terms which he uses to attack and defend, whatever their truth value, indicate the sorts of actions which were considered unacceptable, and the range of issues which could provoke anxiety about Rome's imperial activities.

I look first at Gaius Verres, governor of Sicily 73–71 and, on his return to Rome, the target of a prosecution by Cicero for extortion. Famously, Verres went into exile after Cicero had delivered his introductory speech at the first hearing and the witnesses had been heard, but Cicero wrote up and published five further speeches which purport to have been delivered and describe, in overwhelming detail, Verres' wrongdoing. Verres'

[1] The only other prosecution of any kind that Cicero undertook in his entire career was that of Bursa, in 52. For a summary of the position of provincial governors, see A. W. Lintott, *Imperium Romanum: Politics and Administration* (London: Routledge, 1993), 43–69.

period as governor is thus extremely well documented, and he is an excellent case-study of how an orator could set about demonstrating that someone was a bad governor. And when Cicero attacks his enemies Piso and Gabinius in the speeches he delivered after his return from exile he exploits what he describes as shortcomings in their periods as provincial governors in order to justify publicly what was in effect a personal quarrel; but the justification can only work if the activities which he ascribes to the pair were generally felt to be unacceptable.

Cicero also defended men accused of extortion, and does so by appealing to a positive image of the *imperium*-holder which transcends and even obliterates any minor transgressions at the expense of provincials. In the most substantial of the defences to survive, the speech *pro Flacco*, Cicero's positive presentation of his client Flaccus is complemented by the way he describes the two chief prosecutors. These two men, Decimus Laelius and Gaius Appuleius Decianus, are not magistrates or ex-magistrates; the former is a young Roman of aristocratic family, at the beginning of his political career, who is using the well-tried strategy of making his name and talents known to the electorate through a high-profile prosecution, and the latter a middle-aged Roman citizen domiciled in Asia Minor, Flaccus' province. Since they are not holders of *imperium*, Cicero cannot, obviously, use the model of a bad Roman *imperium*-holder in his attempt to blacken their characters and thus deny authority to their prosecution. His tactics do, however, show marked similarity to those used against Verres, Piso, and Gabinius, albeit tailored to his particular victims; which suggests that codes of appropriate behaviour in the provinces were not limited to figures in authority, but could be extended, by comparison, to any Roman who had dealings overseas.

1.1. VERRES

The prosecution of Verres was a big gamble for Cicero to take: failure would mean a considerable if not decisive set-back to his political career as well as the acquisition of a powerful enemy. These problems were compounded by the fact that the prosecution, which in itself was always a potentially unsavoury act, did not fit the one time when it was acceptable behaviour, that is when the prosecutor was a young man, at the beginning of his career (such as Flaccus) and new to the courts.[2] Cicero was 36, and had been active forensically for ten years; moreover, his position as a 'new man' made him particularly vulnerable. Verres, if acquitted, would have been in a strong position to stand for the consulship of 68, and might well have been successful.

Verres' departure into exile after the first hearing deprived Cicero of the opportunity to display his oratorical skill in the detailed exposition of Verres' crimes, and his publication of the vast second hearing is an attempt to make up for this, as well as to convince any doubters that Verres really was guilty. The sheer mass of material made its arrangement particularly important, if the reader were not to give up in confusion. The first speech of the second hearing is ordered chronologically, covering Verres' career before he went to Sicily; thereafter the order is thematic, with embezzlement and judicial corruption in the second speech, the (mis)management of corn in the third, art theft and attendant sacrilege in the fourth, and military failure and judicial murder in the final speech.

The movement of the five speeches overall is thus one of increasing emotional tension: from the largely dry and technical subject matter of the second and third speeches, to vivid and affecting descriptions of the theft of valued religious artefacts and art treasures, and of shameful military failure and unjust executions. The order is related to what would seem important in the city of Rome: a series of unfair judgements in Sicilian courts is of comparatively little concern, except insofar as it illustrates Verres' general unfitness to possess *imperium*, and while corn was of major political importance, Verres had indeed secured supplies; the charge against him was that he had done so in a corrupt and unjust fashion.[3] But the theft of religious statuary raises the possibility that Verres is

[2] J.-M. David, *Le Patronat judiciaire au dernier siècle de la République romaine* (Rome: *BEFAR* 277, 1992), 525–47; D. F. Epstein, *Personal Enmity in Roman Politics, 218–43 B.C.* (London: Croom Helm, 1987), 90–100.

[3] See G. Rickman, *The Corn Supply of Ancient Rome* (Oxford: Oxford Univ. Press, 1980), 38–42; P. Garnsey, *Famine and Food Supply in the Graeco-Roman World* (Cambridge: Cambridge Univ. Press, 1988), 200.

endangering the Roman state's favoured position with the gods by his impiety; his military failure strikes a direct blow at Roman interests; and his punishment of Roman citizens forms a pathetic climax to the indictment. From a Sicilian point of view, Cicero moves from the actions which had the greatest ill-effects on the province, to conclude with a series of events which affected only a small number of people; but for his Roman audience, the worst is saved until the end.

Verres is one of Cicero's most memorable creations; he becomes an exemplary figure for later generations, the epitome of the corrupt provincial governor.[4] The characterization is created through a series of brilliant vignettes of Verres as he goes about his official business.[5] One of the most revealing comes early in the final speech, when Cicero begins his discussion of Verres' actions as a military commander.

Insofar as we can reconstruct Hortensius' actual defence from Cicero's remarks, it seems that one of his major arguments in favour of Verres was that he had been successful in defending Sicily from various military threats, in particular that of a slave revolt (Verres' period as governor coincided with the height of Spartacus' rising in southern Italy) and the danger of a pirate attack.[6] Cicero 'foresees' Hortensius' argument (2. 5. 2):

What shall I do, gentlemen of the jury? What line of attack shall I use? Where shall I turn? All my attacks run against a wall, that of the name of 'a good general'. I know the trope, and see the arguments which Hortensius will deploy: the dangers of war, the position of the state, the shortage of generals . . .[7]

[4] See Juvenal, *Satires* 2. 26, 3. 53, 8. 106.

[5] See the studies by R. G. M. Nisbet, 'The Orator and the Reader: Manipulation and Response in Cicero's *Fifth Verrine*', in T. Woodman and J. G. F. Powell (eds.), *Author and Audience in Latin Literature* (Cambridge: Cambridge Univ. Press, 1992), 1–17, repr. in his *Collected Papers on Latin Literature*, ed. S. J. Harrison (Oxford: Oxford Univ. Press, 1995), 362–80, on *Verrines* 2. 5. 92–5, and by C. E. W. Steel, 'Being Economical with the Truth: What Really Happened at Lampsacus?', in J. G. F. Powell and J. J. Paterson (eds.), *Cicero the Advocate* (Oxford: Oxford Univ. Press, forthcoming), on *Verrines* 2. 1. 63–85. A. Haury, *L'Ironie et l'humour chez Cicéron* (Leiden: E. J. Brill, 1955), 117–22, summarizes Cicero's use of humour and irony in the speeches.

[6] For a summary of the historical background, see R. Seager, 'The Rise of Pompey', *CAH* 9, 2nd edn. (1994), 208–28, 221–3.

[7] quid agam, iudices? quo accusationis meae rationem conferam? quo

Cicero himself uses very similar arguments three years later in his speech for the Manilian law,[8] and it was potentially a very effective tactic, since it appealed directly to a Roman audience's self-image of itself as a military invincible people.[9] Cicero's anxiety to counter it is understandable.[10]

He begins by explaining, and dismissing, what Verres is said to have done to deal with the danger of a slave revolt, and then turns to a more general description of Verres as a military commander (2. 5. 25–31). On the basis of his response to the slave menace, the jury can see for themselves Verres' 'judgement, care, and alertness', and Cicero then turns to consider what overall type of general Verres is. His qualities are not those of famous generals of the past (2. 5. 25):

> There are many kinds of generals, and my chief aim has been to show you what kind Verres is, so that, in view of the scarcity of brave men you may not remain unaware of his remarkable qualities. He does not aspire to the wisdom of Quintus Maximus nor to the speed in action of the elder Africanus or exceptional judgement of the younger, nor to the planning and control of Paulus, nor to the vigour and courage of Marius; you must understand, please, that it is quite another type of general that you should carefully keep and preserve.[11]

me uertam? ad omnis enim meos impetus quasi murus quidam boni nomen imperatoris opponitur. noui locum; uideo ubi se iactaturus sit Hortensius. belli pericula, tempora rei publicae, imperatorum penuriam commemorabit . . .

[8] *de imp.* 27: 'Fellow citizens, would that you had so great a supply of brave and upright men that you found the choice of who to put in charge of this complex situation and important war difficult!' (utinam, Quirites, uirorum fortium atque innocentium copiam tantam haberetis ut haec uobis deliberatio difficilis esset quemnam potissimum tantis rebus ac tanto bello praeficiendum putaretis!)

[9] See P. A. Brunt, '*Laus Imperii*', in P. D. A. Garnsey and C. R. Whittaker (eds.), *Imperialism in the Ancient World* (Cambridge: Cambridge Univ. Press, 1978), 159–91, repr. in Brunt, *Roman Imperial Themes* (Oxford: Oxford Univ. Press, 1990), 288–323.

[10] This is true even though Verres had already gone into exile by the time that the speeches of the second hearing were disseminated: to make certain of a reputation-enhancing achievement, Cicero must convince Rome that Verres deserved to be in exile.

[11] summa illuc pertinet, ut sciatis, quoniam plura genera sunt imperatorum, ex quo genere iste sit, ne qui diutius in tanta penuria uirorum fortium talem imperatorem ignorare possit. non ad Q. Maximi sapientiam neque ad illius superioris Africani in re gerunda celeritatem, neque ad huius qui postea fuit

Cicero then turns to explain what he means, which he does through a brilliant parody of the military calendar. In the winter, Verres retreats to winter quarters, as any general would: he chooses the city of Syracuse, famed for its pleasant climate, and there retreats to bed. 'Here this good general lived during the winter months in such a way that it was difficult for anyone to see him out of bed, let alone out of the house; and in this way the short days were taken up with feasting and the long nights with sex and adultery.'[12] He is alerted to spring by the first rose (a conventional symbol of the banquet), rather than by changes in the weather or by using his astronomical knowledge, as a competent soldier would, and then 'surrendered himself to activity and travel; he showed himself so tough and energetic in this that no one ever saw him on horseback'.[13] Then follows a clever surprise sentence to explain this statement: it is not that Verres went campaigning on foot, but 'as was the custom of Bithynian kings, he was carried in a litter with eight bearers' and Cicero goes on to describe its luxury—cushions stuffed with rose petals, garlands round Verres' neck and head, a delicate bag of rose-petals for his nose, and direct transit from litter to bed at the various towns on his itinerary.[14]

Instead of hearing legal cases, Verres spends his time carousing and chasing the wives of local notables. 'His dinner parties were not conducted with the quietness appropriate to those of praetors and generals of the Roman people, nor with

  singulare consilium, neque ad Pauli rationem ac disciplinam, neque ad C. Mari uim atque uirtutem; sed aliud genus imperatoris sane diligenter retinendum et conseruandum, quaeso, cognoscite.

  [12] 2. 5. 26. 4–7: 'hic ita uiuebat iste bonus imperator hibernis mensibus ut eum non facile non modo extra tectum, sed ne extra lectum quidem quisquam uiderit; ita diei breuitas conuiuiis, noctis longitudo stupris et flagitiis continebatur.'

  [13] 2. 5. 27. 10–13: 'dabat se labori atque itineribus; in quibus eo usque se praebebat patientem atque impigrum ut eum nemo umquam in equo sedentem uiderit'.

  [14] 2. 5. 27. 13–14: 'nam, ut mos fuit Bithyniae regibus, lectica octaphoro ferebatur'. For a Roman magistrate to use a litter was already a cliché of inappropriate luxury: see Gellius, *NA* 10. 3. 5 (a quotation from a speech of C. Gracchus) and Catullus 10. 15 ff., with C. Fordyce, *Catullus* (Oxford: Oxford Univ. Press, 1961), 119–20, and D. C. Braund, 'The Politics of Catullus 10: Memmius, Caesar and the Bithynians', *Hermathena*, 160 (1996), 45–57.

the restraint which should be used at the parties of magistrates, but with shameful and excessive rowdiness',[15] and Cicero then likens the scene the following morning to the aftermath of a battle: 'anyone who saw it would think he was looking on the appalling effects of Cannae rather than a praetor's dinner party'.[16] The ironical presentation of Verres as a military man continues, but Cicero has chosen the name of a notorious Roman *defeat* for his comparison.

The calendar then moves to summer, but the stress moves somewhat away from military considerations, as Cicero describes this season as 'the time which all praetors in Sicily usually spend travelling' since the island's grain production can most clearly be seen during the summer. Verres, however, innovates (2. 5. 29–2. 5. 31):

Then, I assert, when other praetors were racing around, this new type of commander set up a fixed camp in the most beautiful spot in Syracuse. He put up his tents, made from sailcloth stretched over poles, on the shore at the very edge of the harbour, where the bay first of all turns in towards the city from the line of the coast. He transferred his lodgings to here from the official residence, which had been the palace of King Hiero, with such thoroughness that no one saw him away from the beach throughout this period. There was no access to the camp to anyone unless he was a partner or helper in Verres' unrestrained behaviour. Here came the women with whom he consorted—it is remarkable how many of them there were in Syracuse; here came the men who were worthy of his friendship and to participate in his partying life. Among men and women of his sort his son, no longer a child, spent his time with the result that even if his nature rejected his parent's way of life exposure and practice would make him resemble his father . . . [*a description of dissension among Verres' mistresses follows*]. During this time, this man spent his time revelling with his women, dressed in a purple cloak and an ankle-length tunic, and no one minded that he was away from the forum and legal processes came to a standstill . . . it was not justice and the courts which seemed to be absent from the forum but violence, cruelty, and the bitter and unjust seizure of goods.[17]

[15] 2. 5. 28: 'erant autem conuiuia non illo silentio populi Romani praetorum atque imperatorum, neque eo pudore qui in magistratuum conuiuiis uersari soleat, sed cum maximo clamore atque conuicio'.

[16] 'ut quiuis, cum aspexisset, non se praetoris conuiuium, sed Cannensem pugnam nequitiae uidere arbitraretur'.

[17] tum, inquam, cum concursant ceteri praetores, iste nouo quodam genere

This concludes Verres' year, and Cicero uses his description as
a peg on which to hang some general reflections of Verres' style
of magistracy, which lead into a comparison with Cicero's own
attitude to being a magistrate. 'Immortal gods! How different
are the dispositions and plans of different men!'[18] Cicero
approached being a quaestor, and aedile elect (his position at
the time of the trial of Verres), in such a way that 'I felt myself
bound by a scrupulous regard for all my duties' and goes on to
explain that he felt himself to be on a stage with the world as his
audience and so all his actions must stand up to the most
minute scrutiny.[19] A list of his duties as aedile follows, with the
religious side of duties given prominence, and he concludes as
follows (2. 5. 37):

As a result of all these considerations, gentlemen of the jury, as I hope
that the gods will be favourable towards me, [I declare that] even
though honours bestowed by the Roman people are extremely
pleasant, I none the less take not nearly as much pleasure in it as an
anxious effort to ensure that this aedileship may not seem to have been
given to one candidate because one had to be chosen, but to have been
entrusted to the right person by the judgement of the people.[20]

imperator pulcherrimo Syracusarum loco statiua sibi castra faciebat. nam in
ipso aditu atque ore portus, ubi primum ex alto sinus ab litore ad urbem
inflectitur, tabernacula carbaseis intenta uelis conlocabat. huc ex illa domo
praetoria, quae regis Hieronis fuit, sic emigrabat ut eum per illos dies nemo
extra illum locum uidere posset. in eum autem ipsum locum aditus erat
nemini, nisi qui aut socius aut minister libidinis esse posset. huc omnes
mulieres, quibuscum iste consuerat, conueniebant, quarum incredibile est
quanta multitudo fuerit Syracusis; huc homines digni istius amicitia, digni
uita illa conuiuiisque ueniebant. inter eius modi uiros et mulieres adulta
aetate filius uersabatur, ut eum etiamsi natura a parentis similitudine
abriperet, consuetudo tamen ac disciplina patris similem esse cogeret . . . ac
per eos dies, cum iste cum pallio purpureo talarique tunica uersaretur in
conuiuiis muliebribus, non offendebantur homines neque moleste ferebant
abesse a foro magistratrum, non ius dici, non iudicia fieri; . . . non enim ius
abesse uidebatur a foro neque iudicia, sed uis et crudelitas et bonorum
acerba et indigna direptio.

[18] 2. 5. 35: 'o di immortales! quid interest inter mentes hominum et cogita-
tiones!'
[19] 2. 5. 35: 'sic eos accepti ut me omnium officiorum obstringi religione
arbitrarer!'
[20] ex his ego omnibus rebus, iudices,—ita mihi omnis deos propitios
uelim,—etiamsi mihi iucundissimus est honos populi, tamen nequaquam
capio tantum uoluptatis quantum et sollicitudinis et laboris, ut haec ipsa

This part of the speech is worth considering in some detail because it exemplifies, in a brief compass, the most important themes in Cicero's characterization of Verres throughout the *Verrines*.

First of all, there is the crucial point that Verres is attacked on the basis of his being a bad magistrate. That is his crime, of which all the separate incidents in Sicily and elsewhere are manifestations. This is perhaps too obvious to be worth stating, since he is, after all, on trial for actions committed while he was a magistrate. But it is worth noting that Cicero does not present Verres in relation to a general model of 'how the empire should be run': the whole characterization depends on the assumption that the key figure in imperial government is the individual magistrate, acting as an agent of the Roman people who have elected him. It is on this basis that Cicero can compare Verres directly with himself. The particulars of the aedileship are very different from those of a propraetorship; but they are both magistracies, whose holders should be bound by the *religio omnium officiorum*, the scrupulous care to perform all duties.

This is of course a very vague formulation, since it leaves open how exactly a magistrate should behave. As I argue later, the flexibility inherent in Cicero's imperial model is both a source of oratorical strength, and ultimately a cause of political failure. Here he develops the idea of the bad magistrate in a number of directions.

Verres both is bad, and does bad things. His sexual appetites are deplorable not simply in themselves, but because he is led by them to neglect his duties as a magistrate (camping on the beach all summer when he should be inspecting his province) and to act in ways that are inconsistent with the dignity of Roman magistrates, such as throwing noisy parties. Moreover, sexual desire leads him to pursue respectable women: this is even worse than his consorting with the prostitutes with which Syracuse is so well endowed, since it manifests a particularly deplorable tendency in a Roman magistrate, an inability to keep his hands off provincials' property. This lack of *abstinentia* is particularly prominent in the fourth speech of the second

aedilitas, non quia necesse fuerit, alicui candidato data, sed, quia sic oportuerit, recte conlocata et iudicio populi in loco esse posita uideatur.

hearing, where Verres abuses his position to extract art treasures from hapless Sicilians.

Lust interacts with laziness to produce an anti-*imperator*, giving himself over to hedonism when he should be out, if not on campaign, at least about his duties. Verres' moral weakness is epitomized by his costume: in place of the toga he should be wearing in his civilian capacity, or military garb on campaign, he is wearing a Greek cloak and a long tunic. The implications of this are twofold. On the one hand, Verres is behaving as a Greek (a picture compounded by the presence on the beach of a Rhodian flute-player); in response to the Hellenized environment of Sicily, he is showing signs of going native and as a result is not behaving as a Roman should. But the costume also has overtones of effeminacy in its length—Verres cossets himself rather than exposing himself hardily to the elements;[21] and the hint is strengthened by the next words, *in conuiuiis muliebribus*, 'in a gathering of women'—but the adjective *muliebris*, when used of a man, implies effeminacy.[22] Verres' masculine identity is under threat, and as so often the implication of unrestrained sexual appetites confirms, paradoxically, that his manhood is precariously based.

The implication that Verres is in some sense Greek might seem to be a very effective way of casting doubt on his status as a Roman *imperator*, but in fact Cicero is sparing in his use of this technique. He does exploit the *political* side of easternness at one point, where he likens Verres to a tyrant (2. 3. 76):

[21] Cf. Numanus Remulus' scornful description of the Trojans' costume: 'et tunicae manicas et habent redimicula mitrae' (Virgil, *Aen.* 9. 616), with N. M. Horsfall, 'Numanus Remulus: Ethnography and Propaganda. *Aeneid* 9.598 ff', in *Latomus*, 30 (1971), 1108–16, repr. in S. J. Harrison (ed.), *Oxford Readings in Vergil's Aeneid* (Oxford: Oxford Univ. Press, 1990), 305–15. One of the marks of Catiline's followers, in Cicero's description of them, are their long-sleeved ankle-length tunics: 'quos . . . uidetis, manicatis et talaribus tunicis' (*Cat.* 2. 22). Cf. also A. Lurie, *The Language of Clothes*, 2nd edn. (London: Bloomsbury, 1992), 46 (on the continued wearing of shorts by small boys in Britain), 'Besides, historically, bare knees have always suggested manly toughness: they are associated with the warlike costumes of the ancient Britons, the ancient and modern kilted Scots, empire-building explorers and heroic footballers. To cover them would be a sign of national weakness.'

[22] e.g. *de orat* 3. 41, 'mollis uox aut muliebris'; *Tusc* 2. 15, 'eneruatum muliebremque sententiam'.

In the third year he behaved in a royal manner. They say that the barbarian kings of Persia and Syria usually have a number of wives, who are given towns in this way: this town provides for the wife's girdles, that one for her necklaces, a third for her hair-ornaments. The result is that whole populations do not simply share in the secrets of the king's lusts, they also service them. Now recognize that the unrestrained passions of that man, who called himself king of the Sicilians, operated in the same way.[23]

This passage works because of the opposition it sets up between nasty foreign habits and the implied restraint that a Roman should show, crystallized in the reference to Verres' styling himself a king, that anathema to right-thinking Romans; one can compare the description of Verres' litter in the passage quoted above. Using a litter is arguably already a topos of the bad magistrate; in the *Verrines* passage, it is also linked explicitly with kingship.

Cicero draws attention to Verres' tyrannical behaviour frequently, particularly in the final speech, which is in part concerned with abuse of the judicial process leading to arbitrary execution, an act which is a defining characteristic of a tyrant. By using the model of a tyrant, Cicero can make it absolutely clear to his readers that Verres has overstepped the appropriate limits to his behaviour while avoiding discussing what those limits actually are: a useful move, since it is far from clear that Verres had behaved illegally.

The tyrannical behaviour which Cicero describes in 2. 3. 76 shows that Verres is more than just a bad governor; he is positively a threat to his province. At points Cicero states explicitly that Verres is a *hostis*, an enemy of the state (2. 1. 38; 2. 2. 17; 2. 4. 21; 2. 5. 169), and he even says that he has been worse for Sicily than Hasdrubal and the Carthaginians or Athenio, the leader of the recent slave revolt—the most emotive names which Cicero could come up with for threats to the Roman position in Sicily (2. 3. 125).

Imperator as *hostis* is the ultimate paradox: the job of a

[23] anno tertio uero in hoc agro consuetudine usus est regia. solere aiunt reges barbaros Persarum ac Syrorum pluris uxores habere, his autem uxoribus ciuitates attribuere hoc modo: haec ciuitas mulieri in redimiculum praebeat, haec in collum, haec in crinis. ita populos habent uniuersos non solum conscios libidinis suae, uerum etiam administros. eandem istius, qui se regem Siculorum esse dicebat, licentiam libidinemque fuisse cognoscite.

Roman commander is of course to fight and defeat the enemies
of Rome. It is a conceptually powerful move for Cicero to
make, particularly given that an important plank of Verres'
defence seems precisely to be that he successfully fulfilled the
military side of the job, in comparison to which any irregularities in his civilian administration are unimportant; but to work
well it needs to be related to specific examples which demonstrate Verres' destructiveness, as well as his incompetence.

The longest example is the description of the pirate attack
on Syracuse, during which they sailed into the harbour and
attacked and burnt Roman ships there (2. 5. 80–105). A
particularly striking image is of the pirates' leader acting as
though he were celebrating a triumph (2. 5. 100): 'What a
heart-breakingly painful scene! The glory of the city of Rome,
the good name of the Roman people . . . held up to ridicule by a
pirate galley! A pirate holding a triumph in the harbour of
Syracuse over a fleet of the Roman people, while his bandits'
oars splashed the face of this slothful and wicked praetor.'[24]
The force of this passage, however, is based on Verres' identity
being firmly Roman, since the horror of the attack is that Rome
has been defeated by non-Romans. So Cicero indicates Verres
by the title of the office he holds, *praetor*, and uses the Greek
terms *pirata* and *myoparo* of the pirates. Verres can show
foreign traits in his own dealings with the unfortunate Sicilians,
but the full enormity of his failure as a military commander can
only be made clear if his readers fix their minds firmly on the
fact that Verres is a Roman general.

Comparison with great generals of an earlier period is
another way in which Cicero makes Verres' shortcomings clear.
An example of this is found in the list of qualities of famous
men that Verres does *not* have, in the description of Verres'
military year quoted above (2. 5. 25). Here the greatest military
figures of the past 150 years and their particular strengths act as
a shorthand for all the imperial successes of the period: the
repulse of Hannibal, led by Maximus Cunctator and the elder

[24] 'o spectaculum miserum atque acerbum! ludibiro esse urbis gloriam,
populi Romani nomen, omnium (Peterson) hominum conuentum atque
multitudinem piratico myoparoni! in portu Syracusano de classe populi
Romani triumphum agere piratam, cum praetoris inertissimi nequissimique
oculos praedonum remi respergerent!'

Scipio; the conquest of Greece by Aemilius Paullus; the destruction of Carthage by the younger Scipio; and Marius' defence of Italy against Celtic invasions. Verres is a comprehensive military failure. Elsewhere Cicero makes the point specifically in relation to two men who were assigned Sicily as their province, Marcus Marcellus and, again, the younger Scipio.

Marcellus captured Syracuse during the Second Punic War, and in commemoration set up a festival called the Marcellia. Verres is alleged to have abolished it and set up one in his own honour called the Verria (2. 2. 51–2; 2. 2. 154; 2. 4. 151). The discussion is in the first place designed to provoke the outrage of the audience because of the disparity of services between Marcellus, who was a hero of a heroic period, and Verres. But he takes the comparison in a number of directions to show the scope of Verres' falling off from past standards.

In the first place, Cicero sets up Marcellus and Verres as opposites: Marcellus preserved Syracuse when he had the opportunity to destroy it, whereas Verres has wantonly created havoc (2. 4. 151):

And I will add that the Syracusans would indeed deserve censure if they cut out of their calendar the day of festival celebration made famous and holy by the tradition of its being the actual day of the capture of Syracuse by Marcellus, and observed a festival day commemorating Verres, when Verres had deprived them of everything that the former day of disaster had left them.[25]

Secondly, his actions are an indication of his lack of religious sensibility, since, on Cicero's telling, the unfortunate Syracusans were being compelled to worship someone who had done a great deal to destroy their religious practices through the theft or forced purchase of numinous items (2. 4. 151): 'so that they should hold solemn worship each year for the man who destroyed their religious heritage and took away their

---

[25] etiam hercule illud in Syracusanis merito reprehenderetur, si, cum diem festum ludorum de fastis suis sustulissent celeberrimum et sanctissimum, quod eo ipso die Syracusae a Marcello captae esse dicuntur, idem diem festum Verris nomine agerent, cum iste a Syracusanis quae ille calamitosus dies reliquerat ademisset.
Cf. 2. 51. 6–7.

gods . . .'.[26] And finally, if trivially, Cicero sets up a pun on Verres' name and the verb *uerro*, to sweep up: the festival thus records Verres' most notable characteristic, taking possession of the property of others (2. 2. 52): 'quare appellentur sane ista Verria, quae non ex nomine sed ex manibus naturaque tua constituta esse uideantur'.[27]

Verres does not just fail to come up to the standards of a great Roman: his actions in fact undermine those of Marcellus (2. 4. 115): 'Compare peace under Verres with war under Marcellus: the arrival of a praetor with the victory of a commander, the former's disgusting retinue with the unbeaten army of the latter, lust with self-control; you will conclude that Syracuse was founded by the man who captured it, and captured by the man who received it an ordered state.'[28]

Similar is Cicero's use of Scipio Aemilianus and the statue of Diana he restored to Segesta at the end of the Third Punic War.[29] Cicero puts this in the context of his returning a number of artefacts to Sicilian cities, including the bull of Phalaris to Agrigentum, which allows him to retell a remark made by Scipio to the Agrigentines, asking them to consider whether it was better to be slaves of their own countrymen or obey the Roman people.[30] In the context of Verres' thefts this is clearly ironical: Verres has brought Roman rule to the level of tyranny,

[26] 'ut ei sacra facerent quotannis cuius opera omnium annorum sacra deosque patrios amiserant'.

[27] Puns on *Verres* and *uerrere* also occur at 2. 18–19, 2. 52, and 4. 53. For puns on *uerres*, a domesticated boar, see below. Ridiculous as these puns seem, the Romans' 'speaking' cognomina must have made them seem less forced than they do to us, even if in this case the name is not actually derived from either of the puns. For the use of unflattering names in Roman invective, see A. Corbeill, *Controlling Laughter: Political Humour in the Late Republic* (Princeton: Princeton Univ. Press, 1996), 57–98.

[28] 'conferte hanc pacem cum illo bello, huius praetoris aduentum cum illius imperatoris uictoria, huius cohortem impuram cum illius exercitu inuicto, huius libidines cum illius continentia: ab illo qui cepit conditas, ab hoc qui constitutas accepit captas dicetis Syracusas.'

[29] 2. 4. 72–83. Cicero begins by reminding his audience of the mythical kinship between Rome and Segesta, through Aeneas, which clearly makes Verres' actions even more appalling. This kinship is also used for emotional effect at 5. 125, to increase the pathos of the execution of one of the naval leaders who came from Segesta.

[30] 2. 4. 73: 'dixisse dicitur aequum esse illos cogitare utrum esset Agrigentinis utilius, suisne seruire anne populo Romano obtemperare'.

and undone completely the work of Scipio.[31] This idea is picked up in the Diana episode. Verres behaves in a tyrannical fashion in order to force the Segestans to sell him the statue, and when, reluctantly, they agree to do so Cicero's description of its departure draws an explicit contrast between Scipio and Verres (2. 4. 77): 'What a difference they would observe between now and then! Then a commander of the Roman people, a distinguished man, was bringing back the gods of Segesta from an enemy city to their own home: now a foul and disgusting praetor of the same Roman people was committing the appalling crime of stealing those same gods from an allied city.'[32] Scipio is an *imperator*, acting with religious propriety after a successful military campaign: Verres, a mere praetor of very dubious character, is stealing from an ally of Rome.

Cicero thus sets Verres' shortcomings in a historical framework: his behaviour does not merely have an influence on current events, but marks, so Cicero implies, a drastic change in the nature of Roman behaviour in Sicily since it fell under their sway. Comparison with exemplary figures of the past suggests a further way in which Verres is a bad Roman: he has not taken full account of the actions of the *maiores* (unlike Cicero, whose citation of these figures is proof that he has). And at one point in the third speech Cicero rather unkindly suggests that a contributory factor to Verres' inability to behave properly is his lack of distinguished ancestry (2. 3. 211; he has just said he will use the living figures of Quintus Catulus and Publius Servilius Isauricus as his points of comparison):

Inquire, Hortensius (since you take pleasure in recent examples), what did they do? Well? Quintus Catulus made use of corn, but he did not exact financial contributions; Publius Servilius, who commanded his army for five years (and had he acted like Verres could have made a vast amount of money), decided that he should not do anything which he had not seen his father or his distinguished grandfather Quintus Metellus doing. Will Gaius Verres be revealed as the man who says that one should be permitted to do whatever is advantageous? Who

---

[31] Verres is compared directly to Phalaris, and said to be worse, at 2. 5. 145.

[32] 'quam dissimilis hic dies illi tempori uidebatur! tum imperator populi Romani, uir clarissimus, deos patrios reportabat Segestanis ex urbe hostium recuperatos: nunc ex urbe sociorum praetor eiusdem populi turpissimus atque impurissimus eosdem illos deos nefario scelere auferebat.'

will defend himself by saying he has done what nobody but a scoundrel has done?[33]

Verres was, like Cicero, a new man; Cicero negotiates the potential charge of the pot calling the kettle black by drawing on the character he has set up throughout the second hearing speeches of a man who has a detailed awareness of the past and of its implications for the present. Verres has neither this acquired knowledge, nor the example of his own ancestors; moreover, he is doing Rome a disservice by transmitting his vices to his son. The presence of the younger Verres was one of the many appalling things about the summer beach camp; and in a long disquisition in the third speech (2. 3. 159–62) Cicero muses on Verres' parenting skills: 'You had children not simply for yourself, but also for the fatherland . . . if an energetic, modest, and good son were born from a lazy, shameless, and worthless father, then the state *would* have had something good from you. But now you have supplied the state with a second Verres to take your place . . .'[34] Verres' family life comes across as a sinister parody of the ideal of transmitting family history and achievements on to the next generation.

Verres is, thus, a deplorable failure within a broad historical context. But Cicero also demonstrates that his day-to-day management is deeply unsatisfactory, above all in the way in which he employs and relates to the members of his staff.

Cicero prepares for his use of Verres' followers as means to discredit Verres by arguing that a governor should be responsible for the actions of his *cohors*.

For if we want to be thought to be honest, we need to demonstrate that this is true not simply of us but of our companions too. First we must do our best to take out with us men who will be concerned for

[33] quaere, Hortensi, quoniam te recentia exempla delectant, quid fecerint. itane uero? Q. Catulus frumento est usus, pecuniam non coegit; P. Seruilius quinquennium exercitui cum praeesset et ista ratione innumerabilem pecuniam facere cum posset, non statuit sibi quicquam licere quod non patrem suum, non auum Q. Metellum, clarissimum hominem facere uidisset: C. Verres reperietur qui, quicquid expediat, id licere dicat? quod nemo nisi improbus fecerit, id aliorum exemplo se fecisse defendat?

[34] 'susceperas enim liberos non solum tibi sed etiam patriae . . . esset ex inerti atque improbo et impuro parente nauus et pudens et probus filius, haberet aliquid abs te res publica muneris. nunc pro te Verrem substituisti alterum ciuitati . . .'

our reputation and possible prosecution; secondly, if we make a mistake in our choice of men by relying on friendship, we must make sure that we punish them or dismiss them and always bear in mind that we must provide an account of our behaviour.[35]

While this is not an unreasonable statement, its convenience for a prosecutor is obvious. But Cicero does not restrict himself to describing the wrongdoing of Timarchides and Apronius and ascribing the responsibility to Verres. The characters of the two make Verres' actual association with them shameful.

None of Timarchides' actions is outstandingly horrifying, and few if any were undertaken on his own initiative: his role is consistently that of the faithful assistant.[36] The passage concerning him that is perhaps most damaging to Verres is Cicero's introduction of him (2. 2. 134–6).[37] There are two ways that this passage damages Verres. First, Cicero stresses Timarchides' servile origins and so shows how inappropriately Verres acted in giving him significant powers; second, Cicero describes how Timarchides had power over Verres himself, thus indicating Verres' weakness as well as his cruelty.

2. 134 begins with Cicero offering his audience an explanation for Timarchides' power, so that they should not be surprised by it: clearly they are to see it as something untoward, and it is cited explicitly as evidence for Verres' *nequitia* (2. 2. 134), as well as a *calamitas* for Sicily. He returns to

[35] 2. 2. 28: si enim innocentes existimari uolumus, non solum nos, sed etiam nostros comites praestare debemus. primum omnium opera danda est ut eos nobiscum educamus qui nostrae famae capitique consulant; deinde, si in hominibus eligendis nos spes amicitiae fefellerit, ut uindicemus, missos faciamus, semper ita uiuamus ut rationem reddendam nobis arbitremur.
Cf. D. C. Braund, 'Cohors: The Governor and his Entourage in the Self-Image of the Roman Republic', in R. Laurence and J. Berry (eds.), *Cultural Identity in the Roman Empire* (London: Routledge, 1998).

[36] Carrying of bribes in the trial of Sopater (2. 2. 69–75), and between farmers and Apronius (2. 3. 69); assignation of censors (2. 2. 133); taking money for the building of statues to honour Verres (2. 2. 144); writing a letter of advice to Apronius when Verres had left Sicily (2. 3. 154–63); leading the raiding assault on the temple of Hercules at Agrigentum (2.3.94); accepting bribes during the trial of the naval officers (2. 5. 116–20).

[37] This is not quite the first place Timarchides is mentioned: that is during the description of the trial of Sopater earlier in the second speech. Cicero starts 134 by urging his audience not to be surprised by Timarchides' power: possibly this seemed more effective when examples of this power had already been given.

Timarchides' status and its effects on the island at the end of
the excursus, comparing him to Athenio, the leader of the slave
revolt which terrified Sicily during Verres' tenure as governor.
He sets up, and corrects, the belief that Athenio was a figure
of power at this time: in reality that place was held by
Timarchides (2. 2. 136): 'Understand, therefore, that for these
three years it wasn't Athenio, who didn't capture a single town,
who was in charge, but the runaway Timarchides who held
sway in every town, and that in Timarchides' power were the
children, wives, possessions and money of the oldest and
closest of Rome's allies.'[38] Timarchides is diminished by being
called a runaway (he was of course not even a slave, but a freedman); and, more significantly, Verres appears as a traitor who
has failed to protect women and children, who have as *socii* a
claim on Roman protection from the enemies of Rome. The use
of the slave revolt has particular point, as one of the defences
for his actions that Verres used was that he had protected Sicily
from the threat posed by the slave revolts.

Yet Timarchides is not simply an extension of Verres: in one
important respect he surpasses him. Verres, it seems, suffers
from an unfortunate handicap: he is not very bright (2. 2. 134):
'the only talent that Verres himself had was an insatiable and
ever-present greed: he had no powers of thought or reflection.
The result was that whatever he did at his own direction (as you
know from his behaviour in Rome) seemed to be a matter of
violence rather than trickery.'[39] Timarchides fills this gap. The
way that Cicero describes the relationship between the two is
very reminiscent of the relationship between the hero and the
cunning slave in many Roman comedies, as is the subject
matter, since the objects of Timarchides' plotting are sex and
money.[40] Indeed, it is arguable that the excursus is supposed to

---

[38] 'itaque in Sicilia non Athenionem, qui nullum oppidum cepit, sed
Timarchidem fugitiuum omnibus oppidis per triennium scitote regnasse;
in Timarchidi potestate sociorum populi Romani antiquissimorum atque
amicissimorum liberos, matres familias, bona fortunasque omnis fuisse.'

[39] 'nam ipsum Verrem tantum auaritia semper hiante atque imminente
fuisse, ingenio et cogitatione nulla, ut quicquid sua sponte faciebat, item ut
uos Romae cognouistis, eripere potius quam fallere uideretur.'

[40] A number of words in 134–5 are chiefly found in comedy: e.g. *corruptela*,
callide, *audacter*, *impudenter*, *indagare*, *quadruplator*. Timarchides' care to look
after himself, both financially and sexually, is reminiscent of comic slaves'

Romans in the provinces

39

seem humorous in its emphasis on Verres' lack of dignity and intellect and his reliance on a comic slave-like character, until Cicero abruptly turns to pathos in his remarks about the slave war.

Verres' reliance on Timarchides is thus a sign not only of his unfitness for office and of his capacity to insult Romans, but also of his basic treachery and failure to protect the state. In the case of Apronius, allegedly his ally in the various corn frauds, Cicero's account of the relationship is on the level not of administrative impropriety, but of personal relationship, and hints at deeper and more sordid intimacy (2. 3. 22–3). Similarity of taste has united the two and of course the taste is for vice: 'studiorum turpitudo similitudoque coniunxit' (2. 3. 22). Apronius is portrayed as a disgusting character, and in an extraordinary use of the fiction that the speech was actually delivered, Cicero supports his judgement by reference to Apronius' appearance (2. 3. 23): 'this will be that Apronius, who shows himself not just by his way of life but also through his body and face to be some sort of gross human quagmire or whirlpool full of all kinds of abomination and horror'.[41] Some readers who had been present at the trial might be able to visualize Apronius; others could visualize a foul and disgusting figure.[42] Verres' intimacy with this monstrous figure would be bad enough even if it were restricted to business activities. But Cicero goes further. First he describes friendship (2. 3. 23): 'such was the harmonious union created by the similarity of their characters that Apronius (whom others found an uncouth savage) seemed to Verres alone to be charming and eloquent'.[43]

ability to serve themselves as well as their masters. See further W. Fitzgerald, *Slavery and the Roman Literary Imagination* (Cambridge: Cambridge Univ. Press, 2000), 10–11, 24–6.

[41] 'is erit Apronius ille qui, ut ipse non solum uita sed *corpore atque ore* significat, immensa aliqua uorago est aut gurges uitiorum turpitudinumque omnium.'

[42] As Corbeill, *Controlling Laughter*, 106–12, argues, Apronius' actual appearance, however innocent, could not undermine Cicero's argument since what matters is Cicero's *interpretation* of that face as an index of inner moral corruption. His argument that the chief point of Cicero's remark about Apronius' *os* is to allege that he indulges in oral sex could be taken further, since Cicero makes it quite clear by his stress on the intimacy that existed between Verres and Apronius precisely who Apronius' partner was.

[43] 'tantamque habet morum similitudo coniunctionem atque concordiam ut

This sentence is doubly barbed. If Apronius is a brutal savage, then their alleged similarity makes Verres one too; and since Verres thinks that the monstrous Apronius is nice and cultured, his famed artistic judgement is called into question. Then Cicero moves on to physical intimacy: Verres cannot live without Apronius (2. 3. 23), they use the same cups, Verres thinks that Apronius' smell is pleasant, Apronius is the only person allowed into Verres' bedroom.[44] Cicero concludes with the stock allegation of shamelessness: Apronius danced.[45] To ram home the point, he was naked, and Verres' adolescent son was in the audience: this is the peg for Cicero's consideration of the damage Verres has potentially done the state in producing an *alter Verres*, which I discuss above. Although the passage contains no direct allegations against Verres, he is tarred by association, and his judgement of people, and in particular of appropriate companions for a governor, is shown to be dangerously faulty.

There is a further set-piece excursus which involved both Timarchides and Apronius. This is the discussion of the letter of advice about dealing with the new governor that Timarchides sent to Apronius (2. 3. 154–7).[46] The letter is open

Apronius, qui aliis inhumanus ac barbarus, isti uni commodus ac disertus uideretur.'

[44] Even wild animals cannot stand Apronius' smell, apparently (2. 3. 23): thus Verres is below them on the scale of discernment. There may also be an oblique reference to the pun on Verres' name: this particular domestic animal doesn't have as acute a sense of smell as its wild counterparts. For a discussion of the belief that foul breath can imply participation in oral sex, see W. A. Krenkel, '*Fellatio* and *Irrumatio*', *Wissenschaftliche Zeitschrift der Wilhelm-Pieck-Universität Rostock*, 29 (1980), 77–88, esp. 80–1.

[45] For dancing as a conventional charge in invective, see R. G. M. Nisbet, *In Pisonem* (Oxford: Oxford Univ. Press, 1961), 78–9.

[46] The fragments quoted form a coherent whole if put together in the order they are given:

Timarchides Verris accensus salutem dicit. fac diligentiam adhibeas, quod ad praetoris existimationem attinet. habes uirtutem, eloquentiam; habes sumptum unde facias. scribas, apparitores recentis arripe; cum L. Volteio, qui plurimum potest, caede, concide. uolo, mi frater, fraterculo tuo credas. in cohorte carus habebere. quod cuique opus est, oppone. te postulante omnes uincere solent. scis Metellum sapientem esse. si Volteium habebis, omnia ludibundus conficies. inculcatum est Metello et Volteio te aratores euertisse. obtuderunt eius auris te socium praetoris fuisse. fac sciat improbitatem aratorum; ipsi sudabunt, si di uolunt.

However, at 2. 3. 159 Cicero says that Timarchides referred to Metellus' son, in its exhortation to Apronius to get into favour with the new governor, and simply presenting it is a coup for Cicero. But nothing in it is criminal, and even the reference to Apronius' being responsible for the farmers' sufferings admits nothing, and could easily be read as the sort of problem that any administration could run into.[47] In order to make the most of this document, Cicero has to interlard his quotations with remarks of his own.

One effect is to reinforce the characterizations of Apronius and Timarchides. Cicero draws attention to Timarchides' status: he is an *accensus*, an attendant, and Cicero compares this to a *scriba*, thus drawing attention to the fact that Timarchides had no official position (and suggesting that Verres was wrong to entrust so much to someone of Timarchides' standing) (2. 3. 154). The contempt is reinforced when Cicero asks why the privilege of mentioning one's status should not also be extended to lictors and messengers. Timarchides is to be viewed merely as one of the minor members of the governor's household. Apronius appears as an entirely confident embezzler, to the extent that Cicero suggests that it is ridiculous for Timarchides to give any instructions at all to him.

A second impression that Cicero is trying to create in this passage is that Verres was controlled by these two. In particular, Cicero suggests that Timarchides assumes that the new governor can be controlled because Verres could be manipulated (2. 3. 156): 'Timarchides is making a serious mistake here, both in thinking that Volteius is venal and that Metellus' administration is under the control of any one person. But the error arises from his own experience: since he has seen that many people made a fool of Verres, directly or through intermediaries, he thinks that the same tactics will work with all magistrates.'[48] *Ludibundos* is the key term. Timarchides used it in his letter, where it seems to be used adverbially to mean so part of the letter is omitted, probably because Cicero did not want to repeat lewd suggestions about the younger Metellus.

[47] Cf. Cicero's letter to his brother on how to govern Asia (*ad Q. fr.* 1. 1).

[48] 'hic uehementer errat Timarchides, qui aut Volteium pecunia corrumpi putet posse, aut Metellum unius arbitratu gerere praeturam, sed errat coniectura domestica. quia multos et per se et per alios multa ludibundos apud Verrem effecisse uidit, ad omnis eosdem patere aditus arbitratur.'

'without difficulty'.[49] But in the new context, much more stress is placed on the connection with *ludere* and its meaning 'to treat without seriousness' or 'to trick' or 'to make fun of'.[50] And it is not just Timarchides and Apronius who have used Verres in this way: many have been able to exploit his weaknesses.

A third, related, point is the comparison between Verres and his successor Metellus. Metellus is not vulnerable in the way that Verres was, and so Timarchides' advice is fundamentally misconceived. The comparison is particularly impressive because Cicero openly acknowledges that he has good reason not to like Metellus. By extending the range of acceptable governors to include someone who, on Cicero's telling, obstructed his inquiries in order to secure Verres' acquittal, he demonstrates quite how far outside acceptable behaviour Verres was as governor.

Cicero's discussion of Verres' henchmen has a number of functions. Most obviously, Verres' dealings with his *cohors* is a practical example of his unfitness to be a Roman magistrate, inasmuch as he has put in positions of responsibility and power individuals who are patently unfit to hold them. Yet, because he talks only about undistinguished members of the entourage—Timarchides a freedman, Apronius a citizen, indeed, but simply a tax-collector—Cicero can fill in Verres' background and working habits in a realistic way, while skating over the question of what other Romans might have played a part in Verres' activities. More senior members of his staff, above all his quaestors and legates, are seldom mentioned, and then, often, simply in order to show their innocence and lack of involvement in what Verres was up to. Failure to use the subordinates appointed to him through election and then sortition is an indication of Verres' unsatisfactory use of his staff; and by making it clear that his quaestors were not involved Cicero can avoid making any further enemies among young and potentially rising politicians.

The mechanics of Verres' relationship with Apronius and Timarchides also show that he is stupid and uncultured, unable to perceive their viciousness and open to manipulation: he is not even fully in control of such subordinates as he chooses to

---

[49] Normally the word is used literally: its meaning in Timarchides' letter may well be colloquial.   [50] *OLD, ludere*, 9.

use. And their prominence also enables Cicero to structure his characterization of Verres as a gradual revelation of his vices. The first speech of the second hearing, which covers Verres' career up until his period in Sicily, naturally deals with a range of crimes; but once Cicero has turned to Sicily, he structures his material as a movement from dry and technical crimes, corruption in the courts and in the management of the corn supply, to the more emotive subjects of religious theft and vandalism and then on to disregard for Rome's military glory and finally judicial murder of Roman citizens. Verres' viciousness really only becomes apparent in the fourth and fifth speeches; up to that point, he has been in the background as the figure ultimately responsible, but Cicero has refrained from dwelling on the gory details and such 'human interest' as he does give is provided by lesser figures such as Apronius and Timarchides, or in the litany of Verres' victims.

The result of this is to make the monstrous Verres of the later speeches into a credible figure, since the way has been prepared for him by the characterization of his subordinates. Moreover, Cicero maintains the style appropriate to a forensic speech. Early in the second *actio*, when he starts his survey of Verres' life, he says (2. 1. 32–3): 'and so I shall pass over the horribly foul and immoral first part of his life. He won't hear anything from me about the sins of his childhood and his disgusting adolescence . . . as far as I am concerned all that period of time before he became a magistrate and entered public life can remain untouched and unscrutinized.'[51] Treatment of someone's youth is a standard part of invective,[52] and Cicero is here deliberately putting down a generic marker, reminding his readers that this is a forensic speech and not invective. The implication is that Cicero will concentrate on facts, and will tell the truth: a move that it is particularly important he should make, given that much of the second hearing is, in effect, invective both in style and likely truth value, and that it would never be tested in a court.

---

[51] 'itaque primum illum actum istius uitae turpissimum et flagitiosissimum praetermittam. nihil a me de pueritiae suae flagitiis audiet, nihil ex illa impura adulescentia sua . . . omne illud tempus quod fuit antequam iste ad magistratus remque publicam accessit, habeat per me solutum ac liberum.'

[52] Cf. *Cael.* 6–9; 2nd *Phil.* 44 ff.

Cicero attacks Verres in a wide variety of ways, because he is drawing on a whole range of beliefs about the desirable behaviour of a Roman magistrate while outside Italy and showing that Verres does not fulfil any of the criteria. He has failed in his duties to the Roman people, most notably the military ones; he has failed to behave towards the people of Sicily as he should; and he has failed in the much broader sense of being a good Roman, maintaining appropriate standards of morality and decorum.

The positive model of the good governor is, of course, riddled with contradictions, since the interests of provincials and of Roman citizens living in the same area often conflict: a happy tax-collector implies an unhappy provincial, and vice versa. And this is quite apart from rivalry among Romans themselves as to the exploitation of overseas territory. These are problems fundamental to Rome's use of the territory over which it had authority, to its imperialism. In dealing with Verres Cicero is in general able to avoid these problems; Verres is brutal and unjust to everyone, thus overriding any potential contested areas; and this is presented as the result of his own viciousness, rather than unavoidable friction in the system.

One area, however, in which there are interesting signs of tension in what Cicero says is in his manipulation of ideas of ethnic identity. As I discussed above, Verres is shown at times behaving in a Greek or more generally an eastern way: the climax, in a slightly illogical way, of his inability to be a proper Roman. And the force of this manoeuvre is obvious, playing with fears that a Roman, once geographically divorced from the city whence he derives his identity, may cease to display that identity in his behaviour: in short, that he may 'go native'. In the rest of this chapter I explore other occasions when Cicero makes use of the tactic, and its ultimate expression of the fear is arguably in the anxieties about the extent of Pompeius' ambitions in the East should he be given the command against Mithradates, which Cicero attempts to counter in the speech *de imperio Cn. Pompei*. But in the *Verrines* it is remarkable how cautious Cicero is in playing with ideas about Greek identity. This is particularly striking when he is talking about Verres' art theft. One might imagine that an effective strategy would be to portray Verres as a sinister and greedy connoisseur, pillaging valuables in order to furnish a suitable background for his easternized luxury. And Cicero does at the beginning of the fourth speech set up Verres as someone with specialized know-ledge—in contrast, of course, with Cicero who barely knows the names of the artists. In particular, Verres is contemptuous of those who are not experts (2. 4. 4): 'at Heius' house there was a shrine . . . where there were four beautiful and highly artistic statues, capable of giving pleasure not only to Verres' expert taste but also to any of us whom he calls amateurs'.[53] Verres' alleged use of the Greek term (*idiotas*) sets up an opposition between him and his Greek, snobbish knowledge, and Cicero and the audience (note *nostrum*) who don't know about art but know what they like. Moreover, Cicero suggests that Verres' knowledge is pointless, because even without it one can appre-ciate the statues. Subsequently Cicero has his cake and eats it, by implying that although Verres lays claim to this dubious foreign knowledge, he is in fact a philistine. So at 2. 4. 33 he acknowledges how surprised he was that Verres knew any-thing about art, as this would imply some degree of humanity: but then he realized that it was for this reason that Verres employed two craftsmen from Cibyra, to be his eyes (while he provided the hands): thus Verres' only interest is in acquisition. This idea is reinforced when Cicero tells an anecdote about a censer: Verres 'borrowed' it, and sent it back minus its embossed decorations. As a result, Cicero remarks sarcasti-cally, the audience can see that 'in homine intellegentiam esse non auaritiam, artifici cupidum non argenti fuisse' (2. 4. 46).[54] The overall effect is not to suggest that Verres has 'gone native', but to draw mocking attention to his inability to do so.[55]

[53] 'erat apud Heium sacrarium . . . in quo signa pulcherrima quattuor summo artificio, summa nobilitate, quae non modo istum hominem ingeniosum et intellegentem, uerum etiam quemuis nostrum, quos iste idiotas appellat, delectare possent'.

[54] 'The man is knowledgeable, not greedy, and his passion was for art and not silver'. A similar story is told about the doors of the temple of Minerva at Syracuse: Verres removed various ivory carvings and golden knobs, destroy-ing it as an aesthetic object and showing his interest was in gain rather than art (2. 4. 125).

[55] There may be a jibe about nationality involved when Cicero uses tragic imagery to describe Verres' greed for art treasures, and likens him to Eriphyle (who betrayed her husband because of her desire for a necklace) (2. 4. 39).

Stirring up hostility to Verres by suggesting he behaves in a Greek manner depends ultimately on Roman prejudices against Greeks. And one of the reasons that Cicero is so cautious in playing this card in the *Verrines* is that he does not want to diminish the jurors' sympathy for Verres' Sicilian victims, who were, of course, Greek. In the various cases where Cicero was defending a magistrate accused of extortion, jeopardizing the jurors' sympathy for the provincials was one of his aims;[56] and in connection with the *pro Flacco* I examine the way he uses hostility against Greeks to attack the Romans who were opposed to Flaccus.

However, maintaining the jurors' sympathy for the unfortunate Sicilians may not be the only reason why Cicero eschews the ethnic card on this occasion. One factor may have been that Cicero himself was perceived, in 70, as so strong a devotee of Greek culture that it would have been imprudent to have attacked anyone else on those grounds. He seems to have been remarkable as a young man for his devotion to Greek culture, even among the increasingly Hellenized Romans of the late Republic. His fluency in Greek was exceptional: he trained by declaiming in Greek as well as Latin at Rome, and Plutarch tells a sententious anecdote about the response of Apollonius when he declaimed in Greek at Rhodes: Greece's last remaining glories, eloquence and culture, were now also going to be the possession of Rome.[57] This last took place during Cicero's extended tour of Athens and Asia Minor, which may have attracted attention for its odd position in his career, when he was in his late twenties and had already made his debut in the Forum. To this can be added his translation of Greek poetry and the fact that Diodotus, a Greek philosopher, resided with him permanently from the mid-80s.[58] Plutarch

Verres is even more inflamed with desire than she, because she had seen the object of her desire, whereas he had only heard of it. But arguably the emphasis lies in the fact that Eriphyle is a woman: his madness may be tragic, but it is not heroic.

[56] Vasaly, *Representations*, 191–205.

[57] Declamation at Rome: Cicero, *Brutus* 310. Rhodes: Plutarch, *Cicero* 4. 4–6.

[58] Neither in writing poetry nor in having a tame philosopher was Cicero unique (see J. P. V. D. Balsdon, *Romans and Aliens* (London: Duckworth, 1979, 54–8)), but both were clear signals of his cultural preferences.

records that he was called 'the Greek' on his return from Asia Minor.

So for Cicero to have attacked Verres extensively for his Greek habits could have laid him open to the charge of the pot calling the kettle black. Even more pertinent is the fact that Cicero might have been vulnerable to specific charges of excessive Hellenism based on his own actions in Sicily. He had been very popular with the Sicilians while quaestor, which could have been turned into a charge of inappropriate familiarity,[59] and a competent orator could have turned his rediscovery of the tomb of Archimedes in the company of the leading men of Agrigentum into a damaging episode.[60] Cicero himself describes how he was rebuked by Metellus for addressing the senate at Syracuse in Greek while collecting evidence against Verres.[61] This was not the best case in which to seek to cast others as Greek Romans.

The most important factor, however, in Cicero's decision not to exploit fears about ethnic identity to the full was probably his perception of what was appropriate to a forensic case. Verres was charged with crimes committed as a Roman magistrate, and so it is as a Roman magistrate that he need be judged: to cast doubt on this aspect of his identity too thoroughly would ultimately detract from the seriousness of his offences.

1.2. PISO AND GABINIUS

I turn now to Cicero's characterization of Piso and Gabinius in the speech *de prouinciis consularibus*. I want to consider here how he attacks both men as bad holders of *imperium*: I shall turn to the wider political ramifications of his invective in Chapters 3 and 4.

Piso is presented in the *prou. cons.* as a militarily dangerous

---

[59] The very fact of Cicero's prosecution could have been presented as evidence for his hostility to Rome: cf. his treatment of Laelius in the *pro Flacco*.

[60] Cicero's self-congratulatory account of the episode is at *Tusculans* 5. 64–6.

[61] 2. 4. 147. The reason Cicero refers to the Syracusan senate is to explain the awkward fact that they at first passed a decree in praise of Verres. Their change of mind, combined with the bronze tablet in honour of Cicero and his cousin Lucius, could have been presented as proof that Cicero had bribed them.

figure. He has destroyed a Roman army (5); he has brought an end to the peace that Macedonia enjoyed (5); and his depredations in Byzantium were worse than those caused by Mithradates (6–7).[62] The mention of Mithradates is particularly pointed. It picks up that of Hannibal in 4, where Cicero says that the effects of the consulships of Piso and Gabinius have been worse for the city of Rome than the invasion of Hannibal. Piso is thus lined up with the greatest of all Rome's enemies as well as a particularly feared recent menace: he is to be seen as one of Rome's external enemies.

This portrayal is neatly reinforced by Cicero's use of 'just war' vocabulary. In a reversal of the normal self-justifying rhetoric which made all of Rome's wars *bella iusta*, the Thracians' attacks have become *prope iustum* as a response to Piso's exactions.[63] His use of *iustum* in 6 to describe the hatred felt towards Piso by the provincials is surely connected to this. Piso is so far from the behaviour to be expected from a governor that provincial disloyalty becomes not only understandable but also almost to be condoned:[64] and the repetition of *iustum* may suggest that he is close to provoking a military response from the provincials, a much more serious prospect than border clashes, and one that reinforces the idea that Piso is an enemy of Rome. As such, war on him is just war, even if undertaken by Rome's enemies.

There are two further aspects to Cicero's characterization of Piso as a non-Roman. One is the ascription of tyrannical characteristics. He is cruel (8), he does not heed legal restrictions on his powers (6), his sexual appetites are so violent that women have killed themselves by jumping down wells to avoid his lust (6).[65] These are clearly in general contrast to the

---

[62] Cicero describes Piso's activities in language which emphasizes their hostile nature: *uexare, hostilem in modum, spoliare, nudare.*

[63] Admittedly, Cicero softens the paradox with *prope*: presumably he felt the need to tread carefully between attacking Piso and undermining Roman military legitimacy. Brunt, *Laus*, 172, interprets slightly differently: 'Whatever the provocation they had received, foreign peoples which attacked Rome could at best be said to wage a *bellum prope iustum* (*de prov cons* 4)'. On the concept of the just war, see Brunt, *Laus*, 175–8; S. Albert, *Bellum Iustum* (Kallmünz: Lassleben, 1980).

[64] Cicero again hedges himself, on this occasion with *paene.*

[65] On Cicero's use of the figure of the tyrant in his speeches, cf. V. Buch-

constitutional behaviour and self-restraint which a Roman should display: both on an institutional and a moral level tyrannical behaviour is to be deplored.

The second point to be made is how Cicero presents Piso as enamoured of Greek culture. The context is that Cicero is offering ironical congratulations to Piso on his failure to send dispatches, which have saved him, unlike Gabinius, from the humiliation of having his request for a *supplicatio* turned down:[66] 'this other one [sc. Piso] is either himself more educated and has been trained by his Greeks more carefully (he now revels in gluttony with them in full view, whereas beforehand he did it behind a curtain) . . .'.[67] This brief comment should be seen in the context of Cicero's extensive abuse of Piso between his return from exile and the delivery of this speech, which survives in the speech of thanks to the Senate on his return and in the defence of Sestius. By drawing on the material in these speeches, the audience could flesh out Cicero's allusions here to Piso's adherence to Epicurean doctrines. However, there is a twist. Cicero does not make being an Epicurean on its own into the grounds for invective. Piso's problem, as is made clear in other speeches, is that his is a radically over-simplified Epicureanism: he thinks that all it means is pleasure. The use of *helluor* is this passage should be taken as a reference to the gross indulgence of bodily appetites which, in Cicero's lurid account, comprises Piso's 'philosophy', and *sui Graeci* indicates his resident philosopher Philodemus.

Cicero uses anti-Greek feeling in building up his attack on

heit, 'Chrysogonus als Tyrann in Ciceros Rede für Roscius aus America', *Chiron*, 5 (1975), 193–211.

[66] Cicero turns next in the speech to demolishing a precedent for the refusal, that which Titus Albucius, governor in Sardinia in 105–104, suffered. This was a very convenient analogy for Cicero: Albucius had been a noted Epicurean, and Cicero describes him as 'a light-weight Greek fellow' (15). It is easy for the audience to read this back both to Gabinius, the formal object of the comparison, and to Piso, whose character and interests are closer to those of Albucius. On Albucius, see N. Petrochilos, *Roman Attitudes to the Greeks* (Athens: Ethnikon kai Kapodistriakon Panepistemion Athenon, 1974), 163–4, and E. D. Rawson, *Intellectual Life in the Late Roman Republic* (London: Duckworth, 1985), 6–7.

[67] 14: 'ille alter aut ipse est homo doctus et a suis Graecis subtilius eruditus, quibuscum iam in exostra helluatur, antea post siparium solebat . . .'. The use of theatrical imagery adds to the shamefulness of Piso's behaviour.

Piso, but the overwhelming impression of his character is not
one of Hellenic over-refinement, but barbarian excess, of a misinterpretation of Greek culture. And Cicero confirms this by
referring to Piso's maternal ancestry. In the *prou. cons.* (7) this
simply involves addressing Piso by the name *Caesoninus
Calventius*: but the alert reader or listener would recall Piso's
grandfather, whom Cicero elsewhere presents as a Transalpine
Gaul.[68] He combines traits from both ends of the ethnic
spectrum: these do not cancel each other out, but serve to
demonstrate how far Piso is from the old-fashioned Roman his
stern appearance seems to indicate.[69]

     Gabinius, by contrast, is a much more straightforwardly
eastern creation. Cicero leaves no doubt about this when he
introduces him not by name but as *Semiramis illa* (9), a
reference to the legendary Assyrian queen.[70] This is a brilliantly damaging insult: the comparison to an eastern woman
suggests that Gabinius is not a proper man and not a proper
Roman. The charge of effeminacy can be fleshed out by recollection of what Cicero says about Gabinius in the *post reditum
in Senatu* and the *pro Sestio*, particularly the description of him
as a dancer and of the care he takes with his hairstyle.[71] He is set
up as someone who does not display his masculinity correctly,
and this serves to undermine his fitness as a Roman magistrate.
The charge of nationality is closely fitted to Gabinius' circumstances, since his province was Syria, and Syria and Assyria
seem to have been confused, or assimilated to each other, in
geographical thought.[72] Semiramis, the most famous Assyrian
woman, was the obvious choice for a comparison which would
not only question Gabinius' qualities as a Roman commander,
but also raise the insidious fear that he had fallen a victim to the
effeminizing East.

     These considerations alone may explain Cicero's choice.
However, further details of the myth can be fruitfully linked

---

[68] *red. sen.* 15. For Calventius, see Nisbet, *In Pisonem*, 53–4.

[69] See Corbeill, *Controlling Laughter*, 169–73, on the difficulties which
Piso's appearance caused Cicero when constructing his invective.

[70] See *LIMC* 7/1: 726.

[71] He is a *calamistratus saltator* (*red. sen.* 13) and the marks of the curling
tongs can be seen on his forehead (*red. sen.* 16); cf. also *pro Sestio* 18.

[72] See Strabo 2. 1. 31 (Semiramis described as a Syrian) and 16. 1. 1–2 (for
the geographical scope of the names).

with Gabinius' situation, or rather how Cicero may want his audiences to perceive Gabinius' situation. The two key facts about Semiramis were, first, her passion for lovers; and secondly, the story that she tricked Ninus into letting her rule for five days, and had him killed during that time so that she could continue as sole ruler. The former, in its suggestion of sexual licence and passivity, can be seen as a straightforward piece of invective, but the second aspect of Semiramis' career is more pointed. Gabinius, a new man like Cicero, owed his entire rise to Pompeius' patronage. Now that he has reached a position of power and autonomy, what will he do? Will he turn against Pompeius, as Semiramis turned against Ninus? Can he be trusted, or is he likely to turn against his erstwhile mentor? This allusion thus makes Gabinius untrustworthy in addition to his other un-Roman traits.

Cicero's stereotyping of Jews and Syrians is much less sophisticated and complex than that relating to the Greeks. He describes them simply as 'nations born to servitude'.[73] However, he relates Gabinius to this crude formulation with considerable skill. Even before he has made it, he likens Gabinius to a Thracian mercenary whom the Cappadocian king Ariobarzanes has hired (9), and places foremost among his activities as a commander in Syria 'the striking of financial agreements with tyrants'.[74] Piso was a tyrant: Gabinius is the servant of tyrants. In itself this is a damaging charge against a Roman general, who should, almost by definition, be giving the orders.[75] But it also fits neatly with the character of the Syrians and Jews. They are born to servitude: Gabinius, it seems, has acquired it.

Gabinius, therefore, behaves with inappropriate servility when dealing with non-Romans. This is balanced (or rather exacerbated) by his inappropriate savagery towards the tax-collectors. His 'greed, arrogance, and cruelty' (11) have, according to Cicero, brought them to the brink of financial ruin. He expands this observation with the reflection that when tax-collectors are unable to collect taxes because of enemy

[73] 10: 'nationibus natis seruituti'.

[74] 9: 'pactiones pecuniarum cum tyrannis'.

[75] J. S. Richardson, '*Imperium Romanum*. Empire and the Language of Power', *JRS* 81 (1991), 1–9.

⏎ 52 — *Romans in the provinces*

activity, they are protected by the censorial law (12): so 'isn't it right to help when they have been prevented from gathering taxes by someone who is a public enemy, even if he isn't called that?'[76] Gabinius, like Piso, is presented as a *hostis*.[77]

Cicero's attacks on Piso and Gabinius are short and allusive: they are most effective if read against his slightly fuller remarks in earlier speeches. And in the *prou. cons.* his invective has a very specific point. It is not simply a case, as in the speech to the Senate on his return, of demonstrating that he has regained the political stature to say monumentally offensive things about senior politicians. He has set up his analysis of which provinces should be given to the consuls of 55 in terms of there being four provinces only under discussion: the two Gauls, Syria and Macedonia. Having done this, he can preserve the Gauls for Caesar by showing that both Syria and Macedonia need new governors.[78]

As a result, the abuse is centred on the incapacity of these two men as officials: there is much less on their private vices than in the other speeches. Gabinius' effeminacy, for example, is referred to only through the allusive name Semiramis, and Piso's voluptuously ignorant pursuit of Greek philosophy is dealt with similarly briefly. The chief charge against Piso here is his allegedly dismal military record, and against Gabinius his hostility to the tax-farmers. But in both cases, their behaviour is presented as the result of depravity and not of incompetence or ignorance. It then becomes easy for the audience to connect their moral failure with inability to behave like Romans: they have allowed their physical distance from Rome to be mirrored by a distance in behaviour, and this confirms their unfitness to continue to act on behalf of Rome.

[76] 'quem is frui non sinit qui est, etiam si non appellatur, hostis, huic ferri auxilium non oportet?'

[77] On Gabinius' relations with the *publicani* see D. C. Braund, 'Gabinius, Caesar, and the *publicani* of Judaea', *Klio*, 65 (1983), 241–4; R. S. Williams, '*Rei publicae causa*: Gabinius' Defense of his Restoration of Ptolemy Auletes', *CJ* 81 (1985), 25–38.

[78] See Ch. 4 for a more detailed analysis of Cicero's strategy and aims in this speech.

1.3. THE *PRO FLACCO*

In preparing his defence of Flaccus, Cicero may have felt that he was being hoist with his own petard. The enthusiasm and care with which the chief prosecutor, Decimus Laelius, had gathered his evidence must have been reminiscent of Cicero's own diligence when preparing his case against Verres some ten years earlier: and Laelius could present himself as a young man taking on the establishment even more strongly than Cicero had done, being at the conventional age to undertake a high-profile prosecution and opposed not by one but by the two leading advocates of the day.[79] And in his speech, to judge by Cicero's response, he went back to Flaccus' career before the contested governorship, dealing with his life from his youth onwards, just as Cicero had spent one-fifth of the *Second Hearing* against Verres lambasting his behaviour as a legate in Asia Minor and then as urban praetor.[80] Cicero faced an ironically arduous task in defending Flaccus.

His response is, as it were, to fight fire with fire. For the most part he does not defend Flaccus' actions or seek to argue that he did not do what he is accused of having done: he tries to discredit the evidence as a whole by attacking the witnesses' credibility and the actions of the prosecution. Flaccus himself is hardly mentioned during most of the speech, since the treatment of the charges is based on arguing that the witnesses to them are either congenitally untrustworthy or have personal grudges against Flaccus which undermine their testimony. When Cicero does make him the centre of attention, as happens in the introduction (1–5) and conclusion (94–106), he is presented as a man intimately connected with the safety of the Roman state: he is its saviour, because of his part in suppressing the Catilinarian conspiracy, and the current prosecution is to be seen as a political attack by those who sympathized with Catiline.[81] To emphasize Flaccus' role in the events of 63 is a

[79] Hortensius also defended Flaccus at this trial: *Flacc.* 41, 54.

[80] On the background to the speech, see the commentaries of T. B. L. Webster, *Pro Flacco* (Oxford: Oxford Univ. Press, 1931), and A. Du Mesnil, *Ciceros Rede für Flaccus* (Leipzig, 1883), and the account by Classen, *Recht*, 180–217.

[81] Note the beginning to the peroration (94. 13–15): 'but why do I waste my time arguing about Falcidius' letters and Sextilius Andro and Decianus'

high-risk strategy for Cicero to use, given the unpopularity of the executions with many and Cicero's own precarious position as a result.[82] And he does not rely simply on his skill in restating the danger to the state in an emotionally compelling way, but supports his presentation of the prosecution as an attack on the state by characterizing two of the prosecutors as bad Romans, who can therefore be expected to act contrary to the interests of the state. A central feature of the un-Romanness is the possession of Greek traits which the audience is to understand as the result of the time they have spent in Asia Minor. They have been corrupted by association with non-Romans.

In contrast with the neglect of Cicero's techniques of characterization of the prosecution, the stereotyping of the Greek witnesses from Asia Minor has received considerable attention.[83] However, I have not found any treatment which pays due attention to the flexibility of Cicero's use of stereotypes to attack the Greeks. Yet the effectiveness of Cicero's characterization in this speech depends in large part on his ability to suit the stereotype exactly to his argumentative strategy. Before considering Decianus and Laelius, I shall show how he moulds his presentation of the Greeks themselves.

In 62–6 Cicero sets the prosecution's use of evidence from Greeks from Asia Minor against testimony favourable to Flaccus from Athens, Sparta, other parts of mainland Greece and Massilia, in order to salvage this evidence from the apparently blanket condemnations of Greeks that he had made earlier in the speech. However, this is more than a technique which allows him to have his cake and eat it in respect of evidence: it also reinforces the contempt that Cicero has already expressed for the Greeks of Asia Minor by invoking the authority of mainland Greece.

census rating, and say nothing about the safety of all of us, the destiny of the state and the most fundamental affairs of state?' For Flaccus' part in suppressing the conspiracy (he helped to arrest the Allobroges' envoys) see Broughton, *MRR* 2. 167.

[82] See E. S. Gruen, 'The Trial of C. Antonius', *Latomus*, 32 (1973), 301–10, for the difficulties Cicero had in defending Antonius earlier in the year.

[83] This aspect seems to have struck Quintilian most strongly too: his sole reference to this speech occurs in a passage where he praises Cicero's technique in attacking provincial witnesses (*Institutio oratoria* 11. 1. 89). Vasaly, *Representations*, 198–205, provides modern bibliography.

He does this by offering a carefully constructed account of past Greek history in 64 which shows that Asia Minor is not inhabited by real Greeks, and in fact has been subject to mainland Greece. He begins with an idiosyncratic view of the division of the Greeks into three races (64): 'and does anyone, who has taken the care to know a bit about this subject, not know that there are in fact three races of Greeks? One of these is the Athenians, which was considered to be the Ionian race, and the other two were called the Aeolians and the Dorians.'[84] The threefold division is a commonplace: the oddity lies in the prominence given to the Athenians, who are indeed normally regarded as *part* of the Ionians, but not as its entirety. Cicero's point is surely that since Athenians and Ionians are coterminous, anyone who claims to be an Ionian and is not an Athenian is not an Ionian, and thus not a Greek. And as the inhabitants of Asia Minor were for the most part non-Athenian Ionians this typology means none of them are Greek, and they are thus conveniently excluded from the glory that was Greece that Cicero goes on to describe.[85] Indeed, one of the achievements of Greece was the subjugation of Asia (64): 'the whole of Greece—this Greece—was pre-eminent in reputation, glory, learning, many skilled occupations and even in the extent of its empire and its military fame, and as you know holds and has always held a small part of Europe. It conquered the coastal strip of Asia in war and built cities there, not so that it could rule Asia by means of colonies, but in order to hold it in a state of siege.'[86] It seems clear that Cicero is implying that relations between mainland Greece and Asia remained hostile after the

---

[84] 'quamquam quis ignorat, qui modo umquam mediocriter res istas scire curauit, quin tria Graecorum genera sint uere? quorum uni sunt Athenienses, quae gens Ionum habebatur, Aeolis alteri, Doris tertii nominabantur.'

[85] The name 'Ionian' was potentially a problem for Cicero, since its derivation from a district of Asia Minor increased the implausibility of his analysis. While he does not address this issue, he has already emphasized that the Athenians are autochthonous (62), and thus rules out in advance the possibility that they came originally from Asia Minor.

[86] 'atque haec cuncta Graecia, quae fama, quae gloria, quae doctrina, quae plurimis artibus, quae etiam imperio et bellica laude floruit, paruum quendam locum, ut scitis, Europae tenet semperque tenuit, Asiae maritimam oram bello superatam cinxit urbibus, non ut munitam coloniis illam †gentem† (Bχc; augeret b¹k; generaret Σ; gubernaret i, Stangl; constringeret Clark), sed ut obsessam teneret.'

initial period of colonization, and that the hinterland remained Asian.[87] This small ethnographical digression also sets contempt for and domination of Asian Greeks in a historical context: the Romans are not the only people to feel and act in this way, which adds justification to their behaviour. Cicero makes it clear, by prefacing the fact of the conquest of the Greeks with a list of their achievements, that it was an admirable act on their part, which should in turn reinforce the audience's readiness to support Cicero's earlier division of the Greeks into good and bad. The Greeks who conquered were not only, in this account, culturally superior (their normal favourable profile): they were also militarily competent, which is an unexpected quality to find in a Roman description of Greeks. They are fitting precursors of Rome.

Cicero's manipulation of ethnic identity does not stop here, since he proceeds to switch back to treating the Asian Greeks as Greeks. He quotes various Greek proverbs about Phrygians, Carians, Mysians which emphasize their servility and worthlessness and observes that in Greek comedy the chief slave is often Lydian. Then, by merging the two types of Greek back together he says that the Asians condemn themselves (65. 24–6): 'And so, what offence can you take if we use *your* judgements to make up *our* minds about *you*?'[88] Another example of a Greek being distinguished favourably from other Greeks occurs in 31, where Cicero cites the death of a certain Atyanas at the hands of the pirates as evidence that Flaccus did need his fleet. In this case, however, Cicero cannot invoke differences between Greeks from different places: Atyanas came from Adramytium on the coast of Mysia, and although Cicero does not mention this explicitly it would be clear even to listeners

---

[87] Du Mesnil, *Flaccus*, 157. It is not clear whether Cicero is referring to the period of Greek colonization, or to the Delian league/Athenian empire: but that hardly matters. All he needs to establish in his audience's minds is a vague recollection that Asia Minor was, at some point in the past, subject to the Greek mainland (or part of it). On Asia and Attica, cf. C. Connors, 'Field and Forum: Culture and Agriculture in Roman Rhetoric', in W. Dominik (ed.), *Roman Eloquence: Rhetoric in Society and Literature* (London: Routledge, 1997), 71–89, esp. 84–6.

[88] 'quam ob rem quae uobis fit iniuria, si statuimus uestro nobis iudicio standum esse de uobis?' The use of italic in the translation is an attempt to reproduce in English the effect of the Latin word order.

whose geography was weak that Atyanas came from the Asian litoral. In order to make his death as shocking and deplorable as possible—and thus increase the threat posed by the pirates and justify Flaccus—Cicero must distinguish him in some way from his fellow-citizens. He describes the death thus (31): 'what if a noble man from Adramytium was killed by the pirates, a man whose name is known to practically all of us, Atyanas who was an Olympic victor at boxing? To the Greeks—and we are talking about what they consider to be valuable—this achievement is almost greater and more glorious than it is to triumph at Rome.'[89] Atyanas is not concealed by the anonymity which renders most Greek witnesses in this speech unreliable: he is known to everyone, says Cicero, no doubt massaging the facts considerably. And he was as distinguished in the Greek world as a *triumphator* is in Rome. Cicero can at the same time suggest that Atyanas' death is a serious matter, and, by means of the ironic aside 'quoniam de eorum grauitate dicimus', suggest that even matters of great weight in the Greek world are really quite trivial: they make a games contest equivalent to the greatest achievement open to a Roman.[90] And it also suggests that the Greeks do not take war and politics seriously enough.

These examples are quite straightforward: Cicero needs on occasion to modify or ignore the ethnic prejudices he exploits so effectively in much of this speech. It is perhaps worth noting how easily he seems able to do this: even a Mysian such as Atyanas can be salvaged without too much difficulty. It is clear that he is dealing with a very generalized and usually latent prejudice against foreigners, which can be made explicit but is not invincible in the case of individuals. It is also the case that his ethnic remarks are linked to class: one of the reasons that the Greeks are unreliable is that they give too much promi- nence in political activity to the worthless and impoverished among them (16–17). Thus Cicero can exploit fear of the rabble

[89] 'quid si etiam occisus est a piratis Adramytenus homo nobilis, cuius est fere nobis omnibus nomen auditum, Atyanas pugil Olympionices? hoc est apud Graecos, quoniam de eorum grauitate dicimus, prope maius et gloriosius quam Romae triumphasse.'

[90] Balsdon, *Aliens*, 33 n. 22, gives other examples of Roman mockery of the Greeks' alleged obsession with athletics.

in Rome to strengthen his condemnation of the Greeks. And he needs only to mention Atyanas' noble birth in order to distinguish him from his compatriots.

It is against this background that Cicero's attacks on Laelius and particularly on Decianus should be examined. On the one hand, there is an apparently rigid distinction drawn between Asian Greeks as a whole and mainland Greeks, or between Greeks and Romans; on the other, individuals are able to shift categories very easily if they behave in ways that are inconsistent with the ethnic identity that has been set up for them. Cicero exploits this flexibility to question the Romanness of his opponents. The purpose of this manoeuvre is not simply to make the jury unsympathetic or hostile to the prosecution. As Cicero states that Greeks cannot comment on Roman imperial government (especially in 27), he casts doubt on the justification of the prosecution. If he can suggest that it is conducted by quasi-Greeks, for Greeks, surely he undermines its claim to the attention and sympathy of a Roman court.

1.3.1. Decianus

Decianus was a Roman citizen who had spent his life in Asia Minor.[91] Nowhere in the extant speech does Cicero give him his full name, C. Appuleius Decianus: thus by nomenclature he is made to seem similar to the Greek witnesses, who each have a single name.[92] He was the son of C. Appuleius Decianus, a tribune of the plebs in 98, who became notorious when he lost a prosecution because he expressed sympathy with Saturninus.[93] This Appuleius also unsuccessfully prosecuted Flaccus' father (77) and was himself condemned, probably on a charge of *maiestas* after his term of office, and went into exile, apparently to Pergamum.[94]

There are three passages where Cicero deals with Decianus. The first is preserved only in one sentence in the Bobbio scholia: 'quid uero Decianus'. Webster suggests plausibly that

---

[91] See C. Nicolet, *L'Ordre Équestre à l'époque républicaine*, vol. 1 (Paris: de Boccard, 1966), 706–7; vol. 2 (Paris: de Boccard, 1974), 781–3.

[92] See Balsdon, *Aliens*, 146–51, for Romans as the people of *tria nomina*.

[93] Evidence in Broughton, *MRR* 2. 4–5.

[94] For Decianus' family background see E. Badian, 'P. Decius P.f. Subulo', *JRS* 46 (1956), 91–6.

this may refer to Decianus' father, as a counter to accusations made by the prosecution about the elder Flaccus.[95] The second is a discussion of the evidence given by the Greek Lysanias (51). Cicero does not actually say what charges Lysanias was making: the paragraph is designed to show that his evidence, whatever he says, is worthless, and at the same time to paint a most unpleasant picture of Decianus. He accomplishes this by explaining that Lysanias is in effect being blackmailed by Decianus. Lysanias borrowed money from Decianus on the security of his family farm, and was, we must understand, unable to pay the interest; Decianus has now taken possession of the farm. He, says Cicero, has compelled Lysanias to give evidence in return for the prospect of getting his farm back. Cicero goes on to suggest that not only does this mean that Lysanias will say whatever Decianus wants, but that there is absolutely no point in his addressing Lysanias' charges before he has given evidence, since that will simply make him change his statement (51: 'he will change everything and make up some other story').[96] The reader who can examine the passage at leisure is left feeling that Lysanias' evidence against Flaccus must have been fairly damning. Nor does Cicero restrict himself to undermining the witness. Decianus also comes across badly. Charging exorbitant rates of interest was not perhaps in itself enough to blacken someone, and given that many of the jurors might themselves do so it would not perhaps have been wise to try to make it seem appalling.[97] But Cicero makes the affair seem unsavoury by his strong punning hint that Decianus was motivated by a desire for sexual control over Lysanias (51): 'you knew him at Temnus when he was an ephebe, and because his nakedness pleased you, you wanted him always to be naked.'[98] Cicero implies that Decianus has achieved his ambition by stripping Lysanias financially bare and that Lysanias has had to prostitute not only his evidence but also his body. Badian suggests that Cicero may have been conscious of

[95] Webster, *Pro Flacco*, 56.

[96] 'totum enim conuertet atque alia finget'.

[97] One of the most notorious cases of exorbitant interest was after all the rate of 48% per annum that the upright Brutus levied on a loan to the city of Salamis in Cyprus: see further Ch. 5.

[98] 'quem tu cum ephebum Temni cognosses, quia tum te nudus delectarat, semper nudum esse uoluisti.'

the unsavoury anecdotes about Decianus' (probable) biological grandfather at this point.[99] This is an attractive idea, though as he acknowledges, charges of sexual misdemeanours are commonplaces in invective.[100] It is also unclear whether Cicero would have been sure of the details before he started to explore the historical background of leading Roman orators for the *Brutus*: it is surprising that he does not make *more* use of Decianus' family background if he was au fait with it, as a neat parallel could be drawn between Gracchan and Catilinarian politics. (Of course, he may have done so in the missing early part of the speech.) The idea also depends on Badian's being right to identify Decianus' biological grandfather with Decius Subulo, which may be an over-enthusiastic swipe with Ockham's razor. But whether or not Decianus' ancestry is involved with this passage, the accusation of homosexual misdemeanour adds to the portrayal of Decianus as a Greek: the use of the word *ephebus* is pointed.

The third, most detailed, passage concerning Decianus is the discussion of the charges that Decianus himself has made against Flaccus (70–83). Decianus may be a Roman citizen, but he is a stranger to Rome. Cicero emphasizes this with a stunning surprise sentence (70): 'You've spent thirty years in the forum: but in the forum at Pergamum.'[101] Until the *sed tamen* clause, any listener would assume that Cicero was talking about the Forum: that is, the Roman forum. Cicero thereby draws attention to Decianus' marginal status. He reinforces this by remarking on the infrequency of Decianus' visits to Rome, and by describing his movement with the verb *peregrinari*: that is, to travel to a foreign country. He brings a new face and an old name (70): Cicero reminds his listeners that Appuleii have in the past been active in the capital, and this encourages a question as to why this is no longer the case: a historically aware listener might remember that Decianus' father went into exile—especially if reference had already been made to this in the missing part of the speech.

Cicero next draws attention to Decianus' appearance: in addition to his new face and his old name he brings to the

[99] Badian, 'Decius', 96.

[100] See Nisbet, *In Pisonem*, 194–5; Corbeill, *Controlling Laughter*, 104–6.

[101] 'annos iam xxx in foro uersaris, sed tamen in Pergameno.'

capital *purpuram Tyriam*, in the form of the clothes he is wearing. Purple was of course the defining mark of the Roman
magistrate; it also had powerful regal overtones. As such it is
completely inappropriate for an obscure Roman citizen living
in the provinces. The remark is part of Cicero's attempt to
make Decianus seem ridiculous. Moreover, as Cicero is careful
to point out, the purple dye is Tyrian: that is, the most expen-
sive variety.[102] By drawing attention to it Cicero is suggesting
that Decianus is a decadent and non-Roman easterner. But the
subtle defamation does not stop there. Cicero continues (70): 'I
envy you the fact that you can look smart in one set of clothes
for so long.'[103] Decianus only has one set of fine clothes, or
looks sufficiently shabby to make that plausible: Cicero is
suggesting poverty. He may also be suggesting that Decianus'
personal hygiene leaves something to be desired, as *lautus* can
also mean 'washed' and thus 'clean'.[104]

Cicero then suggests that Decianus is culturally Greek. He
has chosen not to locate his business activities in cities where
there is a large population of Roman citizens and Roman jurisdiction: why not? Because (71), 'you like leisure, you hate
disputes and crowds and praetors, and you rejoice in Greek
freedom'.[105] This is another damning sentence. Decianus likes
Greek *libertas*—which consists, it seems, of laziness and dis-
honesty, and he rejects Roman authority as represented by the
praetor. Cicero sets up the paradox of a *negotiator* who likes
otium: further proof of Decianus' un-Roman slackness. It is not
just the washing that he neglects. And why should he hate
lawsuits, the crowd, and the praetor unless he often finds

[102] Purple could be produced from a variety of organic and inorganic
sources, but Tyrian purple, made from crustaceans, had the finest and most
durable colour. Pliny the Elder (*NH* 37. 294), in his list of the best products
of various environments, makes this dye the most valuable product from
'creatures that belong to both land and sea'. For the use of purple dye, see
M. Reinhold, *History of Purple as a Status Symbol in Antiquity* (Brussels:
Latomus, 1970); J. L. Sebesta, '*Tunica Ralla, Tunica Spissa*: The Colors and
Textiles of Roman Costume', in J. L. Sebesta and L. Bonfante (eds.), *The
World of Roman Costume* (Madison: Univ. of Wisconsin Press, 1994), 65–76.

[103] 'in qua tibi inuideo, quod unis uestimentis tam diu lautus es.'

[104] *Pace* Reinhold, *Purple*, 44 n. 3, who suggests that *lautus* 'is a reference to
the color-fast properties of sea purple'.

[105] 'otium te delectat, lites, turbae, praetor odio est, Graecorum libertate
gaudes'.

himself being prosecuted? This picture of a shady businessman has a specific function in undermining the evidence Decianus has given against Flaccus, since it concerns a lawsuit heard in the province in which Flaccus, as presiding magistrate, found against Decianus. It also undermines the prosecution as a whole, since Decianus is not just a witness but also a counsel.

The paradox of Decianus—the Greek Roman, the lazy businessman—is complemented by the paradoxical nature of his victims, the inhabitants of Apollonis in Lydia. They are in general good allies (71): 'very friendly towards the Roman people and most reliable of allies'.[106] In particular, they are very different from the normal run of Asian Greeks (71): 'out of the whole of Asia, these are the most honest and religious men and the furthest removed from the luxurious habits and frivolity of the Greeks',[107] and also, by implication, very different from the overly Hellenized Decianus, with his *luxuria* of fancy clothes and his love of *otium*, surely a sign of *leuitas*. Moreover, the Apollonians are farmers, hard-working and admirably parsimonious (71): 'householders content with their own property, ploughmen, and countrymen. Their land is naturally very fertile and made more so by careful cultivation.'[108] That is, they fit one of the stereotypes that Romans fondly believed of their own past. In talking about Decianus and the Apollonians, Cicero has reversed the ethnic identities: Roman becomes Greek and vice versa. But in another way, the story he unfolds matches the overall impression of the speech, of the good Flaccus under attack from untrustworthy Greeks. Here we have the good Apollonians under attack from the untrustworthy and quasi-Greek Decianus. This tactic also has the advantage of removing Flaccus from the scene: instead of the injustices of the governor towards a citizen we get the injus-

[106] 'amantissimos populi Romani, fidelissimos socios'.

[107] 'homines sunt tota ex Asia frugalissimi, sanctissimi, a Graecorum luxuria et leuitate remotissimi'.

[108] 'patres familias suo contenti, aratores, rusticani; agros habent et natura perbonos et diligentia culturaque meliores.' See Vasaly, *Representations*, 214. Her point about the Apollonians' remoteness (they 'seem to inhabit a kind of isolated, Golden Age land') can be put more strongly, as Cicero explicitly draws attention to the remoteness of the place through its connections with myth (see below).

tices of a citizen of dubious status against a good provincial community.

Decianus' presence among the Apollonians thus seems paradoxical: he is in the wrong Greek community. And Cicero reinforces this by his discussion of the reasons for Decianus' choosing to live in this place (71–2):

> It was here [sc. Apollonis] that you wanted a farm. I would have preferred it—and it would have been more like you, if you now wanted fertile land—had you got it somewhere near Crustumerium or Capena. But let that be as it may: there is a saying of Cato, 'to balance feet against money'. It is certainly a long way from the Tiber to the Caicus—where even Agamemnon and his army would have got lost, if they hadn't found a guide in Telephus.[109]

The use of a remark of Cato to justify Decianus' purchase is unquestionably humorous through its inappropriateness: the Hellenized city-dweller being given advice drawn from the archetypal Roman peasant made good. This would be the case even if Cicero did not deliberately misinterpret Cato's remark. But as it is, he pretends that Cato meant that land prices are cheaper the further one gets from Rome, whereas Cato's point was that hard work can make up for (not having any) money.[110] This misinterpretation has a further humorous point, since it is entirely suited to Decianus: he is just the sort of person who would think in terms of saving money rather than hard work. Cicero's interpretation of Cato also suggests that Decianus is in financial embarrassment: he couldn't afford to buy a farm in Crustumerium or Capena, Cicero's suggestions of appropriate areas. Decianus hasn't the resources to be a proper Roman, it seems, and can only make the desirable shift from commerce to agriculture in a remote and thus cheap area.[111]

[109] In hisce agris tu praedia habere uoluisti. omnino mallem, et magis erat tuum, si iam te crassi agri delectabant, hic alicubi in Crustumino aut in Capenati parauisses. uerum esto; Catonis est dictum 'pedibus compensari pecuniam.' longe omnino a Tiberi ad Caicum, quo in loco etiam Agamemnon cum exercitu errasset, nisi ducem Telephum inuenisset.

[110] Du Mesnil, *Flaccus*, 171.

[111] 'Trade, if it is on a small scale, should be considered demeaning. If, however, men trade on a large and expansive scale, importing many things from all over the world, and distributing them to many people without misrepresentation, that is not entirely to be criticized. Indeed, if ever such men are satiated, or rather satisfied, with what they have gained, and just as they

Cicero then shifts cultural register entirely by invoking the mythical figures of Agamemnon and Telephus.[112] Telephus was the son of Auge and Hercules who was brought up in Mysia with his stepfather, the local king Teuthras. He fought the Greeks who came to attack Troy and was wounded: the wound failed to heal, and an oracle stated that it could only be cured by what had inflicted it. Telephus travelled to Greece to seek help and was there persuaded to help the Greek invasion force (who had had an oracle saying that they would only capture Troy with Telephus' help). He agreed, and was healed by rust from the spear of Achilles which had harmed him.[113]

The superficial point of the reference is to show that Apollonis is so remote that even Agamemnon would have got lost there had he not had Telephus as his guide. The implication for Decianus is that he had no good reason to be there. This reinforces the idea that Decianus has 'gone native'; it also prepares the audience for Cicero's narrative of the events at Apollonis, which reveals that Decianus was motivated solely by lust and greed. But Cicero did not need to refer to Agamemnon and Telephus in order to make this point.

One of the key issues concerning Telephus in Euripides' play seems to have been his nationality: was he Greek (through his parents) or Mysian (through upbringing and abode)?[114] Given that Cicero's reference occurs in a passage in which he is manipulating questions of ethnic identity, it is very tempting to see whether this aspect of the analogy is used. Arguably it is. The Apollonians, as the local inhabitants, take the place of Telephus. This confirms their ethnically flexible character: just

have often left the high seas for the harbour, now leave the harbour itself for land in the country, it seems that we have every right to praise their occupation. However, there is no kind of gainful employment that is better, more fruitful, more pleasant and more worthy of a free man than agriculture.' (Cicero, *de off.* 1. 151; trans. M. T. Griffin and E. M. Atkins).

[112] See *LIMC* 7/1: 856–7.

[113] On Euripides' *Telephus*, the most famous Greek handling of the myth, see E. W. Handley and J. Rea, 'The Telephus of Euripides' (London: *BICS* suppl. 5, 1957) and C. Collard, M. J. Cropp, and K. H. Lee, *Euripides: Selected Fragmentary Plays* (Warminster: Aris and Phillips, 1995), 17–52. Versions in Latin by Ennius and Accius would have made the story familiar to a Roman audience.

[114] Handley and Rea, 'Telephus', 33; E. Hall, *Inventing the Barbarian* (Oxford: Oxford Univ. Press, 1989), 174–6.

as Telephus is really a Greek, though at first sight he is a Mysian, so the Apollonians are almost like Romans despite being the inhabitants of a Lydian town. The analogy can also be extended to the characterization of Decianus. He is the counterpart to Agamemnon: this suggests that he is Greek and that he is dealing with matters that he does not really understand.[115] The comparison also raises an element of suspense. Is the relationship between Decianus and the Apollonians going to be as productive and harmonious as that between Agamemnon and Telephus? The answer, as revealed in the subsequent narrative, is emphatically 'no'.

The story of Decianus' activities in Apollonis that unfolds is of bewildering complexity but plausible detail.[116] Fortunately it is not necessary to disentangle the story here to see how Cicero continues to manipulate the issue of Decianus' ethnic identity. He cunningly suggests that Decianus is not quite a match for Greek intellect. He does not realize that the apparently honorific decree that the Pergamenes voted him in fact damns him with faint praise (76): 'You didn't understand that they were making fun of you when they recited this decree to you: "a man of great distinction, outstanding wisdom and remarkable intellect"? Believe me, they were.'[117] It may seem ironical that it takes Cicero, who presents himself as so contemptuous of the Greeks, to interpret their activities correctly when a Hellenized Roman cannot: but it fits his self-presentation throughout the speech as someone who knows what the Greeks' real motives are when others may be fooled into thinking that the Greeks have real grievances, and this allows him to express such disdain for the actions of the prosecution. And Decianus, it seems, is stupid as well as a bad Roman, hood-

[115] It is difficult to see any close analogy between Decianus' behaviour in Apollonis, where he steals the wife of a distinguished local and attempts to take possession of her property, and the more disreputable aspects of Agamemnon's career. However, Cicero may be trying to add to his picture of Decianus as an undesirable figure by the connection alone, as Agamemnon was not an unflawed hero.

[116] See Webster, *Pro Flacco*, 93–4, and A. J. Marshall, 'Romans under Chian Law', *GRBS* 10 (1969), 254–71, esp. 267–9, for discussion of what was actually going on, and compare Cicero's speech *pro Tullio* for a similar tale of rural terrorism and self-help.

[117] 'tu ludi te non intellegebas, cum tibi haec uerba recitabant; "clarissimum uirum, praestantissima sapientia, singulari ingenio"? mihi crede, ludebant.'

winked because he is *cupidus gloriae* (75); an admirable Roman
trait is, in Decianus' case, expressed in a derisory ambition.
Cicero, however, has the wit to appreciate the Pergamenes'
uenustas and *facetiae*, those two fashionable terms: thus he
manages to claim the cultural high ground as well as the moral.
At this point, ethnic stereotypes are not being used simply to
arouse ill-feeling against the prosecution, but also to undermine their competence.

1.3.2. *Laelius*

The elements in the portrayal of Laelius which link him to the
Greeks are much less obtrusive, and this is hardly surprising:
while we do not know anything of his earlier career there is no
reason to think that this case was not an example of an aristocratic young Roman making his name with a high-profile
prosecution. Crude jibes about dirty clothes and sexual pecca-
dilloes would be out of place: instead Cicero follows his
standard practice with aristocratic young prosecutors of
employing extreme politeness while subtly attacking them.[118]
     The first mention of Laelius illustrates this (2):

> If it was going to be the case that someone would plot the destruction
> of Lucius Flaccus, I never thought, gentlemen of the jury, that it
> would be Decimus Laelius: that the son of an excellent man and him-
> self possessing excellent prospects of the highest honours, would take
> up a prosecution which was more suited to the hatred and madness of
> the criminal classes than to his own good qualities and the standards
> of a well-brought-up young man.[119]

On the one hand, Cicero makes polite reference to Laelius' distinguished father and his own glorious prospects and present
character: on the other, his prosecution is described as something which is appropriate to the madness and hatred of the
criminal classes. Cicero thus reduces the impact of Laelius'
advantages as a prosecutor, that is the *auctoritas* he derives

---

[118] Cf. his treatment of Torquatus in the *pro Sulla*, Laterensis in the *pro
Plancio,* or Atratinus in the *pro Caelio*.

[119] quod si esset aliquando futurum ut aliquis de L. Flacci pernicie
cogitaret, numquam tamen existimaui, iudices, D. Laelium, optimi uiri
filium, optima ipsum spe praeditum summae dignitatis, eam suscepturum
accusationem quae sceleratorum ciuium potius odio et furori quam ipsius
uirtuti atque institutae adulescentiae conueniret.

from distinguished ancestors and his own talents.[120] Indeed, he turns Laelius' good qualities into marks of disapprobation by his hostile description of Laelius' motives. Despite having all the advantages which should have taught him how to behave, he has strayed; and although Cicero, in keeping with his generally polite tone, does not make his point explicit, there is a very clear implication that Laelius' actions are made worse by his failure to live up to the standards imposed on him by his ancestry.

Since Cicero has, in the first sentence of the speech, linked the prosecution of Flaccus with the peril that the state is in, there is certainly an implication that Laelius, through his prosecution of Flaccus, is a threat to the state as well as to Flaccus. In this case Laelius is dangerous because he has aligned himself with the internal enemies of the state. Later Cicero describes how he has, if not aligned himself with, at least exploited the hostility of the external enemies of Rome (18–19). Cicero describes in great detail the effort that Laelius made to gather his evidence: here (18):

A fine young man, of noble family, eloquent, arrives in a Greek town with a big elaborate escort and calls a public meeting; he stops prosperous and respectable citizens from opposing him with the threat of being summoned as a witness to Rome and he wins over the poor and irresponsible with hopes of handouts and travelling expenses and even by private generosity.[121]

This picks up the description of Laelius' activities in general in 13–15. Laelius is said to have deliberately gone about his task in such a way as to get evidence that is misleadingly hostile to Flaccus. This involved playing on the hatred of 'the dregs of cities' (*faex ciuitatum*, 18) for the Roman empire, and offering these people 'the opportunity to do damage' (*facultas laedendi*, 19) to it. This description of Laelius' researches picks up and reinforces the doubts about him that Cicero created in the

---

[120] On the importance of the *auctoritas* of advocates during trials see May, *Character*; Berry, *Pro Sulla*, 293–4.

[121] adulescens bonus, honesto loco natus, disertus cum maximo ornatissimoque comitatu uenit in oppidum Graecorum, postulat contionem, locupletis homines et grauis ne sibi aduersentur testimoni denuntiatione deterret, egentis et leuis spe largitionis et uiatico publico, priuata etiam benignitate prolectat.

opening paragraphs with his suggestion that he is at the very least unwittingly colluding with the remnants of those who sympathized with Catiline.

Laelius is not, therefore, a good Roman. He is certainly not like a Roman of the past. After Cicero's first description of Laelius' evidence-gathering tactics, he exclaims (15): 'if only we had held to the excellent habits and self-discipline that we got from our ancestors! But somehow they are slipping away from us',[122] and then proceeds to explain how wisely an earlier generation of Romans controlled popular gatherings. The current loss of that ability must refer to the disturbances due to the clashes between the consuls of 59, Caesar and Bibulus, and to the operations of the Caesarian tribune Vatinius. But instead of developing the contrast between past and present at Rome, he turns to *Greek* habits of popular assembly (16): 'the whole of Greek politics is run by reckless public assemblies which meet sitting down'.[123] The key word here is *sedentis*: it indicates both their slackness and their willingness to spend large amounts of time on the dangerous activity of holding public assemblies. And, as Cicero explains, the results have been disastrous: the achievements of Greece have been swept away *hoc uno malo* (16). It is clear that Cicero is in fact referring to Athens: and having given the impression that rowdy assemblies happened all over Greece, and therefore suggested that they are a perma-nent ethnic characteristic, he acknowledges explicitly that he is thinking about Athens (17). He can then use Athens' specific cultural prestige to make the behaviour of contemporary Asian Greeks seem even worse (17): 'if at Athens this sort of thing tended to happen . . . what restraint do you think there was in a public meeting in Phrygia or Mysia?'[124]

The benefits for Cicero of discussing the faults of the Greek democratic processes are obvious in the context of the whole speech: he can devalue any votes of assemblies which criticize Flaccus. By bringing in Roman practice he appeals to his

[122] 'o morem praeclarum disciplinamque quam a maioribus accepimus, si quidem teneremus! sed nescio quo pacto iam de manibus elabitur.'

[123] 'Graecorum autem totae res publicae sedentis contionis temeritate administrantur.' Roman assemblies stood.

[124] 'quod si haec Athenis . . . accidere sunt solita, quam moderationem putatis in Phrygia aut in Mysia contionum fuisse?' Cf. the discussion above of 62–6.

audience's sense of the superiority of Rome in order to increase
their disapproval for the Greek system as he describes it. But he
risks undermining that feeling with his tacit acknowledgement
that Rome at the moment is also foolish in its use of popular
assemblies. However, the reference to current problems works
to make Laelius seem dangerous. The exclamation about the
decline in Roman standards comes immediately after a description of how Laelius dealt with Greek assemblies. The listener,
who does not of course have time to unravel the argument, is
given a strong though illogical impression that Laelius' activities in Greece are a manifestation of the disastrous abandon-
ment of the wisdom of the *maiores*, and even that he is somehow
responsible for fomenting the disturbances in Rome or at least
in sympathy with those who do. In the wider context of the
whole speech, Laelius becomes part of the *pericula* (1) facing
the Roman state. After all, says Cicero, Athens possessed
wealth, an empire, and glory (16) and lost them all through
democracy: it seems clear that he is trying to line up Rome with
Athens and Laelius with the forces of disastrous democracy.

This impression is also given when Cicero describes Laelius'
tactics in gathering evidence (13). He draws attention to the
size of his retinue: 'what an escort he had when he was conduct-
ing his investigations! I say "escort": I should rather say
"army"!'[125] The figure of *correctio* draws attention to the
sinister idea of military force. He returns to this with a request
that the jury bear Laelius' tactics in mind if they hear anything
'about violence, force, weapons or troops',[126] and a reminder
that a limit has been set to the number of investigators by the
lex Iulia de repetundis. This must be a hint that Laelius could be
prosecuted under this law. This adds to the impression that all
Laelius' evidence must be disregarded, because it has been
extracted by force.

Against this general picture of Laelius as a potential danger
to the entire state, Cicero ascribes to him two particular
traits which, in the context of the speech, perhaps characterize
his un-Romanness as Greek. These are his greed and his
eloquence.

[125] 'qui comitatus in inquirendo! comitatum dico; immo uero quantus
exercitus!'
[126] 'de ui, de manu, de armis, de copiis' (13).

When Cicero returns to the issue of Laelius' motivation and behaviour (after the lacuna, and the first attack on Greek witnesses in 6–12) he describes him as having taken up the prosecution 'fired by an incredible desire'.[127] This picks up one of his charges against the Greeks, that their evidence is irretrievably compromised because it has been bought: they are people 'for whom all prospects of honour, profit, influence and favour depend on a shameless lie'.[128] Greek desire is thus for money. Cicero does not specify what Laelius' desire is for, and there is an obvious, and innocent, object: that is to advance his political career by a successful and high-profile prosecution.[129] None the less, in this close juxtaposition with undesirable *cupiditas*, unsavoury conclusions can be drawn. And it is certainly the case that Laelius' researches, whatever their motivation, and Greek greed are in a symbiotic relationship: Laelius is providing the opportunity, in this particular case, for the Greeks to indulge their desire for gain.

The other characteristic is eloquence. In 18 Laelius is described as *disertus*: in itself, a complimentary term; but in context, damning. Laelius uses this skill to get the votes he wants from the assemblies of Asia Minor. The audience has already been told that the concern of a Greek witness is not with justice, but with avoiding being trapped verbally (11). This means that the people who are chosen as witnesses are not the best men, but 'impudentissimus *loquacissimusque*' (11). Charges of excessive cleverness and ease in speaking were a standard part of Roman characterizations of the Greeks,[130] and the success of Cicero's ethnic stereotyping depends here on his

---

[127] 'inflammatus incredibili cupiditate' (13).

[128] 'quibus . . . laus, *merces*, gratia, gratulatio proposita est omnis in impudenti mendacio' (12). In the previous sentence, where Cicero makes the distinction between Roman and Greek absolutely clear by offering, as a contrast, his laudatory description of how a Roman gives evidence, one of the ways in which a Roman does *not* act is *cupide*. Compare also 66 where, at the very end of his discussion of the Asian Greek witnesses, Cicero summarizes their unreliability with the three vices of *leuitas*, *inconstantia*, and—in final position—*cupiditas*.

[129] It is of course true that *cupiditas* is not inevitably a bad quality: e.g. pro Sulla 40, 'animum meum tum conseruandae patriae *cupiditate* incendisti.' But the word does usually imply disapprobation, and this is almost invariably the case when it is not modified by a genitive expressing the object of desire.

[130] Petrochilos, *Attitudes*, 35–7.

audience adopting a suspicious attitude towards rhetoric. Then to describe the chief prosecutor as 'eloquent' is a barbed remark: while *disertus* is a positive term, and *loquacissimus* distinctly not, Laelius and his witnesses are at different ends of the same scale. His eloquence is a sinister and effective counterpart to their gabbiness.

It should be stressed that both *cupiditas* and eloquence can be and usually are admirable qualities for a Roman to possess and display. However, both are expressed in relation to certain ends, and when the ends are undesirable and even dangerous, as in this case, the qualities become tarnished by association. It is quite clear that Cicero is using them to build up his picture of Laelius as a figure who is a threat to Rome. It is more debatable whether they suffice to give Greek colouring to Laelius. It is, however, a line of interpretation open to a listener or reader to pursue, precisely because Laelius is displaying these qualities in the same arena as the Greeks are displaying them. His eloquence and *cupiditas* are closely intertwined with theirs. The fact that Cicero attacks Laelius' Roman-ness much more subtly than he does Decianus' is a reflection of Laelius' higher social standing and greater importance. It would both be more dangerous for Cicero to alienate him completely and might well backfire by offending the sensibilities of the jury. Moreover, Laelius' Roman identity *is* more pronounced, and more dangerous, than Decianus': he comes before the court as a member of the elite and a potential senator and magistrate, aspirations which Decianus cannot share, and which are an essential part of his claim to authority, and, unlike Decianus, he is domiciled in Rome. And of course there is a rhetorical advantage to be gained from making the prosecutors distinct in character in terms of variety and interest.

Despite the smoothness and absence of overt hostility in Cicero's expression of Laelius' character and behaviour, the consequence of his tactics is to make Laelius a more sinister figure than Decianus. Whereas the overriding tone of Cicero's remarks about Decianus is humorous, and thus leaves the audience feeling that Decianus is a risible and thus not very dangerous figure, Laelius is presented, without the use of ridicule, as someone extremely competent and thus dangerous. This approach does not just protect Cicero from the anger of a

potentially distinguished Roman: it is an appropriate response
to the rhetorical situation which Cicero faced, since Laelius was
the chief prosecutor and possessed a great deal more *auctoritas*
than Decianus did. The danger to Flaccus is far more serious
than that posed by provincials alone.

1.4. CONCLUSIONS

The five men whose characterizations are explored in this
chapter were all opponents of Cicero for reasons other than
ideological: that is, he was not attacking them simply because
they had behaved badly overseas, but because forensic or political circumstances made them his opponents. Consequently, it
would be a mistake to look to these speeches for a coherent or
systematic analysis of imperial problems: Cicero's aims are to
get Syria and Thrace named as consular provinces, to secure
the acquittal of Flaccus, and to display to a reading audience
his oratorical brilliance in driving Verres into exile. Piso and
Gabinius were not enemies of Cicero's choosing, but their
failure to help him respond to the threat from Clodius made
them so; and a quarrel which was based entirely in politics at
Rome is expressed in *de prouinciis consularibus* in terms of proconsular misconduct because that is, in the particular circumstances of the speech, the most effective way of damaging the
pair. Laelius and Decianus made themselves targets by
prosecuting a man Cicero was defending: again, it was the
forensic situation and the nature of the alleged crime which
made the behaviour of Laelius and Decianus in Asia relevant,
rather than any outrage Cicero might have felt independently.
In the case of Verres alone is there, possibly, a principle at
stake. Cicero had personal connections with Sicily as the result
of his own period there, and despite the potential advantages to
his career—actual by the time he wrote the speeches of the
second hearing—of the prosecution, it is perhaps overly cynical
entirely to dismiss the concern for the Sicilians' suffering, as
well as for the damage to Rome's interests, which he claims was
motivating him. Certainly his stance shows such a motive could
be viewed as credible and admirable. Yet, even in this case, the
characterization of Verres takes place within a forensic context.
    None the less, the ways in which Cicero presents these five as

unsatisfactory imperial figures are highly indicative of how
Rome's empire was conceptualized towards the end of the
Republic and how these concepts could be manipulated in an
oratorical context. Two features stand out in particular. One
is the focus on the individual magistrate and the elision of
supporting imperial structures. Verres, Piso, and Gabinius
each appear in a vacuum, autonomous and morally corrupt.
This raises a crucial issue for the entire study. Imperial
administration under the Republic did indeed involve very few
people, and placed the governor in a position of absolute,
though temporally and spatially limited, power, and so it is
natural and easy to think that imperial problems are the result
of individual failings. But this is not only a natural analysis, but
also a very convenient one, inasmuch as it presents a complex
situation very simply and in a way that is unlikely to disturb the
audience. If the only thing wrong with the empire is the misbehaviour of individuals, then there is no need to feel concern
about the system of imperial administration more generally; no
need to consider whether the relationship between Senate and
individual magistrate involves a satisfactory distribution of
power, or whether governors are under irreconcilable pressures
from provincials and Roman citizens in their provinces.

The second feature worth noting is the variety of ways in
which Romans in the provinces can be presented as unsatisfactory. Cicero constructs his five bogeys in specific and
different ways, both to exploit the perceived characters of the
men he is attacking—hence, for example, the differences
between the hypocritical Piso and the effeminate Gabinius—
and to fit with the roles they are to play in the world he constructs in each speech. The very autonomy of the magistrate is
a fruitful source of anxiety about what a magistrate should do.
The terms in which Cicero attacks his opponents demonstrate
that there is a wide, and contested, range of appropriate
conduct: magistrates, quite literally, made it up as they went
along. And it is against this background that the anxieties about
maintaining one's Roman identity make sense. Without an
institutional structure and a continuous and stable Roman
official presence throughout the empire it is particularly
difficult for magistrates to be sure they are presenting themselves to provincials, and to the unseen audience in Rome, in

the right way; and it is a fruitful and effective tactic for an opponent to play on the corresponding fears of the audience at Rome that their representatives abroad are in fact not maintaining a reliable Roman identity. Decianus and Laelius, moreover, demonstrate that these concerns need not be restricted to magistrates; any Roman who acts in the provinces risks having his identity and behaviour as a Roman scrutinized.

I return to these fears and their particularly acute expression in relation to the extraordinary commands of the late Republic in Chapter 4; but first I shall look at another aspect of the creation of Roman identity in an imperial context, which is the acquisition of Roman citizenship by provincials.

2

How to become a Roman: the cases of Archias and Balbus

IN the previous chapter I looked at the oratorical presentation of Romans outside Rome, and at the ways in which Cicero attempts to convince his audience of the goodness or badness of particular individuals in imperial contexts. In this chapter I turn to a phenomenon which is in some senses the reverse: non-Romans at Rome. In particular, I examine a pair of speeches in which Cicero argues that a particular (non-slave) individual who had acquired Roman citizenship during the course of his adult life had acquired it legally: *pro Archia* and *pro Balbo*. It is here that one might expect a stereotype of the good Roman to be spelt out, since an obvious tactic, it might seem, in such cases would be to argue that Archias or Balbus had assimilated themselves to some putative 'Roman way of life' and had as a result become worthy citizens.

The reality is rather different. In place of a rhetoric of assimilation, there is a rhetoric of service to Rome and to particular Romans which sidesteps the whole issue of cultural change. Acquiring the citizenship is not the natural result of absorbing Roman patterns of behaviour, but is a specific reward for particular services. Cicero's failure to use arguments based on assimilation can be seen as a sign that his jury, and readers, felt uneasy at the prospect of non-Romans becoming Roman. Furthermore, the model that he does set up, of foreigners serving the Roman state with enthusiasm, confirms Rome's dominance over its subjects. The Romans do not simply conquer: they make their subjects glad to have been conquered.[1]

---

[1] Cf. *prou. cons.* 31, Cicero's upbeat summary of the state of Rome's empire in 56: 'possum de omni regione, de omni genere hostium dicere: nulla gens est quae non aut ita sublata sit ut uix exstet, aut ita domita ut quiescat, aut *ita pacata ut uictoria nostra imperioque laetetur.*'

2.1. BACKGROUND

2.1.1. How to become a Roman citizen

The Roman state was unique among the major political powers of the ancient world in its willingness to give others its citizenship, and projected this part of its self-image right back to its origins.[2] Yet the vast majority of new citizens were freedmen, enfranchised automatically at the time at which they were manumitted.[3] Grants of citizenship to particular free, non-Roman individuals were extremely uncommon during the Republic, and the incorporation of large numbers of freedmen into the citizen body was matched by anxiety about alien groups within the city, which expressed itself on occasion in expulsions.[4] The theoretical possibilities of enfranchisement were not in practice exploited.

The great exception to the very cautious enfranchisement of free non-Romans is the extension of the citizenship to the whole of Italy south of the Po in the aftermath of the Social War. But in a sense this episode merely confirms the point, since the citizenship was extended only after a bitter and destructive war, which was the culmination of serious Italian grievances at their status in relation to Rome which went back well over thirty years.[5]

[2] Sherwin-White, *Citizenship*; C. Nicolet, *The World of the Citizen in Republican Rome*, trans. P. S. Falla (London: Batsford, 1980), 17. For an earlier perception of Rome's exceptional generosity with its citizenship, see Philip V's letter to Larissa of 214 (*SIG*, 3rd edn. 543).

[3] See e.g. J. A. Crook, *Law and Life of Rome* (London: Thames and Hudson, 1967), 41.

[4] Grants of citizenship to individuals: see E. Badian, *Foreign Clientelae* (Oxford: Oxford Univ. Press, 1958), 152 ff.; Sherwin-White, *Citizenship*, 291–5; expulsions: N. Purcell, 'The City of Rome and the *plebs urbana* in the Late Republic', *CAH* 9, 2nd edn. (1994), 652–3. For a discussion of these tensions in a religious context, see M. Beard, 'The Roman and the Foreign: The Cult of the "Great Mother" in Imperial Rome', in N. Thomas and C. Humphrey (eds.), *Shamanism, History and the State* (Ann Arbor: Univ. of Michigan Press, 1994).

[5] E. Gabba, *Republican Rome, the Army and the Allies*, trans. P. J. Cuff (Oxford: Blackwell, 1976), 70–130; P. A. Brunt, 'Italian Aims at the Time of the Social War', in *The Fall of the Roman Republic* (Oxford: Oxford Univ. Press, 1988); Mouritsen, *Italian Unification*, 87–99, argues that, by 91, citizenship on its own was not what the Italians were seeking: by then they desired freedom from Roman political control.

One of the factors in the Italian agitation in 91 was the increasing Romanization of the peninsula, and cultural convergence made political integration a natural next step. A model of citizenship as a response to assimilation was clearly developing at this period, with the clear expectation that for at least some of the Italians Roman citizenship would lead to active participation in Rome's political life; as indeed political integration of Latin communities earlier in the republican period had rapidly been followed by office-holding at Rome by the new citizens.[6]

Outside Italy, however, enfranchisement was rare. Pompeius Strabo gave the citizenship to a troop of Spanish horsemen during the Social war under the provisions of the *lex Iulia*, to reward them for their services: they became Roman citizens *uirtutis causa*. Other cases are confined to individuals.[7]

2.1.2. The cases

Archias was prosecuted in 62, Balbus in 56: both cases were brought under the *lex Papia* of 65, which demanded the expulsion of non-citizens from Rome.[8] Despite this similarity, the speeches have seldom been considered together (outside discussions of citizenship law), and scholars have used them for rather different purposes.[9] The *pro Balbo* has been comparatively neglected, and such interest as has been shown has been

[6] See in general Sherwin-White, *Citizenship*, 38–95; P. A. Brunt, 'The Romanization of the Local Ruling Classes in the Roman Empire', in D. M. Pippidi (ed.), *Assimilation et résistance à la culture gréco-romaine dans le monde ancien* (Bucharest: Editura Academiei, 1976), 161–73, repr. in P. A. Brunt, *Roman Imperial Themes* (Oxford: Oxford Univ. Press, 1990), 267–81; M. H. Crawford, 'Italy and Rome from Sulla to Augustus', *CAH* 10, 2nd edn. (1996), 414–33.

[7] Pompeius Strabo: *ILS* 8888 (*ILLRP* 515); the speech for Balbus, unfortunately, provides most of the evidence for other enfranchisements (50–5); see also Sherwin-White, *Citizenship*, 291–311.

[8] D. Cloud, 'The Constitution and Public Criminal Law', *CAH* 9, 2nd edn. (1994), 491–530, esp. 526; Gruen, *Last Generation*, 410–11. For the circumstances of Archias' trial, see H. Vretska and K. Vretska, *Marcus Tullius Cicero: Pro Archia Poeta: ein Zeugnis für den Kampf des Geistes um seine Anerkennung* (Darmstadt: Wissenschaftliche Buchgesellschaft, 1979), 3–9, and for Balbus', P. A. Brunt, 'The Legal Issue in Cicero *pro Balbo*', *CQ* 32 (1982), 136–47.

[9] For the issues of citizenship raised by these cases, see Sherwin-White, *Citizenship*, 291–311.

directed largely towards the legal problems it raises.[10] The *pro Archia* is, in contrast, one of the most studied of Cicero's speeches.[11] This is in part due to its pedagogically convenient brevity, but, more importantly, because of the defence of poetry which takes up well over half of the whole speech.[12] It is not surprising that classicists should be attracted by such an eloquent defence of the value and usefulness of humane letters, and the attention that has been devoted to this speech has done much to clarify Cicero's rhetorical practice and methods of argumentation. However, an undesirable consequence of the *pro Archia*'s status as a supremely 'literary' text has been the neglect of the context in which such a defence was made. The oddity of a digression on poetry in a forensic speech has often been noted: but few people have approached the speech from the perspective of how to argue that a Greek poet should keep his Roman citizenship.[13]

In both speeches Cicero argues that his client has performed valuable services for the Roman state, although this is not the legal point of dispute in either case. It is worth considering briefly what were the legal situations with which he was faced,

[10] Loutsch, *L'Exorde*, 357 n.1, gathers together the scant bibliography, and see also J. Spielvogel, *Amicitia und res publica* (Stuttgart: Franz Steiner Verlag, 1993), 137–41.

[11] The speech has the rare distinction of two modern commentaries, those by H. C. Gotoff, *Cicero's Elegant Style: An Analysis of the pro Archia* (Urbana: Univ. of Illinois Press, 1979) and Vretska and Vretska; other substantial treatments are M. von Albrecht, 'Das Prooemium von Ciceros Rede pro Archia poeta und das Problem der Zweckmässigkeit der *argumentio extra causam*', *Gymnasium*, 76 (1969), 419–29; H. Eisenberger, 'Die Funktion des zweiten Hauptteils von Ciceros Rede für den Dichter Archias', *WS* 92, NS 13 (1979), 88–98; C. Damon, *The Mask of the Parasite: A Pathology of Roman Patronage* (Ann Arbor: Univ. of Michigan Press, 1997), 268–76; E. Narducci, *Cicerone e l'eloquenza romana* (Rome and Bari: Editori Laterza, 1997), 3–18.

[12] 12–31: see J. H. Taylor, 'Political Motives in Cicero's Defense of Archias', *AJPh* 73 (1952), 62. This factor is ignored in Porter's strictures on the inability of scholars to justify their interest in this speech (W. M. Porter, 'Cicero's *Pro Archia* and the Responsibilities of Reading', *Rhetorica*, 8 (1990), 137–52, esp. 137–8).

[13] A striking indication of the way that these speeches have *not* been considered as documents on Roman attitudes to ethnicity and identity is their absence from Vasaly's recent book on Cicero's manipulation of ideas about the world, *Representations*: no mention at all of the *pro Archia*; one mention of the *pro Balbo* in a note (134 n. 9), for its use of the idea of a world empire.

with the proviso that it is of course extremely difficult to assess the strength of Cicero's case in the absence of other evidence about the trial. One is restricted to 'common-sense' judgements about the limits of knowledge and belief on the part of the jurors within which Cicero's manipulations could operate.

In the Balbus case, there seems to have been no dispute about how he acquired the citizenship, that is as a gift from Pompeius Magnus in recognition of his services during the Sertorian War. The prosecutor's case was that this grant of citizenship was illegal, since Balbus' original state, the town of Gades, had not agreed to such an enfranchisement. A number of scholars have argued that the case against Balbus was well founded; I am inclined to accept the contention of Brunt, that this argument, insofar as we can reconstruct it, was flawed, but also irrelevant, since the point in question concerns actions under Roman law.[14] The key point is that the link between Pompeius and Balbus was clear to all, which allows Cicero to support the long and complex legal arguments of the speech with Balbus' acknowledged relationship to his patron.

In Archias' case, the issue is more complex, since what is in dispute is not a question of law, as in the Balbus case, but a question of fact, that is whether he had indeed obtained citizenship at Heraclea and then converted that into Roman citizenship under the provisions of the *lex Plautia Papiria*.[15] It is ultimately impossible to be certain, as we cannot check Cicero's assertions.[16] The key point is the absence of much of the written proof of Archias' citizenship that one would expect. His name is not in the archives of Heraclea, nor does it appear in any census lists, though Cicero has explanations for both absences. What he can cite is the list that Metellus compiled of

[14] H. Galsterer, *Herrschaft und Verwaltung im republikanischen Italien* (Munich: Beck, 1976), 162–4; V. Angelini, 'Riflessioni sull'orazione pro L. Cornelio Balbo', *Athenaeum*, 68 (1980), 360–70; contra Brunt ('Legal Issue', 143), 'To impugn Balbus' Roman citizenship, it was necessary to show that it had been conferred on him in contravention of Roman law'.

[15] von Albrecht, 'Prooemium'; Vretska and Vretska, *Pro Archia*, 6–9 for a discussion of the likely arguments used by the prosecution.

[16] *Pace* E. Badian, 'Marius' Villas: The Testimony of the Slave and the Knave', *JRS* 63 (1973), 121–32, 129: 'For once there can be no doubt that the prosecution was a piece of mere chicanery, and that Cicero's client was as innocent as his counsel claimed.'

new citizens under the provisions of the *lex Plautia Papiria* (9);
he can also produce Marcus Lucullus as a witness to the grant
of citizenship at Heraclea, as well as a delegation from Heraclea
to say the same thing.

In addition to this evidence, there is the further argument,
which Cicero uses later in the speech (25–6), that it is far from
clear why Archias should have had to make a false claim to the
citizenship. There were of course practical benefits; but it was
also an honour, whose value to him over the previous twenty-
five years would have been much reduced had he not in fact
been entitled to have it. There seems to have been no question
that he could have been made a citizen of Heraclea and on that
basis claimed the Roman citizenship: the issue was whether he
did. In such circumstances, it would seem more probable that
Archias was the victim of paperwork rather than that he had
been practising an unnecessary deception for a quarter of a
century.[17]

However, there are some odd aspects to the case. In the first
place, as the prosecution presumably pointed out, the evidence
available depends on Archias' patrons, as in the evidence of
Marcus Lucullus and the records of the late Quintus Metellus,[18]
or could have been set up by them (it would not have been difficult for Lucullus to apply pressure on Heraclea).[19] Secondly,
while the explanation for Archias' absence from the census lists
seems reasonable,[20] one might ask why he does not appear on
any lists of citizens of Heraclea subsequent to their destruction
by fire during the Social War.[21] However, the shortness of the

[17] The fact that Cicero employs this argument himself (25–6) does not mean
that it should be dismissed out of hand.

[18] For their connections with Archias, see 6. 13–18.

[19] One might also query how well informed the current generation of
Heraclean notables would be of an enfranchisement which took place some 30
years earlier—particularly if the records were missing.

[20] Though it is worth noting that registration of those absent from Italy at
the time of the census was possible: P. A. Brunt, *Italian Manpower* (Oxford:
Oxford Univ. Press, 1971), 38–9.

[21] *pro Archia* 8: 'quas [sc. tabulas] Italico bello incenso tabulario interisse
scimus omnes'. For the 'everybody knows' topos, and the need for caution in
assessing it, see D. M. Macdowell, *Andokides: On the Mysteries* (Oxford:
Oxford Univ. Press, 1962), 79–80, and J. Ober, *Mass and Elite in Democratic
Athens* (Princeton: Princeton Univ. Press, 1989), 149–50. As there does not
seem to have been Social War campaigning near Heraclea, *Italico bello* must

discussion of the evidence cannot be used either for or against Archias' position, despite attempts to do so.[22] The point at issue was extremely simple: whether or not Cicero's argument was true, there was no further evidence he could cite that might make it any more convincing. In particular, one can see why he might not wish to introduce commonplaces on the reliability of witnesses when two of his key witnesses, M. Lucullus and Q. Metellus, were or had been distinguished consulars.[23] One should not even have to *raise* the issue of their veracity.

The digressions away from legal argument in both these speeches cannot be explained simply in terms of the strength or weakness of each case. In part, digressiveness is, as so often in Cicero's oratory, a response to political implications of the trial. Neither speech is concerned simply with Balbus' and Archias' citizenship. There is fairly general agreement that the prosecution of Archias is an attempt to embarrass L. Lucullus, in the context of continuing ill-feeling between him (and more generally, the 'Optimates') and Pompeius; and that the prosecution of Balbus should be seen as an attempt to embarrass the 'first triumvirate' in the aftermath of their re-formation at Luca.[24] But the position Cicero puts forward in his digressions, justifying citizenship in ethical terms, as a reward for services rendered, as well as by legal argument, is also a powerful rhetorical device, which sets up the grant of citizenship as a way of confirming Roman domination over its empire.

refer simply to time rather than cause; the implication that the records were lost on active service, as it were, gives a heroic pardon to what was probably administrative incompetence.

[22] von Albrecht, 'Prooemium', 427, offers a summary of these.

[23] Quintus Caecilius Metellus Pius, cos. 80, *pontifex maximus* (81–63), held a triumph on the basis of his campaigns in Spain against Sertorius; M. Terentius Varro Lucullus, cos. 73, held a triumph on the basis of his campaigns in Thrace.

[24] For the political background to Archias' trial, see Taylor, 'Political Motives', and Gruen, *Last Generation*, 267–8; for Balbus', Gruen, *Last Generation*, 312–13.

2.2. ARCHIAS

2.2.1. Singing for the Romans

The legal argumentation of the *pro Archia* is complete by the
end of 11; what follows is usually termed a digression, in which
Cicero considers why poetry is valuable. The digression clearly
falls into two parts: one, 12–16, in which Cicero explains why
he personally takes such pleasure in literature; the other, 17–30,
in which he argues that honour should be shown to those, such
as Archias, who produce literature because of the value which
he and other statesmen have found in it.[25] Cicero concludes the
second part by discussing the value which poetry has as a spur
to glorious action through its capacity to preserve the memory
of such action, with particular reference to his own recent
achievement in suppressing the Catilinarian conspiracy, which
enables him to bring the two parts of the digression together as
he brings it to a close.

Why does Cicero place such emphasis on the praise of
poetry? One place to begin an analysis is with the issue of
what precisely the *doctrina* and *litterae* upon which Cicero
apparently places such high value consist in. What were
Archias' literary productions? The question has to be answered
almost entirely from the evidence of the *pro Archia*, since
the poet is only mentioned twice elsewhere (as opposed to a
reference to this speech).[26] Nor does any of his poetry definitely
survive, although it is possible that some of the epigrams transmitted in the Greek Anthology under this name are by him.[27]

In the *pro Archia*, Cicero ascribes the following works to
Archias. He was an extemporizer of great fluency and facility,
who could produce different poems on the same subject;[28] he

---

[25] Vretska and Vretska, *Pro Archia*, 17–18, though I would not put as much
emphasis as they on Archias' importance in the second part of the digression.
On the connections between the main argument of the speech and the digression, see von Albrecht, 'Prooemium', and Eisenberger, 'Funktion'.

[26] Cicero, *ad Att.* 1. 16. 15 (Archias is not yet writing the hoped-for poem
on Cicero's consulship); *de diu.* 1. 79 (Archias' poem on the actor Roscius).

[27] A. S. F. Gow and D. L. Page, *The Greek Anthology: The Garland of
Philip, and Some Contemporary Epigrams*, vol. 2 (Cambridge: Cambridge
Univ. Press, 1968), 432–5.

[28] 18. Gow and Page, *Garland*, 435 n. 4, suggest on the basis of this passage

wrote on the Cimbric War as a young man (19); he wrote, in
more than one book, on the Mithradatic War (21, and note
libri); and he had begun an epic on Cicero's achievements
during his consulship (28). This list has been used to construct
a picture of a dependent poet, diligently writing at the behest of
his Roman patrons.[29] However, it is worth considering quite
how impressive a bibliography this really was.[30]

The extempore poems were probably not recorded, and
despite Cicero's claim for 'a great number of excellent verses'
the improvisatory format means that it is most likely that these
were short epigrams, such as those under the name of Archias
in the Greek Anthology, whether or not those are indeed by
this Archias. This was not an impressive genre: practised by
aristocrats such as the elder Catulus, certainly, but as an intellectual diversion and no more.[31] It is significant, I think, that
Cicero prefaces his glowing description of Archias' extemporizing skills with an appeal for the jurors' attention: 'I shall take
advantage of your goodwill, since you are listening to me so
carefully despite the unfamiliarity of my subject matter'.[32] This
may just be an encouragement to the jurors to maintain their
concentration despite the general oddity of the subject matter.
But if we allow it a specific relevance, then it suggests that the
jury would not naturally consider a skill in poetic improvisation
to be grounds for a claim to Roman citizenship, and so need
particular reassurance about the relevance of what Cicero is
saying.

There are good grounds for doubting that Archias finished
the epic on the Cimbrian Wars.[33] Cicero's words are 'Cimbricas

that a collection of artfully varied epigrams about the same subject which are
transmitted under the name 'Archias' might belong to this Archias.

[29] T. P. Wiseman, '*Pete nobiles amicos*: Poets and Patrons in Late Republican Rome', in B. K. Gold (ed.), *Literary and Artistic Patronage in Ancient
Rome* (Austin: Univ. of Texas Press, 1982), 28–34, 31–4; B. K. Gold, *Literary
Patronage in Greece and Rome* (Chapel Hill: Univ. of North Carolina Press,
1987), 73–86, with due scepticism as to Archias' productivity; Rawson,
Intellectual Life, 221 n. 33, 'Archias did eulogise a number of great Romans,
including Lucullus.' [30] Cf. Eisenberger, 'Funktion', 94.

[31] Gellius, *NA* 19. 9.

[32] 18. 22–3: 'iudices—utar enim uestra benignitate, quoniam me in hoc
nouo genere dicendi tam diligenter attenditis'.

[33] So Vretska and Vretska, *Pro Archia*, 150, though their doubts could be
more strongly expressed.

res adulescens attigit' (19). *Attingo*, when used of writing,
means 'I take up' or 'I engage in': it does not carry any implication of bringing such work to completion, and there are cases of
its being used with adverbs which make clear the activity was
not taken too seriously.[34] Given that Cicero is arguing at this
point for the importance and scale of Archias' contribution to
Roman glory, we would expect him, if anything, to exaggerate
what Archias had done. This epic was probably no more than
some scattered fragments.

Archias' work on the Mithradatic War was, it seems, more
substantial: as mentioned above, Cicero refers to more than one
book on the subject. He describes Archias' achievement as
follows: 'the Mithradatic war, which was long, difficult and
fought out over a wide variety of theatres both on land and at
sea, has been treated in its entirety by this man: books which
glorify not only Lucius Lucullus, that brave and distinguished
man, but also the name of the Roman people.'[35] It is worth
noting, however, that the attributes belong to the war and to
Lucullus and not to the poem. This paragraph continues with
a long, elegantly constructed account of the war as an accom-
plishment of the Roman people, which concludes by stating
that the triumphs of this war will be a constant subject of
remembrance and praise as Roman achievements. The paragraph ends with his saying that whoever treats of these subjects
is increasing the reputation of the Romans. That is, Cicero does
not say anything about the content of the poem.

This silence need not be a cause for concern: it is rhetorically
effective to remind the jurors of a recent and ultimately
successful military campaign and then let Archias be affected
by the goodwill that this engenders, whereas concentrating on a
poem, and one in Greek at that, might serve rather to alienate

[34] Cicero, *de or.* 1. 82: 'egomet, qui sero ac leuiter Graecas litteras
attigissem'; cf. *ad fam.* 13. 29. 3 (not on writing): 'sed oppressus tantum *attigit*
negoti quantum recusare non potuit'; also suggestive, Catullus 22. 14–15:
'idem infaceto est infacetior rure | simul poemata *attigit* . . .'; Nepos, *Life
of Atticus* 18. 5: '*attigit* poeticen quoque, credimus, ne eius expers esset
suauitatis'.
[35] 21: 'Mithridaticum uero bellum magnum atque difficile et in multa
uarietate terra marique uersatum totum ab hoc expressum est; qui libri non
modo L. Lucullum, fortissimum et clarissimum uirum, uerum etiam populi
Romani nomen inlustrant.'

the jury by seeming to trivialize Roman military accomplishments. And if the focus of the poem was the achievements of
Lucullus himself, it is understandable that Cicero would not
want to commit himself to an account of the Mithradatic War
that ignored the achievements of Pompeius, given his own
expectations of a useful political partnership with Pompeius.
So Cicero's failure to talk in any detail about Archias'
Mithradatic epic cannot safely be interpreted as a sign that
there was not, yet, much epic to talk about. However, in a letter
to Atticus of the following year Cicero indicates that Archias is
only just thinking of starting the next project: 'Archias has
written nothing about me; and I'm afraid that now that he has
finished his Greek poem for the Lucullus brothers he is considering a Caecilian drama.'[36] This letter also indicates that the
epic which Cicero allowed himself to hope for in public (*pro
Archia* 28) about his own achievements came to nothing.[37]

Cicero would only, in this context, refer to poems which he
could make appear to be contributions to Rome's glory, and
there may have been any amount of poetry which Archias wrote
and which could not be made to seem a valid reason for his
holding Roman citizenship.[38] None the less, on the basis of the
surviving evidence, Archias' completed poetic works amount to
two or more books on the Mithradatic War and, possibly, some
epigrams. This is not an overwhelming output over the space of
forty years.

More interesting perhaps is the way in which Cicero presents
this exiguous productivity: it is central to the glory of the
Roman state. In part, Cicero achieves this simply by stating it,
as when he summarizes the effects of Archias' epic on Lucullus
(passage quoted above). But he also tries to enhance Archias'
status by comparing him with poets who have been regarded as
central to their states' reputation. Most striking is his use of a
comparison of Archias to Homer, having given a brief description of the struggles among cities of the coast of Asia Minor to
claim him as their own: 'And so they sought out a foreigner

[36] *ad Att.* 1. 16. 15: 'et Archias nihil de me scripserit; ac uereor ne, Lucullis
quoniam Graecum poema condidit, nunc ad Caeciliam fabulam spectet.'

[37] Here too he uses *attigit* (28) of Archias' poetic activity.

[38] Though the fact that Cicero does so much with Archias' extemporizing
suggests that he could have made something out of short, written, non-
patriotic poems.

even after his death, because he was a poet: shall we then cast out a living poet, who is ours by law and by his own wish, especially since Archias has for a long time devoted all his enthusiasm and all his talent to celebrating the glorious renown of the Roman people?'[39] Here the statement of Archias' capacity to add to the glory of the Roman people is supported by the implication that he can be compared with Homer, the archetype of the epic poet. If that is the case, then his value to the Roman state hardly needs further support.

Homer is not the only poet whom Cicero cites to show how highly valued poets have been. He mentions Plotius, who might have written a poem in celebration of Marius (20) and Accius (27), as well as the historian Theophanes who wrote an account of Pompeius' campaigns against Mithradates (24). By citing Theophanes as a parallel to Archias, Cicero is deliberately and rather pointedly skating over the differences between their patrons, and the fact that Theophanes' and Archias' accounts of the Mithradatic War were at one level in competition.[40] As in his discussion of Archias' Mithradatic epic, Cicero is unwilling to side openly with either Pompeius or Lucullus. Most important, however, is Ennius, whose description of poets as *sancti* is cited in 18, to whose works 22 is devoted, and with whom the general section on poets and their patrons concludes in 27. The comparison of Archias to Ennius is even more emphatic than that to Homer: it places Archias specifically at the centre of Rome's cultural achievements, given that Ennius was still, at this period, *the* epic poet of Rome. And Cicero reinforces this point by stressing the communal value of Ennius' poetry:

But Ennius' poetry did not enhance simply the man who was praised, but also the name of the Roman people. Cato . . . is elevated to the skies; great honour is added to the affairs of the Roman people. And all those Maximi, Marcelli, Fulvii are not embellished without praise which is shared by all of us. And so, our ancestors admitted into the

---

[39] 19: 'ergo illi alienum, quia poeta fuit, post mortem etiam expetunt; nos hunc uiuum qui et uoluntate et legibus noster est repudiamus, praesertim cum omne olim studium atque omne ingenium contulerit Archias ad populi Romani gloriam laudemque celebrandam?'

[40] S. P. Haley, 'Archias, Theophanes and Cicero: The Politics of the *Pro Archia*', *CB* 59 (1983), 1–4.

state the man who had accomplished this, a man from Rudiae; shall we throw out of our state a man from Heraclea, sought out by many states and legally part of ours?[41]

As Damon points out, Cicero's desire to emphasize the relationship between Ennius and the Roman people, as opposed to that between Ennius and his various patrons, leads him to describe Ennius' acquisition of Roman citizenship, which in fact was the result of the intervention of a Fulvius, as due to the action of the citizen body as a whole.[42] Moreover, the similarity of vocabulary and ideas to the passage comparing Archias' situation with Homer's, quoted above, reminds the audience of the similarity of the enthymeme: great poets are in demand as ornaments to states; Archias is a great poet; therefore he should be in great demand by the Roman state for whom he has done so much.[43]

The recollection of glorious poetic predecessors enables Cicero to put Archias at the centre of a cultural tradition whose value to a state is taken for granted. Not only does this exaggerate Archias' talents; it also recasts the traditional relationship between poet and individual aristocratic patron into a relationship between poet and the state. Cicero continues the idea of the importance of the poet to the state when he turns to his own relation with Archias in 28–30. But at this point the argument rises to a climax: Archias' poetry is not valuable simply in augmenting and disseminating glory: it is crucial to the very survival of the state.[44]

These paragraphs are the conclusion of the digression's ring-composition: Cicero began with his own personal relationship to poetry and now ends with it. In 12–14 Cicero begins with the

---

[41] 22: at eis laudibus certe non solum ipse qui laudatur sed etiam populi Romani nomen ornatur. in caelum . . . Cato tollitur; magnus honos populi Romani rebus adiungitur. omnes denique illi Maximi, Marcelli, Fuluii non sine communi omnium nostrum laude decorantur. ergo illum qui haec fecerat, Rudinum hominem, maiores nostri in ciuitatem receperunt; nos hunc Heracliensem multis ciuitatibus expetitum, in hac autem legibus constitutum de nostra ciuitate eiciamus?

[42] Damon, *Parasite*, 270.

[43] 19: 'ad populi Romani gloriam laudemque' ~ 22: 'populi Romani nomen; communi omnium nostrum laude; legibus noster est' ~ 'legibus constitutum; alienum' ~ 'Rudinum hominem; expetunt' ~ 'expetitum'.

[44] Eisenberger, 'Funktion', 97–8.

importance of poetry in enabling him to be an orator: 'or do
you think that I could have available the material to speak on
such a range of subjects every day, if I did not steep my mind in
learning, or that my mind could bear such strains, if I did not
relax with this same learning?'[45] Cicero is here conflating two
quite different uses of *doctrina*: one as a source of the material
from which the orator can construct his speeches, the other as a
means to relaxation which fits the orator for further oratorical
battles. While poetry does feature among the types of literature
which an orator can read with profit, Cicero's choice of vocabulary to describe Archias' work, as *doctrina* and *studia*, tends to
conflate his poetry with learning more generally, whose value to
an orator would be much less debatable.

It is after all far from obvious that a Roman orator could find
anything of direct use in Greek epigrams and recent Greek
epic, or indeed that it would be desirable if he did.[46] Cicero
avoids these problems in part through not spelling out in detail
how Archias has been helpful to him, but also by shifting
the argument entirely, away from poetry as a means to great
oratory to poetry as the motive for being a great orator. The
shift is accomplished in the following crucial sentences:

And I should be permitted [sc. to pursue these studies] all the more,
since it is from them also that my oratorical ability derives, which,
such as it is, has never failed my friends in times of trouble. And if it
seems insubstantial to some, I am conscious from what source I have
got the parts of it which are most important. Because unless I had
convinced myself from childhood onwards by means of the advice of
many people and by large quantities of reading that nothing in life was
more worth pursuing than fame and honour, and that in that pursuit
all bodily agony and all dangers of death or exile were to be considered
as trifles, I would never have taken a stand, on behalf of your safety, in
so many important battles and against these daily attacks by depraved
men.[47]

[45] 12: 'an tu existimas aut suppetere nobis posse quod cotidie dicamus in
tanta uarietate rerum, nisi animos nostros doctrina excolamus, aut ferre
animos tantam posse contentionem, nisi eos doctrina eadem relaxemus?'
[46] Excessive facility at speaking is one of the traits which make up the
hostile stereotype of the Greek: see Sect. 1.3.2.
[47] 13–14: atque id eo mihi concedendum est magis quod ex his studiis haec
quoque crescit oratio et facultas quae, quantacumque est in me, numquam
amicorum periculis defuit. quae si cui leuior uidetur, illa quidem certe quae
summa sunt ex quo fonte hauriam sentio. nam nisi multorum praeceptis

The shift is facilitated by the ambiguity in the second of the sentences that I quote. *quae . . . leuior* can only refer back to *oratio et facultas*, which leads the audience to expect that the *illa . . . quae summa sunt* are the most accomplished parts of Cicero's oratorical skill. However, the following sentence's stirring presentation of the ideal of the statesman only makes sense if *illa . . . quae summa sunt* shift to being the most elevated parts of Cicero's way of life. The *nam* of the third sentence helps this manoeuvre by giving a specious veneer of logic.[48] This careful shift enables Cicero to harness, for Archias' benefit, the long-standing appreciation of poetry as an incentive to glory through its remembrancing powers, an appreciation which would not automatically extend to Archias (who would be more likely to be slotted into a category of dependent Greek intellectual) nor to his poetic output. And it also allows Cicero to recast his undisputed oratorical skills as the sort of heroic activity which is celebrated in epic. Neither move would be unchallenged were it obvious: hence the care to conceal the shift.

In 14 Cicero alludes in passing to his resistance to the Catilinarians as one of the consequences of his realization that *laus* and *honestas* were the only things worth pursuing. He returns to and refines this argument in 28–30. Since glory is the only thing which virtue wants as its reward, if glory is not to be obtained there is no reason why virtue should exercise itself: 'virtue wants no other reward for the effort and danger it incurs than that which consists in praise and glory. But if this is taken away, what reason is there, members of the jury, for us to exert ourselves hugely when the course of life is so short and insubstantial?'[49] Archias is a key part of this process: his is the poetry

multisque litteris mihi ab adulescentia suasissem nihil esse in uita magno opere expetendum nisi laudem atque honestatem, in ea autem persequenda omnis cruciatus corporis, omnia pericula mortis atque exsili parui esse ducenda, numquam me pro salute uestra in tot ac tantas dimicationes atque in hos profligatorum hominum cotidianos impetus obiecissem.

[48] Vretska and Vretska, *Pro Archia*, 127, are right to gloss *quae summa sunt* as 'Lebensgrundsätze', but by translating them as such in the sentence crucial to the shift they obscure Cicero's care in constructing his argument here.

[49] 28: 'nullam enim uirtus aliam mercedem laborum periculorumque desiderat praeter hanc laudis et gloriae; qua quidem detracta, iudices, quid est quod in hoc tam exiguo uitae curriculo et tam breui tantis nos in laboribus exerceamus?'

recording Cicero's great deeds which provides Cicero's reward of *laus* and *gloria*. This concluding example of the value of a poet also brings together the two conflicting models of poetic activity which have already appeared: one which involves a poet writing in praise of a single patron and the other where the individual patron is replaced by the state. The unfamiliarity of the second position is eased by 28–30, because Cicero indicates that there is a close connection between his position and the fate of the state: 'all the actions which I took, with your assistance, during my consulship, to ensure the salvation of this city and empire and to preserve the lives of the citizens and the existence of the state as a whole, these has Archias begun and touched upon in his poetry'.[50] This is not quite the same as suggesting that Archias' epic on Lucullus is in effect an epic to the glory of the Roman people, since Archias' putative poem on Cicero's consulship would celebrate not their achievements but their survival as a civic body. But Cicero's favoured identification between himself and the *res publica* does reap double benefits: he can present Archias as a figure of value to the whole community, while inserting himself into a tradition of heroic Romans whose deeds were celebrated in verse. In this speech Cicero does not emphasize his achievements at the expense of the state and even suggests that the state itself is the fitting recipient of Archias' praise in his summary of Archias' achievements: 'he who has constantly honoured you, your generals and the achievements of the Roman people, who has also indicated that he will grant an everlasting witness of praise to those recent internal dangers which have threatened me and you'.[51] Just as the poet–patron relationship involves the exchange of services, of poetic commemoration and thus everlasting life in return for material support, so, the jurors are encouraged to think, should the relationship which Cicero has suggested exists between Archias and the state be confirmed by their material support for Archias, that is, their allowing him to remain as a Roman citizen.

[50] 28: 'nam quas res nos in consulatu nostro uobiscum simul pro salute huius urbis atque imperi et pro uita ciuium proque uniuersa re publica gessimus, attigit hic uersibus atque inchoauit' (*urbis* suppl. Naugerius).

[51] 31: 'eum qui uos, qui uestros imperatores, qui populi Romani res gestas semper ornauit, qui etiam his recentibus nostris uestrisque domesticis periculis aeternum se testimonium laudis daturum esse profitetur'.

So Archias is presented as an Ennian epic poet with the added dimension that his patrons are not simply the individual Romans but also the state as a whole.[52] But this does not exhaust Cicero's tactics for making Archias' poetic activity seem attractive. It is time to consider how Cicero deals with Archias as a Roman.

2.2.2. Becoming a Roman

At first sight it might seem that Cicero tries to present Archias as a Roman. So, he is called in the opening paragraphs Aulus Licinius (1, 4), the name he held by virtue of being a Roman citizen, and his concluding argument for Archias' actually possessing the citizenship is that he has exercised his legal rights as a citizen, making his will, inheriting, and having the state pay his expenses while accompanying Lucullus (11). However, alongside the powerfully persuasive assumption that Archias is indeed a citizen, Cicero presents an image of Archias as a Greek. In this section I shall explore what exactly makes up this Greekness, and then consider why Cicero might have adopted this somewhat paradoxical strategy.

To begin with, Aulus Licinius vanishes after the opening paragraphs, and Archias takes over.[53] And Cicero does nothing to conceal or distract attention away from Archias' Hellenic origins: he comes from Antioch, a 'populous and wealthy city, awash with learned scholars and the pursuit of liberal arts',[54] and came to Italy after a highly successful career in Asia Minor and mainland Greece. Archias' Italian allegiances lie very much in the Greek south of the peninsula: the four cities which Cicero says gave Archias their citizenship (5) are all Greek foundations, and he draws attention to Archias' affection for Heraclea (likewise a Greek city) which Archias cited when claiming his Roman citizenship in 89 under the *lex Plautia Papiria* (10): 'other people have crept into the citizenship lists of these towns [sc. Rhegium, Locri, Naples, and Tarentum], not only after the grant of Roman citizenship but even after the *lex Papia*. Should we then expel someone who didn't make use

---

[52] Damon, *Parasite*, 268–76.

[53] The *A. Licini* in 9 is a quotation from the register of citizens' names.

[54] 4: 'celebri quondam urbe et copiosa atque eruditissimis hominibus liberalissimisque studiis adfluenti'.

of the lists he was on, because he wanted always to be a Heraclean?'[55] Devotion to one place is of course a commendable civic virtue and one which supports Cicero's argument that Archias deserves to be a Roman citizen, as well as actually being one: the allegiance he has shown in the past to Heraclea is now matched, on a larger scale, by his devotion to Rome. And Archias' allegiance to this particular town is given a specific positive gloss by the contrast which Cicero sets up between it and all the other places, whose citizenship Archias did not cite when converting, though he could have done, and whose citizenship is so easily given that even actors are honoured in this way. Although Cicero says nothing explicit about Heraclea, the contrast implies that it has higher standards, and this reflects back on Archias. So Cicero makes no attempt to hide the fact that Archias' Roman citizenship very much comes about through his involvement with the Greek cities of Italy.

Archias' essential Greekness is the specific focus of two passages later in the speech, during the digression on poetry. The first is in 18–19, where Cicero is developing the argument that honour should be paid to poets because of the delight they provide to statesmen. One argument he employs for the special status of poets is that their art, unlike all others, cannot be reduced to a series of rules, since inspiration is also necessary. He continues:

For this reason our fellow countryman Ennius rightly calls poets 'holy', because they seem to be entrusted to us as though by gift and grant of the gods. And so let this name of 'poet' be holy to you, gentlemen of the jury, as cultured, educated men, a name which no barbarian has ever harmed. Rocks and deserts respond to the voice, savage animals are often swayed by song and stand still: shall we, brought up in civilization, not be moved by the voices of poets?[56]

---

[55] 'quid? cum ceteri non modo post ciuitatem datam sed etiam post legem Papiam aliquo modo in eorum municipiorum tabulas inrepserunt, hic qui ne utitur quidem illis in quibus est scriptus, quod semper se Heracliensem esse uoluit, reicietur?'

[56] qua re suo iure noster ille Ennius 'sanctos' appellat poetas, quod quasi deorum aliquo dono atque munere commendati nobis esse uideantur. sit igitur, iudices, sanctum apud uos, humanissimos homines, hoc poetae nomen quod nulla umquam barbaria uiolauit. saxa atque solitudines uoci respondent, bestiae saepe immanes cantu flectuntur atque consistunt; nos instituti rebus optimis non poetarum uoce moueamur?

Simply on the level of a general description of the effects of poetry, this is a powerfully persuasive passage. Gotoff draws attention to the verbal and specifically poetic artistry of the final sentence.[57] On a conceptual level, Cicero sets up the distinction between civilization and barbarity only to deny its importance, since everything, regardless of its level of civilization, should respond with the same awe to poetry. As well as appealing to the jurors' *humanitas*, this tactic also allows Cicero to suggest the magnitude of Archias' own poetic achievement: this would be particularly important given how little Archias had actually written.

This passage is effective if read only as a hyperbolic description of the power of poetry, and by avoiding an explicit reference to myth Cicero does not run the risk of excluding any of his audience.[58] None the less, there is a specific candidate for the poet who can affect nature by his singing, namely Orpheus. Archias is thus being compared to the archetype of the divinely inspired and irresistible poet.[59]

However, there is a problem in Cicero's account of Orpheus, which anyone who picked up the reference at all would surely observe: one of the fixed parts of the myth was Orpheus' violent death at human hands.[60] Indeed, Cicero is so emphatically

[57] Gotoff, *Elegant Style*, 177.

[58] The only *named* occurrences of Orpheus in Cicero's writings are in the *ND* (1. 107; 3. 45). Cf., however, *Verr.* 2. 5. 171, where Cicero exclaims that even were he to be describing Verres' crimes to desert rocks, they would be affected. Here Cicero is ascribing to himself the Orpheus role (though he becomes so effective as a result of what Verres has done, rather than because of his own skill).

[59] *Pace* Narducci, *L'eloquenza romana*, 12, who explains this passage by reference to Democritus and Plato. Orpheus does not appear in extant Latin poetry until the *Eclogues*, but there he is 'already as a symbol of artistic perfection, represented by the power of his singing over nature' (P. E. Knox, *Ovid's Metamorphoses and the Traditions of Augustan Poetry* (Cambridge: PCPhS suppl. vol. no. 11; 1986), 48). The main elements of the myth (for which see *LIMC* 7/1; 81–3) would be familiar to any educated Roman; for Orpheus as a symbol of poetic inspiration see C. Segal, *Orpheus: The Myth of the Poet* (Baltimore: Johns Hopkins Univ. Press, 1989). Funerary epigrams for Orpheus are preserved in the Palatine Anthology, including one by Antipater of Sidon (7. 8), the friend of Catulus; it would be an elegant compliment by Cicero had Archias ever produced something similar.

[60] *LIMC* (vol. 7/1; 82).

wrong in arguing that no poet has ever suffered harm from barbarians that the mistake draws attention to itself.

Cicero hardly ever makes mistakes in his deployment of Greek myth: certainly not one as simple as this. One interpretation is to see this as a deliberate error, which is to be detected as such and as a result remind the audience, as the reference to rocks and animals alone might not do, of Orpheus' fate.[61] Archias is, like Orpheus, a poet under threat; but the jury is not to behave as the Thracians did, and will not allow him to suffer at their hands. From the Romans, the poet's name will be safe: as it ought to be. If the jury do this, they will be showing a higher level of culture and civilization than Orpheus' Greek tormentors: an unexpected reversal of the normal cultural hierarchy between Rome and the Greek world, and one appealing to anyone who picked up Cicero's point. Moreover, it is Archias' poetry which brings about or at least provides the opportunity for this display of *humanitas*. Unlike the Thracian maenads, the Roman governing classes, in the microcosm of a jury, know how to treat a poet.

However, the idea of Rome showing a superior level of culture to the Greeks is extremely paradoxical: and Cicero may allow his audience to continue thinking of themselves as straightforward, no-nonsense people who are on the 'barbarian' side of the divide. It is possible to take *barbaria* as a reference to rocks, deserts, and wild beasts.[62] Orpheus' period in the wilderness did not harm him; problems arose only from other people, who should not have displayed any barbarousness.[63] On such a reading, then, the audience would be encouraged to accept Greek assessments of their Roman barbarity but show, through acquittal, that they still know how to behave justly, using their

[61] In the allusion in *Verr.* 2. 5. 171 (cited above), there is no need to recall Orpheus' death; indeed, the apparent identification between Cicero and Orpheus rather suggests that one should not.

[62] I can find no other use by Cicero of *barbaria* or any related words of landscapes. But Horace talks of *barbaras Syrtis* (*C.* 2. 6. 3) (Nisbet and Hubbard, *A Commentary on Horace Odes, Book 2* (Oxford: Oxford Univ. Press, 1978), 97, may be right to say the epithet refers to the inhabitants: the key point for my argument is that it is used of a place) and it is common in later writers.

[63] The Thracians were, from a Greek point of view, barbarians. But a Roman audience may not have made such distinctions, particularly in the context of a story which requires a contrast between Greek and Roman.

own experience of *res optimae*. Cicero prepares for the idea that protecting poets is compatible with being Roman by his reference to Ennius' use of the word *sanctus* to describe poets. Not only does he emphasize that Ennius is 'one of us', *noster Ennius*, and therefore a reliable guide; he also appeals to the Romans' self-image of themselves as a particularly religious race.[64] They, of all people, know what is due to the gods, and *nobis* in the same sentence can be read as specific to Romans, rather than mankind in general (as the contrast with *deorum* at first sight suggests). The fact that Archias' identity as a Greek is not concealed is essential in bringing these issues into sharper focus. It is because he is Greek that not attacking him becomes, on this interpretation, an opportunity for barbarian Romans to show over-civilized Greeks what true *humanitas* consists of.[65]

The second passage in which ethnic identity is very obviously exploited is 23, where Cicero counters a possible argument against the usefulness of Archias' poetry, which is that it is written in Greek.

If anyone thinks that there is less of a crop of glory from Greek verses than from Latin ones, he is making a serious mistake. Greek is read among practically all nations, whereas Latin is circumscribed by its own fairly narrow boundaries. If our achievements are limited only by the edges of the world, we ought to want our glorious reputation to penetrate as far as our soldiers' weapons have gone. Not only is such a record impressive for the people themselves whose affairs are chronicled, it is the greatest possible spur for those who risk their lives in the pursuit of glory to face dangers and struggles.[66]

---

[64] D. C. Feeney, *Literature and Religion at Rome* (Cambridge: Cambridge Univ. Press, 1998), 116–17; M. Beard, J. North, and S. Price, *Religions of Rome* (Cambridge: Cambridge Univ. Press, 1998), 108–13; Polybius believed them (6. 56. 6–15).

[65] The allusion can itself be read as a test case for *humanitas*: anyone who picks up the Orpheus reference should, clearly, act as Cicero urges.

[66] 23: nam si quis minorem gloriae fructum putat ex Graecis uersibus percipi quam ex Latinis, uehementer errat, propterea quod Graeca leguntur in omnibus fere gentibus, Latina suis finibus exiguis sane continentur. qua re, si res eae quas gessimus orbis terrae regionibus definiuntur, cupere debemus, quo hominum nostrorum tela peruenerint, eodem gloriam famamque penetrare, quod cum ipsis populis de quorum rebus scribitur haec ampla sunt, tum eis certe qui de uita gloriae causa dimicant hoc maximum et periculorum incitamentum est et laborum.

Archias, as a poet writing about Rome's achievements in Greek, is an essential part of Rome's imperialism. It is not enough simply to conquer countries: they need also to be brought into a proper frame of mind about their own conquered state, so that they perceive their part in Rome's *gloria* and *fama*. Archias' role is to be a persuasive interpreter of Roman culture. It is also worth noting the wide significance that Cicero assigns to Archias' work. The people as a whole will benefit as well as those who do the fighting; and the latter are so described that they are not restricted to those in charge of armies. The ordinary soldiers, *homines nostri*, are also to be spurred on to great actions by Archias' poetry. This is as far as I know an unprecedented statement of the general importance of Greek culture. It is the culmination of Cicero's extraordinary redescription of a Greek poet whose output was intimately linked with the aspirations and desires of his particular patrons as a figure of great importance to the state as a whole in its imperialist ambitions.

The overall argument of the speech, or at least of the digression, that Archias deserves to hold the citizenship in return for the services he has done the state, fits into the long-standing tradition of granting citizenship to outsiders in return for actual or potential benefits to the state. This argument is in sharp contrast to the other justifications for extending the citizenship, which are pragmatic, or present it as a response to cultural assimilation. The fact that Cicero does not draw any connection between Archias' claim to the citizenship and the Social War is striking, given that it would have been possible to present the entire case as a result of the confusions in sorting out enfranchising the whole of Italy, and thus sidestep the whole issue of Archias' origins. One of the consequences of enfranchising the whole of Italy was that a large number of towns in southern Italy which were, culturally and linguistically, entirely Greek, now became Roman;[67] an aspect of the results of the Social War which seldom receives much attention, since the communities which initiated and led the revolt were all situated further north, as was the fighting. Yet the absorption of this part of Italy changed the composition of the citizen body quite as radically as including Etrurians or

[67] Crawford, 'Italy and Rome', 419–20.

Samnites or Campanians. But Cicero does not place Archias' enfranchisement within the context of a mass enfranchisement of men who were from a similar cultural background. His account of the process (6–7) emphasizes at each stage the singularity of Archias' position: he was given citizenship at Heraclea through the intervention of the Luculli; he converted that into citizenship at Rome by personal statement before the praetor. This picture is strengthened by Cicero's quotation from the *lex Plautia Papiria* of the necessary conditions for claiming the citizenship: 'Whoever were members by ascription of allied states, and resided in Italy at the time of the passing of the law, and declared their names before the praetor within sixty days . . .'. There is no reason to doubt that Cicero is quoting accurately; however, as Sherwin-White argues, this clause must be a special provision, specifically designed to plug a loophole in the earlier *lex Iulia* through which men like Archias, who were not resident in the Italian community of which they were citizens, might fall.[68] The effect of the quotation is to conceal the fact that Archias' enfranchisement took place in the context of literally thousands of other enfranchisements, and to suggest that it is in some sense a mark of personal favour: the argument which Cicero proceeds to put forward strongly in the digression.

Archias' value to Rome, as Cicero presents the case, is precisely his Greekness. It is because he writes in Greek that he can assist the project of cultural, as opposed to military, imperialism, as 23 shows; and it is through being Greek that his trial offers to the jury such a pleasing opportunity to demonstrate their cultural superiority to the Greeks by treating a poet as a poet should be treated. Indeed, it is tempting to think that the jury was to see Archias' Greekness as an attractive feature beyond its usefulness. What, after all, could be more satisfying or a better indication of Rome's power than having one of the defeated praising Rome's glory? Conquering a nation is the first step; informing them about

[68] Sherwin-White, *Citizenship*, 152; he remarks further: 'There is a negative element latent in the clause, which has been framed to exclude some *ascripti*. The Romans were not prepared to allow a host of provincials to creep into the fold on the plea that at some time they or their ancestors had been given the freedom of some Hellenic city in the south of Italy.'

Rome's magnificent reputation comes next; but best of all is to get them involved in disseminating that reputation themselves. Were Cicero to portray Archias as one who had adopted Roman customs and behaviour, his particular value, in return for which he could be allowed to be a Roman, would largely disappear.

One further possible consideration informing Cicero's tactics in the speech may be his need to rule out, as clearly as possible, the most likely route for a man in Archias' position to have obtained the citizenship, that is through being a freed slave: almost everyone at Rome who possessed the *tria nomina*, but with a distinctively Greek *cognomen*, would belong to that category.[69] Archias, however, owes his position to his voluntary participation in the great project of Roman world domination; and by emphasizing his relationship with the Roman people over that with his patrons, Cicero also helps to refute the possibility, which might have occurred to some of the jury, that Archias' original connection with them was servile.

2.3. BALBUS: IS PATRONAGE ENOUGH?

Cicero's defence of Archias depends to a large extent on cutting out the individual patron, through whom the citizenship was originally granted, and making Archias a client of the whole Roman state. In contrast, Balbus' chief patrons, Pompeius and Caesar, play a central role in Cicero's speech on his behalf. Balbus himself plays a curiously minor role, although a figure of much greater importance and note in Roman society than Archias.[70] By unravelling the mechanics of this defence, it is possible to see how Cicero responds to the delicate challenge of dealing with the re-formed first triumvirate, while at the same time complementing his reluctance to deal in general terms with the problems posed by citizenship which was apparent in the *pro Archia*.

The simplest way to view the structure of the *pro Balbo* is to

[69] See S. Treggiari, *Roman Freedmen during the Late Republic* (Oxford: Oxford Univ. Press, 1969), 6–8 and 110–28.

[70] On Balbus' wealth and career, see Nicolet, *L'Ordre Equestre*, vol. 2 (1974), 853–5; A. Alföldi, *Oktavians Aufstieg zur Macht* (Bonn: Habelt, 1976), 36–43.

see it in three parts: an extended introduction (1–16), which sets up the rectitude of Pompeius' actions as the issue to be judged; 17–55, which contains the discussion of the legal issue and the citation of numerous other cases where citizenship has been granted to foreigners; and a conclusion (56–5), which once more turns attention to Balbus' patrons, as Cicero urges the jury not to punish a man because of his friends.

The most striking point about this structure is the importance it ascribes to Balbus' patrons. The legal arguments for Balbus' citizenship are strong in themselves; but as far as position goes, the jurors are left to consider whether they wish to condemn an act of Pompeius, and a protégé of both Pompeius and Caesar.

Cicero suggests that the primacy of Pompeius is the real target at the trial: the point at issue, he explains, is whether or not Pompeius granted the citizenship to Balbus legally. This dominates his first statement of the case, at 5–8: the fact of being granted the citizenship can only be considered as a sign of honour for Balbus and if there has been any wrongdoing it is Pompeius' alone:

All these facts are a source of praise for Cornelius and entirely his own doing: no grounds for a charge adheres to them at all. Where then does the charge come from? Because Pompeius gave him the citizenship. Is this a charge against *Balbus*? Of course not, unless one considers an honour to be a disgrace. Whose then? In reality, nobody's, but according to the prosecutor's suit, against him alone who made the grant.[71]

And the final sentence of the speech concludes the summing up of the case for the jury similarly: 'finally, gentlemen of the jury, keep this consideration fixed in your minds, that you are not, in this trial, coming to a judgement about any wrongdoing of Lucius Cornelius, but about a benefit conferred by Gnaeus Pompeius.'[72] It is true that this is not an entirely unreasonable summary of the case. But Cicero is seldom so bound by legal

[71] 6–7: haec sunt omnia cum plena laudis tum propria Corneli, nec in iis rebus crimen est ullum. ubi igitur est crimen? quod eum Pompeius ciuitate donauit. huius crimen? minime, nisi honos ignominia putanda est. cuius igitur? re uera nullius, actione accusatoris eius unius qui donauit.

[72] 65: 'postremo illud, iudices, fixum in animis uestris tenetote, uos in hac causa non de maleficio L. Corneli, sed de beneficio Cn. Pompei iudicaturos.'

points as not to be able to construct his speech around quite
different issues should he so wish; in this case one can point to
two significant advantages which the focus on Pompeius gave
him. In the first place it meant that he need not talk about
Balbus a great deal; on his presentation, Balbus' character is
guaranteed already by Pompeius' action. I return below to the
advantages of giving Balbus a low profile. The second advantage was that Pompeius was an excellent subject for Cicero to
praise. Not only were his achievements truly impressive and
easy to make appealing, he had already been praised extensively
by Cicero. The allusions to the speech *de imperio Cn. Pompei*
are obvious and significant.

In the first place the allusions allow Cicero to recall
Pompeius' glory days as a military commander. Pompeius had
done very little as a soldier since his return from the East in
62,[73] and his popularity had suffered considerably through his
participation in the first triumvirate.[74] Cicero is here reminding
the jury why it was that they admired, or at least ought to
admire, Pompeius. This benevolence would then, ideally, be at
the service of Balbus, particularly given that his citizenship was
obtained during Pompeius' campaigns against Sertorius, the
grounds for his second triumph.

But the allusions refer not only to the deeds themselves, but
also to Cicero's earlier treatment of them in the *de imp.* 27–48.
Cicero's discussion of Pompeius in the *pro Balbo* (9–15) asks to
be read against the *de imp.* quite clearly: the general similarity
of subject would push an alert reader in this direction, and it is
supported not only in the similar general arrangement around
a list of Pompeius' attributes (*scientia, uirtus, auctoritas*, and
felicitas in the *de imp.*, *usus rerum, ingenium, pudor, integritas,
religio, diligentia* in the *pro Balbo*) but also in specific verbal
reminiscences.[75] This impression is reinforced by what looks

---

[73] He had been involved in securing the grain supply in 57–56: see Garnsey,
Famine, 201.

[74] T. P. Wiseman, 'Caesar, Pompey and Rome, 59–50 B.C.', *CAH* 9, 2nd
edn. (1994), 368–423, 375 and 392.

[75] The praise of Pompeius in 9–13 of the *pro Balbo* is a recapitulation,
with variations, of the praise of Pompeius in the *de imp.*: so for example *pro
Balbo* 9: 'cuius plerique aequales minus saepe castra uiderunt quam hic
triumphauit' ~ *de imp.* 28, 'saepius cum hoste conflixit quam quisquam cum
inimico concertauit, plura bella gessit quam ceteri legerunt'; *pro Balbo* 9:

like a deliberate correction of the earlier speech's insistence on
Pompeius' luck in the sentence, 'even the very chances and out-
comes of events have been not the controllers of his plans but
his companions: in this one man the greatest good fortune has
struggled with the greatest virtue so that everybody agrees in
ascribing more to the man than to the goddess'.[76] What are the
effects of the allusion? A diligent *reader* of Cicero might have
returned to an earlier scroll, and admired the virtuosity with
which Cicero repeats the substance while abbreviating and
varying the actual words. But the real importance lies not so
much in detailed verbal correspondences, or their absence, but
in the simple fact of recalling the situation ten years earlier.
Then, Pompeius was granted a powerful command in order to
defeat Mithradates: he accomplished this, and much more,
with his annexation of Syria and reorganization of Asia Minor.
By recalling the start of such a benign and effective intervention
into Rome's imperial affairs, Cicero suggests that Pompeius'
earlier intervention in granting citizenship to Balbus was a
similarly good thing. As Cicero says towards the beginning of
the speech, everything connects: 'everything which the man
who has a firm mental grasp on all the virtues does turns out
well'.[77] The specific reference is to Pompeius' oratorical skill,
admirable in one who has had so little time to devote to the
art, but is clearly to be understood as true of all Pompeius'
actions.[78] The correspondence between the *de imp.* and the *pro*

events obey Pompeius ~ *de imp.* 48: even winds obey Pompeius; *pro Balbo* 9:
the enthusiasm of imperial subjects for Pompeius ~ *de imp.* 41: the keenness of
the allies on Pompeius; *pro Balbo* 13: the whole world is witness to Pompeius'
achievements ~ *de imp.* 30–1.

[76] 9: 'quin etiam ipsi casus euentusque rerum non duces, sed comites eius
consiliorum fuerunt: in quo uno ita summa fortuna cum summa uirtute
certauit ut omnium iudicio plus homini quam deae tribueretur'. For
Pompeius' luck, see *de imp.* 47–8.

[77] 3: 'ei qui omnis animo uirtutes penitus comprehendisset omnia quae
faceret recte procedere' (*recte procedere* Peterson, following Mueller and
Madvig); for a discussion of the textual problems here, see Loutsch, *L'Exorde*,
366 n. 35.

[78] The sentiment is a Stoic commonplace (*SVF* 3. 557–66), and Cicero indicates its philosophical provenance immediately before with the words, 'ut
mihi iam uerum uideatur illud esse quod non nulli litteris ac studiis doctrinae
dediti quasi quiddam incredibile dicere putabantur'. Its application to

Balbo also evokes a memory of Cicero's activity in 66, and thus
indicates how long he has been connected with Pompeius:
important for the speech as a sign of Cicero's continuing
support for the first triumvirate.

Cicero also indicates the importance of Caesar to Balbus, and
Balbus to Caesar: he too will be distressed, and have his judgement impugned, should Balbus be deprived of his citizenship.
Balbus was by now far more closely linked with Caesar than
with Pompeius, and, formally, was his *praefectus fabrum* while
campaigning in Gaul. As in the speech *de prouinciis consularibus*
Cicero can exploit the impression made by Caesar's conquests:
in this speech he draws attention to the pain that the jury will
inflict on Caesar if they vote to convict Balbus:

> But, since Gaius Caesar is so far away and in those places which by
> their location mark the edge of the world and by his achievements the
> edge of the Roman empire, please, gentlemen of the jury, I appeal to
> you by the immortal gods, do not allow this bitter news to be carried
> to him, so that he hears that his own *praefectus fabrum*, that a man on
> the most intimate and friendly footing with him, has been condemned
> by your votes not because of any crime of his own doing, but as a
> result of his friendship with Caesar himself.[79]

The news, the reader is to understand, will be unpleasant for
Caesar; the quasi-military force of Balbus' title may also
suggest that Caesar will be disadvantaged in some military
capacity, which might seem more serious. It is worth noting too
that Cicero is relying on slightly different constructions of
Pompeius and of Caesar. Pompeius' character and achievements guarantee Balbus' citizenship, and so to vote against
Balbus diminishes Pompeius' *dignitas* and is a sorry indication
of the failings of contemporary society (15. 5–8); but there is no
suggestion that Pompeius will be personally grieved by Balbus'
conviction. Caesar's grief, by contrast, is in itself presented as

Pompeius is paradoxical: perhaps deliberately so. See below for further discussion of possible covert sniping at Pompeius in this speech.

[79] 64: sed quoniam C. Caesar abest longissime, atque in iis est nunc locis
quae regione orbem terrarum, rebus illius gestis imperium populi Romani
definiunt, nolite, per deos immortalis, iudices, hunc illi acerbum nuntium
uelle perferri, ut suum praefectum fabrum, ut hominem sibi carissimum,
non ob ipsius aliquod delictum, sed ob suam familiaritatem uestris oppres-
sum sententiis audiat.

something which should deter the jury. This difference makes Caesar much the more formidable figure.

The focus on Pompeius and Caesar is complemented by the lack of attention paid to Balbus. He is strikingly absent from the exordium,[80] and the speech's ending openly directs our attention away from Balbus and to Pompeius. In the *pro Archia* Archias' own desires and emotions are obscure, but his actions, and indeed what Cicero presents as his intrinsic nature as a poet, are very much to the point. By contrast, it is difficult to gain any precise idea of what Balbus has done to justify his citizenship. Cicero's summary of the grounds for his being granted the citizenship early in the speech is as follows:

The prosecutor admits everything else: that Cornelius was with Quintus Metellus and with Gaius Memmius, in both navy and army, in Spain during a most strenuous campaign; that when Pompeius arrived in Spain and had Memmius as his quaestor, Cornelius never left Memmius, that he was besieged at Carthage and present at those major and hard-fought battles, on the Sucro and the Turia, that he stayed with Pompeius until the very end of the war. These qualities are Cornelius' own: dutifulness towards our state, hard work, industry, fighting, courage worthy of a great general, hope of rewards for the dangers he faced. The rewards themselves depend on the act not of the man who obtained them, but of him who granted them.[81]

Balbus is, as throughout this speech, addressed by his Roman name Cornelius: this in itself makes him a colourless figure, since whatever the jury knew about him, they would naturally attach to his distinctive appellation, 'the stammerer'. And Cicero does not cite any notable deeds that Balbus may have done in the fighting in Spain. On his account, Balbus contributed by his presence alone: *fuisse, numquam discessisse, esse obsessum, interfuisse, fuisse.* This is an unimpressive

---

[80] Loutsch, *L'Exorde*, 364–5.

[81] 5. 1–6. 11: cetera accusator fatetur, hunc in Hispania durissimo bello cum Q. Metello, cum C. Memmio et in classe et in exercitu fuisse; ut Pompeius in Hispaniam uenerit Memmiumque habere quaestorem coeperit, num-quam a Memmio discessisse, Carthagine esse obsessum, acerrimis illis proeliis et maximis, Sucronensi et Turiensi, interfuisse, cum Pompeio ad extremum belli tempus fuisse. haec sunt propria Corneli, pietas in rem publicam nostram, labor, adsiduitas, dimicatio, uirtus digna summo imperatore, spes pro periculis praemiorum; praemia quidem ipsa non sunt in eius facto qui adeptus est, sed in eius qui dedit.

formulation, even if Balbus had done nothing worthy of note. He is given a number of qualities, but instead of saying that these constitute grounds for obtaining the citizenship Cicero adds a further attribute, the *hope* for rewards. As Cicero emphatically says, the granting of the rewards cannot be influenced by the person who benefits. All that Balbus can claim as his own, *propria*, are his virtue and activity and the intangible *spes*.

What are the consequences of this description? It maintains the focus on the patron and away from the client which I have already discussed. And insofar as the audience is allowed to perceive Balbus, it is as an entirely passive figure. He cannot influence his fate with regard to Rome: the Romans have complete control. What Cicero does allow him to do is have relations with the Roman state. *Pietas* is, unfortunately, an emendation:[82] if we accept it, then we have the striking picture of Balbus expressing a highly appropriate and Roman emotion from a position outside the state (which *nostram* underlines).[83] One does not have to rely on *pietas*, however: *in rem publicam nostram* seems secure, even if a word other than *pietas* has dropped out. This produces the appealing picture, for a Roman, of provincials who feel these admirable sentiments towards Rome and surrender themselves entirely to the beneficence of Roman commanders who may, but are not compelled to, reward them. This picture would lose much of its charm if Balbus were to seem to be Roman: as in the *pro Archia*, the possession of citizenship by a provincial turns out to be a demonstration of Rome's power over that provincial.

An important strand of argument in the speech for letting Balbus' citizenship stand is that Rome benefits greatly by having this tool with which to ensure the loyalty of its provincial subjects: 'but if our generals, the Senate and the Roman people are not allowed to entice the bravest and best of the inhabitants of states allied and friendly with us into facing dangers on our behalf by offering rewards, we will have lost a

---

[82] *Corneli pietas* (Mueller), in place of *Cornelii hic* (*GE*), *cornelitas* (*P¹*), *Cornelii talis* (*P²*, other manuscripts).

[83] The *OLD* elides the oddity and the difficulty of the phrase entirely, citing it, without indicating the insecurity of the text, as the first example of *pietas* used for the feelings of a citizen towards his state.

most valuable advantage, and often a source of great protection in troubled and dangerous times'.[84] The use of the word *elicere* is particularly telling, since it sets up an unequal relationship between the two parties. *Elicere* is to get something from someone who might not otherwise give it by means of particular tactics; it is often used in cases where the giver is deceived, and there is never a suggestion that the giver is acting in his or her own advantage.[85] In this passage, it contains not only the realistic acknowledgement that provincials are not going to work for the Roman state without some reward, but also the implication that the Romans are pulling an advantageous fast one, getting provincials to risk their necks on behalf of the Roman state, *pro salute nostra*.

For these arguments and implications to work, it is important that Balbus should seem still positively Spanish. As in the *pro Archia*, Cicero needs to conceal any signs of assimilation on the part of his client in order to set him up as a pleasing example of the state's control over its empire. The examples of other non-Romans who have received the citizenship which Cicero cites to support his case are treated in a similar fashion. At the end of a long list of people and communities that Pompeius and other generals have enfranchised, he concludes with a general hope: 'and if those who by their own efforts and danger protect our state are worthy of other rewards, they are certainly particularly worthy of being given the citizenship of the state for which they have faced dangers and weapons'.[86]

The essential otherness of those who are enfranchised appears even more strongly in Cicero's final example, a comparatively extended discussion of the priestesses of Ceres:

Our ancestors, gentlemen of the jury, wanted the rites and ceremonies of Ceres to be carried out with the utmost sanctity, rites which came

---

[84] 22: 'atqui si imperatoribus nostris, si senatui, si populo Romano non licebit propositis praemiis elicere ex ciuitatibus sociorum atque amicorum fortissimum atque optimum quemque ad subeunda pro salute nostra pericula, summa utilitate ac maximo saepe praesidio periculosis atque asperis temporibus carendum nobis erit'. Cf. 20; 24.

[85] Cf. Caesar, *BG* 6. 8. 2; Livy 37. 13. 10.

[86] 51: 'etenim cum ceteris praemiis digni sunt qui suo labore et periculo nostram rem publicam defendunt, tum certe dignissimi sunt qui ciuitate ea donentur pro qua pericula ac tela subierunt'. The double meaning of *ciuitas* means the sentence needs to be expanded when translated.

from Greece and had always been tended by Greek priestesses and were in every respect called Greek. But although they chose the woman to perform and manage the rites from the Greek-speaking world, they none the less wanted a citizen to manage the rites, on behalf of citizens, so that she might pray to the immortal gods with foreign imported knowledge but with the attitude of a native citizen.[87]

Cicero rams home the Greekness of the priestess with five uses of *Graecus* and *Graecia*, and even though she, unlike all the other examples, is said to be to some extent assimilated into Roman culture, this is in the first place simply to serve Rome better and, secondly, an automatic consequence of her being enfranchised and not the grounds for it.[88] She is valuable to Rome precisely because she is not, fully, a Roman.

The prevalence of the model of citizenship as a reward is, paradoxically, emphasized at the one point at which the alternative, citizenship as a response to Romanization, is allowed, briefly, to surface. It does so when Cicero turns to the attitude of the Gaditanes themselves to the enfranchisement of Balbus and argues that they are very much in favour of it. One reason for their feeling this way, Cicero argues, is that Balbus has got the Romans to take more interest in his home town. In particular, this applies to Caesar: 'I pass over the number of honours which Gaius Caesar bestowed on this nation when he was praetor in Spain, the fact that he settled disputes, ordered, with their permission, their law code, extirpated a particular kind of ingrained barbarity from the customs and behaviour of the Gaditanes, and, at Cornelius' request, conferred much attention and many benefits on the state.'[89] Caesar is presented

[87] 55: sacra Cereris, iudices, summa maiores nostri religione confici caerimoniaque uoluerunt; quae cum essent adsumpta de Graecia, et per Graecas curata sunt semper sacerdotes et Graeca omnino nominata. sed cum illam quae Graecum illud sacrum monstraret et faceret ex Graecia deligerent, tamen sacra pro ciuibus ciuem facere uoluerunt, ut deos immortalis scientia peregrina et externa, mente domestica et ciuili precaretur.

[88] It is true that the Romans seem to have been particularly self-conscious about, and careful of, the distinction between themselves and the Greeks in a religious context: the cult of Ceres was worshipped *Graeco more* since its (alleged) introduction in the early 5th cent.: Feeney, *Literature and Religion*, 26–7.

[89] 43: 'omitto quantis ornamentis populum istum C. Caesar, cum esset in Hispania praetor, adfecerit, controuersias sedarit, iura ipsorum permissu statuerit, inueteratam quandam barbariam ex Gaditanorum moribus

here as the civilizing face of Roman imperialism, the peaceful improvement of societies by exposing them to Roman law and Roman morality. Balbus is the facilitator of this benevolence, but not the man who actually does it, and it is open to the audience to reflect that Cicero passes over entirely the effects upon Balbus himself of exposure to the Romans.

Why does Cicero treat Balbus in this way, ignoring almost entirely his character and achievements and presenting his enfranchisement as a bland example of the fine tradition of a Roman general's granting of citizenship in return for unspecified services rendered? It cannot simply be that this is an appealing model: his description of Caesar's actions shows that Rome as the civilizing force could also be presented in a self-congratulatory way.

One factor is Balbus' own unpopularity in Rome. Cicero gives a glimpse of it in one of his letters to Atticus late in the year 50, where he lists what has resulted from Caesar's pre-eminence: 'my exile, the loss of the *ager Campanus*, the adoption of a patrician by a plebeian and of a Gaditane by a Mytilenaean, the wealth of Labienus and Mamurra . . . and the Gardens of Balbus and his house at Tusculum'.[90] And from the charges against which Cicero does defend Balbus in this speech it is possible to confirm and complement the picture produced by his own later complaints. Cicero acknowledges, through his defence, that Balbus has been attacked for his wealth, his luxury, his Tusculan villa, his acquisition, by a successful prosecution, of membership of the rural tribe *Clustumina*, and his adoption by Theophanes.[91] He does not attempt to offer a defence of the particular charges, but dismisses them all as the results of envy, echoing his statement earlier in the speech, at the end of his praise of Pompeius, that it is only because of the contemporary tendency to feel envious of virtue that he need extend his defence. This allows him to make a transition to a

---

disciplinaque delerit, summa in eam ciuitatem huius rogatu studia et beneficia contulerit.'

[90] *Att.* 7. 7. 6: 'me expulsum et agrum Campanum perisse et adoptatum patricium a plebeio, Gaditanum a Mytilenaeo, et Labieni diuitiae et Mamurrae . . . et Balbi horti et Tusculanum'.

[91] 56–7. For Balbus and Theophanes, see Gold, *Literary Patronage*, 99–101; on Balbus' wealth, Shatzman, *Senatorial Wealth and Roman Politics*, 329–30.

further category of Balbus' enemies, those who attack him
because they are enemies of Balbus' friends:

> None the less, it is not that difficult to placate the feelings of those who
> envy Cornelius himself. They envy him in the way that men do: they
> nibble away at him at banquets, they carp in conversation: they bite
> him not with the tooth of enmity but with this slanderous one. But
> there are people who *are* enemies of Lucius Cornelius' friends, or
> envy them, and they are a reason for much greater apprehension on
> Cornelius' part. For has a personal enemy of Cornelius ever been
> found, or could there rightly be such a one?[92]

Cicero's distinction between envy and enmity in order to
dismiss the importance of the former seems at first sight
breathtakingly implausible: the dislike felt towards Balbus
really did exist and, insofar as the jurors might share it, could
well lead to his loss of citizenship. But it enables Cicero to
bring the debate away from Balbus and back to the issue of his
patrons, to Pompeius and to Caesar, and to what does seem to
have been the real aim of the prosecution, the embarrassment
of the first triumvirate.

Balbus' position in society was so closely linked to his
relationships with Pompeius and Caesar that an attack on him,
particularly on a charge that could have been used at any time
over the previous nine years, could only be interpreted as an
indirect attack on his patrons. There is no need to interpret
the prosecution as a left-over manoeuvre from the period
before the remaking of the alliance at Luca.[93] This trial must
be several months after that conference, and the prosecution
would have abandoned it had it no longer been strategically
sensible. In fact it makes particular sense in the post-Luca
period, precisely because effective political opposition was
then much harder: an attack on an unpopular subordinate is
precisely the sort of move that could be effective. Either
Pompeius had to disown Balbus, or he had to stand up and

---

[92] 57–8: quamquam istorum animos, qui ipsi Cornelio inuident, non est
difficillimum mitigare. more hominum inuident, in conuiuiis rodunt, in
circulis uellicant: non illo inimico, sed hoc malo dente carpunt. qui amicis
L. Corneli aut inimici sunt aut inuident, ii sunt huic multo uehementius
pertimescendi. nam huic quidem ipsi quis est umquam inuentus inimicus
aut quis iure esse potuit?

[93] See Loutsch, *L'Exorde*, 357 n. 2.

speak on behalf of him and thus openly support someone who was widely disliked. Indeed, the prosecution may have been trying to exploit the fact that Balbus was now Caesar's protégé in order to drive a wedge between the two, forcing Pompeius, in Caesar's absence in Gaul, to protect someone who had, it seems, shifted his allegiance from Pompeius to Caesar.

A further factor which made Balbus a good tool to make Pompeius unpopular was his foreign status. Men like Balbus and Theophanes were a new phenomenon: non-Romans who played an important *political* role at Rome, as opposed to the quite familiar activity of Greeks in the cultural sphere. By drawing attention to Balbus' transition from a foreigner to a figure of great importance in Rome, the prosecution was highlighting the arrogance and innovation of Pompeius', and of Caesar's, behaviour, in employing provincials, whom they chose as a direct result of their military activity. One can see how this could be presented as a perversion of the desirable pattern of imperial activity, of Romans exploiting provinces for the benefit of Rome, since Pompeius and Caesar were using the provincials, or rather a particular provincial, for their own personal benefit, and moreover allowing him to cross over the boundary between non-Roman and Roman. Cicero's construction of Balbus' citizenship as a benefit to the whole state certainly suggests that this was a line of argument being used by the prosecution.

Cicero's own presence at this trial as a defence counsel would inevitably be interpreted by his audience as a further indication of the U-turn he had done after Luca. The first public manifestation of this was the speech *de prouinciis consularibus*, to which he refers in this speech (61), together with a justification, on the grounds of the good of the state, of his recent change of political tack. As in the *prou. cons.*, the general support which Cicero gives needs to be read together with a number of indications of dissent.

One such indication is in the passage following Cicero's distinction between envy and enmity. Balbus has no personal enemies himself because he has never regarded political differences as a ground for hostility (58). Cicero's example of this is Balbus' behaviour towards him when he was exiled: 'not only did Cornelius not triumph over the collapse of my

fortunes and your wearing of mourning, but he relieved my
people in my absence with every attention: tears, services, con-
solation'.[94] This example makes quite clear how shallow and
improbable is the current entente between Cicero and the first
triumvirate, since Cicero would not have found himself in exile
had not Pompeius and Caesar acquiesced in Clodius' plans.
This tension is confirmed as Cicero goes on to argue that
Balbus' services to him ought to make Balbus popular with all
who wished for Cicero's recall. Whether or not we want to see
Cicero as making, here, a genuine pitch for the widest possible
coalition of support for Balbus (rather than putting together a
group whose point is its obvious implausibility), it is clear that
Cicero is pointing out that he is not an isolated figure. As in the
prou. cons., albeit on a much smaller scale, he is reminding
Pompeius and Caesar that he has a political position other than
that of an appendage to them.

This passage on Cicero's exile is the only place in the speech
where he points to a personal connection with Balbus. As a
result, he does not bring to bear his own *auctoritas*, nor does he
suggest that Balbus' conviction will lead to any suffering or loss
of prestige on his own part. This is a further indication of the
gap which he is setting up between himself and the other advocates, Pompeius and Crassus. And if there is no personal reason
for Cicero to get involved in the case, then his presence
becomes that of the first triumvirate's hired eloquence. It is
very tempting to read the beginning of the speech, in which
Cicero praises Pompeius' eloquence and deprecates his own
contribution, as a slyly ironic allusion to this. 'What is my role
to be?', he asks in response to his sketch of the other's talent.[95]
It is not difficult to supply an answer, in the gaps between
Cicero's ingenuous praise of Pompeius' skill at speaking, given
that he has had hardly any time since adolescence to devote to
it, and his failure to comment on Crassus' speech until 17,
where his assessment, 'Marcus Crassus, who had explained the
whole case to you most carefully, according to his ability and
sincerity', is easily read as a back-handed compliment.[96]

---

[94] 58: 'non modo non exsultauit in ruinis nostris uestrisque sordibus
Cornelius, sed omni officio,—lacrimis, opera, consolatione,—omnis me
absente meos subleuauit'.   [95] 1: 'quae sunt igitur meae partes?'
[96] 17: 'M. Crassus, qui totam causam et pro facultate et pro fide sua dili-

2.4. BECOMING A ROMAN CITIZEN

In both these speeches Cicero employs the well-established model of citizenship as a reward for services rendered to the Roman state: it bestows status, but does not result in partici-pation, and is granted within the context of some form of patron–client relationship. This model is appealing to a Roman audience because it makes the granting of citizenship an aspect of Rome's imperial success; it also allows Cicero to avoid the potentially worrying reflections which could accompany the granting of citizenship on a very large scale, as at the end of the Social War, with consequent radical changes in the composi-tion of the citizen body and ultimately, in what 'being a Roman citizen' meant. Citizenship as *beneficium* shows only the posi-tive and unproblematic aspects of extending the franchise in an extensive empire controlled by a society which had a long, unquestioned, but highly eccentric tradition of increasing its citizen numbers by absorption from below. Instead of being a destabilizing force within the state, because of the changes which followed from a vastly increased citizen body, granting of citizenship is presented as another means of controlling the empire and harnessing the diverse talents of provincials to the direct service of the Roman state.

These two speeches also demonstrate Cicero's flexibility in adapting this model to the specific circumstances of each case. Archias' personal identity and talents, as a Greek and as a poet, are central to his value to the Roman state: as a writer from the culturally important, but politically vanquished, Greek east he has a crucial role to play in disseminating a persuasive account of the Roman world order to its Greek-speaking subjects. And by stressing that citizenship is, in Archias' case, a specific reward for his particular talents and achievements, Cicero

gentissime uobis explicauit'. We expect Crassus to be mentioned by name in the proem, as happens with Pompeius. Instead, the other person mentioned is *Lucius* Crassus (3), as an examplar of a great orator who could not have pleaded the case better than Pompeius. Are we supposed to contemplate how far the current Crassus fails to match his namesake as an orator? For M. Crassus' abilities as a speaker, see *ORF* 342–5. Loutsch, *L'Exorde*, 367 n. 37, takes a different line, pointing out that Cicero is said to have written speeches for Pompeius and exclaiming, 'Quelle tentation d'imaginer Cicéron faire ici l'éloge d'un discours sorti tout entier de sa propre plume!'

glosses over entirely the fact that his enfranchisement is part of a mass enfranchisement of communities which were in many respects still Greek.

Cicero's approach to Balbus is rather different, since the problem, in this case, was not that he was one of a large number of new citizens whose Roman identity was dubious; he is an isolated figure, but one who has transcended the patron–client relationship to become an important political player at Rome, albeit one who was still, in 56, operating outside the overt structures of political power as represented by the Senate and office-holding. His power was clearly a cause of his considerable unpopularity; Cicero attempts to lessen this by presenting a bland and anonymous figure, the passive recipient of the traditional reward for services to the Roman state. The trial of Balbus is really, according to Cicero, about Pompeius and Caesar, who are being attacked through Balbus; but the latter should really be seen by the jury simply as a sign of Roman power, supported and extended through the willing co-operation of provincials. This is a most misleading portrait of the ambitious and politically adroit Balbus; but, as in the case of the speech for Archias, Cicero has adopted a strategy which uses a familiar model of Roman citizenship in order to harness for his client the favourable emotions inspired by the control of a large empire while eliding the problems and anxieties to which generosity with the franchise gave rise.

3

Controlling the uncontrollable:
Cicero and the generals

IN this chapter I turn to the key imperial issue of the late Republic: the generals who rewrote the rules for holding commands, added huge tracts of land to the empire, and, on most accounts, precipitated the end of the Republic.[1] The plight of provincial victims of misgovernment, or of aspirants to the citizenship whose claims were subject to challenge, simply did not have the same influence on events. It was not the provincials who brought about the transformation in the form of Roman government. And even though this assessment depends on the benefit of hindsight, it is clear that at the time commands of the sort granted to Pompeius and Caesar were felt to be a new phenomenon. While *repetundae* and citizenship cases continued to be dealt with through the standing courts, the allocation of provinces and the military commands which went with them became a matter for tribunician law, and heated, even violent, public debate, rather than, as before, one of the functions of the Senate.

Cicero's participation in these debates provides some of the best evidence for these commands: his speech *de imperio Cn.*

---

[1] I am particularly interested in this chapter in the Gabinian and Manilian laws which gave to Pompeius the commands against the pirates and then against Mithradates, and the law of Vatinius which gave Caesar his command in Cisalpine Gaul and Illyria. But tribunician laws were regularly used in the 50s to determine the allocation of provinces: the Clodian laws of 58, determining the provinces of the consuls Piso and Gabinius, and sending Cato the Younger to Cyprus; and the laws of Trebonius in 55, extending Caesar's command in Gaul and giving Syria and Spain, respectively, to the consuls Crassus and Pompeius. See Millar, *Crowd*, 142–3; 170: 'But, in a way that was by now almost customary, their dispositions [sc. of the Senate concerning consular provinces in 56] were overridden by tribunician legislation early in 55'. On the definition of the 'extraordinary commands', see R. T. Ridley, 'The Extraordinary Commands of the Late Republic', *Historia*, 30 (1981), 280–97.

Pompei, in which he argues that Pompeius should be given a powerful command against Mithradates, and the speech *de prouinciis consularibus*, where he argues that Caesar's command in Gaul should not come to an end. The latter speech was, it is true, delivered in the Senate during the traditional annual debate to determine the provinces to be allocated to the consuls of the following year: but Caesar's command, the real issue being debated, had been created by a law of the tribune Vatinius.

In both these speeches Cicero argues in favour of extraordinary commands, a highly paradoxical position for him to take up given that, overall, his political beliefs are thoroughly conservative.[2] And, in both cases, he supports an uncharacteristic position not because of a sudden change of mind, but in order to further or protect his own career, a subject I shall return to in the next chapter. In this chapter I consider how he makes extraordinary commands seem acceptable and desirable to his audience. These commands raised a whole range of constitutional issues: one pressing question was how to control this concentration of power. Cicero's response depends not on countering openly the objections of his opponents, but on presenting Pompeius and Caesar as dutiful servants of the Roman state. And if Pompeius and Caesar really are like this, then the possibility that they could come into conflict with the Senate cannot arise. I also look at Cicero's portrayal of Murena in his defence of him against charges of electoral bribery. Murena was a praetorian general of no particular distinction: how Cicero handles him provides a useful indication of what exactly is distinctive in the presentations of Pompeius and of Caesar.

3.1. THE *LEX MANILIA*: THE CONSTITUTIONAL DEBATE

One useful approach to the speech that Cicero made in support of giving Pompeius an extraordinary command is to try to

---

[2] See, in general, L. Perelli, *Il pensiero politico di Cicerone: tra filosofia greca e ideologia aristocratica romana* (Florence: La Nuova Italia, 1990); N. Wood, *Cicero's Social and Political Thought* (Berkeley: Univ. of California Press, 1988).

establish the state of the debate to which Cicero was contributing, and as a result isolate the issues that were contentious.
In turn, this may make it possible to get outside the Ciceronian
frame, and answer a perennial interpretative problem that his
speeches pose: does he concentrate on a particular issue because
it is controversial, and the audience must be won over to his
view, or precisely because it is not controversial and therefore
opens up a straightforward vein of persuasion?

Cicero gives a summary of the arguments used by the main
opponents of the Manilian law, and a refutation of sorts,
towards the end of the speech (51–63). He is of course a suspect
source: yet the fact that he does not come up with any satisfactory answers to the criticisms made by Hortensius and
Catulus may suggest that he has not misrepresented their arguments to any serious extent, though that does not guarantee
that he has given a complete summary of their positions.

Cicero summarizes Hortensius' opposition as follows: 'what
then does Hortensius say? If everything is to be entrusted to
one man, Pompeius is the most appropriate candidate, but
everything should not in fact be entrusted to one man.'[3]
Catulus' position is slightly more complex and has two
elements. The first, alluded to by Cicero in passing, and more
as a compliment to Catulus than a serious focus of argument, is
that the accumulation of power in one man leaves the Roman
people vulnerable should anything happen to that man: 'this is
the man who received an impressive return for his worth and
standing when he asked you in whom you would place your
trust if you entrusted everything to Gnaeus Pompeius and
something happened to him: practically with one voice you all
said that you would place it in Catulus himself.'[4] Cicero goes on
to say that he differs from Catulus in wanting the state to
benefit from the abilities of great men when that is possible;[5]

---

[3] 52: 'quid igitur ait Hortensius? si uni omnia tribuenda sint, dignissimum
esse Pompeium, sed ad unum tamen omnia deferri non oportere.'

[4] 59: 'qui cum ex uobis quaereret, si in uno Cn. Pompeio omnia poneretis,
si quid eo factum esset, in quo spem essetis habituri, cepit magnum suae
uirtutis fructum ac dignitatis, cum omnes una prope uoce in eo ipso uos spem
habituros esse dixistis.'

[5] 59: 'sed in hoc ipso ab eo uehementissime dissentio, quod quo minus certa
est hominum ac minus diuturna uita, hoc magis res publica, dum per deos
immortalis licet, frui debet summi uiri uita atque uirtute.'

suggesting that Catulus is advocating an over-cautious and
rather mindless frugality.

The second objection is that innovation is undesirable: 'But
let nothing new happen which is not in accordance with the
practice and ordinances of our ancestors.'[6]

Before looking at how Cicero deals with these objections, it is
worth considering how far it is possible to supplement Cicero's
account of the opposition with Dio's account of the passage of
the *lex Gabinia* the previous year, which gave Pompeius a very
similar command against the pirates.[7] There are two difficulties
in using this evidence: the first is the general problem of how
much reliance we can place upon Dio's account; the second is
the extent to which the differences between the two laws, and
their passage, invalidate the comparison.

It seems clear that Dio consulted a wide range of authorities
in composing his history, and as a result was able to incorporate
much valuable material into his account.[8] However, where
his version of events can be compared with other sources,
faults in chronology and misleading or incorrect inferences
sometimes become evident. Moreover, the speeches are his
own compositions, whatever material he drew on.[9] The discussion of the *lex Gabinia* is very much a set-piece, with
speeches by Pompeius as well as Gabinius and Catulus; yet the
correspondences with the arguments that Cicero indicates were
in the air the following year are sufficiently close to suggest,
if nothing more, that the details that can be extracted from
Dio to supplement the *de imp.* may not all derive from Dio's

[6] 60: 'at enim ne quid noui fiat contra exempla atque instituta maiorum.'

[7] Dio 36. 24–36. His account of the passage of the *lex Manilia* (36. 42. 4–43.
5) is much briefer, and does not include details of the arguments used. Its
dominant feature is an attack on Cicero for his lack of political principle: cf.
F. Millar, 'Some Speeches in Cassius Dio', *MH* 18 (1961), 11–22.

[8] For Dio's value as a source, see F. Millar, *A Study of Cassius Dio* (Oxford:
Oxford Univ. Press, 1964); B. Manuwald, *Cassius Dio und Augustus* (Wies-
baden: Steiner, 1979), esp. 168–79; A. W. Lintott, 'Dio and the History of the
Late Republic', *ANRW* 2. 34. 3 (1997), 2497–523.

[9] Millar, *Cassius Dio*, 83: 'Dio's speeches carry further the tendency
towards generality and lack of apposite detail which characterises his History
as a whole . . . in general their interest must lie not in what they can contribute
to historical knowledge, but in the insight they can give into the mind of a
senator writing under the Severi, the political questions which were upper-
most in his mind and the sort of reasoning he could apply to them.'

imagination.[10] Details of the passage of the law were certainly available, as the presence in Plutarch's *Life of Pompeius* of an extended discussion of the pirate menace and of the passage of the *lex Gabinia*, similar but not identical (and without speeches), demonstrates. Moreover, even material which comes from Dio's imagination should not necessarily be dismissed without further reflection, given his wide reading in and understanding of the period.

The debate surrounding the passage of the *lex Gabinia* is a potentially valuable comparison because of the similarity between the two laws. The Manilian law was clearly designed as a successor to the Gabinian law, taking advantage of Pompeius' presence in the eastern Mediterranean with large resources and applying these to another problem, that of the persistent resistance to Roman rule from Mithradates. The response in Rome was, however, quite different. Whereas Gabinius had faced extreme violence in attempting to get his law passed, and was supported by very few senators,[11] Manilius' law had extensive backing, and the only significant opponents appear to have been Hortensius and Catulus. This change would suggest that feelings had changed very much over the course of the year, and so call into question the validity of using Dio's evidence.

This is, however, not an insuperable problem, since the evidence from Cicero's speech for the positions of Hortensius and Catulus show that there was considerable continuity between the opposition to these laws, consisting largely of anxieties about the wisdom and necessity of such large innovations. What seems to have shifted so many senators into Pompeius' camp was not a change of mind about extraordinary commands but the pragmatic realization, based on the popularity of the Gabinian law and Pompeius' success in carrying out that commission, that the Manilian law was destined to pass and that opposing it would achieve nothing except alienating Pompeius. There may also have been a calculation that the constitutional

[10] Dr Lintott suggests to me, for example, that the proposition of Dio's Catulus, that the *legati* should be chosen by the assembly rather than by Pompeius (36. 36. 1), might be one that was used at the time.

[11] But cf. O. D. Watkins, 'Caesar solus? Senatorial Support for the *lex Gabinia*', *Historia*, 36 (1987), 120–1.

damage had by 66 already been done, and that the State might
at least take advantage of Pompeius' skill and position to solve a
long-standing problem; and the Manilian law would at least
shelve what might have been seen as the 'Pompeius problem',
both the specific issue of his clashes with Metellus in Crete,[12]
and more general worries concerning what Pompeius might
do next, given that the command against the pirates ran for
three years. Setting him the task of dealing with Mithradates
would at least postpone the moment when he would return to
Rome.

There is, however, an interesting difference in the problems
which these laws were setting Pompeius to solve. The pirates
had proved resistant to conventional methods of warfare: there
was every justification for a new *sort* of command in order to try
to eliminate the problem.[13] Mithradates was, on the other hand,
entirely familiar, not only in himself, since he had been causing
problems for Rome for over twenty years, but also as the type
of the powerful eastern ruler who submitted reluctantly, if at
all, to the authority of Rome. It was far from clear why the
Senate's allocation of consular provinces had to be bypassed in
order to deal with *him*.

The particular type of threat which the pirates pose is indeed
one of the factors in the arguments which Catulus is given in
Dio's account of the *lex Gabinia*.[14] But general concerns about
the wisdom of the sort of law are prominent. Catulus' first point
is that it was not right to give one man so many commands one
after another (36. 31. 3). One of the arguments he uses to
support this proposition is that individuals who are given large
commands are often reluctant to stay within the constitution.
He cites Marius and Sulla as examples of men who were transformed into dangers to the state because of the exceptional

---

[12] R. Seager, *Pompey: A Political Biography* (Oxford: Blackwell, 1979),
38–9; Kallet-Marx, *Hegemony to Empire*, 318–20.

[13] For the problem of piracy at this period, see H. A. Ormerod, *Piracy in the
Ancient World* (Liverpool: Univ. Press of Liverpool, 1924), 190–247; H. Pohl,
*Die römische Politik und die Piraterie im östlichen Mittelmeer vom 3. bis zum 1.
Jh. v. Chr.* (Berlin: de Gruyter, 1993); P. De Souza, *Piracy in the Graeco-
Roman World* (Cambridge: Cambridge Univ. Press, 1999), 161–78.

[14] For a discussion of Catulus' speech in Dio, see D. Fechner, *Untersuchungen zu Cassius Dios Sicht der Römischen Republik* (Hildesheim: Olms,
1986), 43–8.

commands that they had held, and then summarizes this phenomenon (36. 31. 4): 'for it is not in human nature that a person (and I don't just mean the young but also the more mature) who has for a long time held extraordinary commands should be willing to stay within the limits set within ancestral custom.'[15] Catulus here goes on immediately to make clear that his remarks are not directed specifically at Pompeius, but neither does he make an exception for him, and it is clear that doubts are being raised about Pompeius' willingness to behave in a constitutional fashion and in particular to accept the authority of the Senate. Another danger in the concentration of power, he argues, is that it reduces the pool of commanders, since fewer get the opportunity to develop their military skills (36. 32. 2): 'but if you take the other course [sc. giving extensive commands to just a very few men] it is absolutely inevitable that you will be faced with serious shortage of those who will train as is necessary and will be able to be entrusted with military affairs'.[16] Were Pompeius to lose his touch, his previous career, which had involved hogging all military opportunities, meant that there would be no one available to take over. This anxiety also lies behind an anecdote which is recorded in Xiphilinus' abbreviation of part of Catulus' speech which is now lost. Catulus asked the crowd whom they would send out if Pompeius were to fail—clearly implying that they would have difficulty in finding anyone—to which they replied, 'You!'[17]

Catulus' second argument is that it is unwise to make elected magistrates unnecessary (36. 33. 2–3):

What is the point of your electing annual magistrates, if you are not then going to make use of them in dealing with this sort of problem? Surely not so that they can wander round in purple-bordered robes and hold the position in name only, while they are deprived of its force. How can you avoid the enmity of these men, and all the others who might choose to enter public life, if you abolish constitutional

[15] οὐ γάρ ἐστιν ἐν τῇ τῶν ἀνθρώπων φύσει ψυχήν, μὴ ὅτι νέαν ἀλλὰ καὶ πρεσβυτέραν, ἐν ἐξουσίαις ἐπὶ πολὺν χρόνον ἐνδιατρίψασαν τοῖς πατρίοις ἔθεσιν ἐθέλειν ἐμμένειν.

[16] ἐκείνως δὲ δὴ πολλὴν τὴν σπάνιν καὶ τῶν ἀσκησόντων τὰ προσήκοντα καὶ τὸν ἐπιτραπησομένων ἀνάγκη πᾶσα γίγνεσθαι.

[17] 36. 36a; cf. *de imp.* 59. 10–14, discussed above.

offices, entrusting nothing to those whom you have elected in accordance with the laws while giving a strange and unheard-of command to a private individual?[18]

The *lex Gabinia* will create a pool of resentful and excluded men, who would in other circumstances expect to hold important positions within the state. This in turn could lead, on Catulus' euphemistic but none the less clear interpretation, to civil discord. Catulus then goes off on a digression about the dictatorship (36. 34). His argument seems to be that there already exists an office outside the normal run of annual magistrates, precisely for emergencies; but if the people hate the idea of a dictatorship, with its restrictions of duration (to six months) and of place (to Italy), what are they doing in creating a new post which is virtually unrestricted in geographical terms and will last for three years? He concludes this part of the argument by recapitulating the dangers of excessive powers in the hands of one man (36. 35. 1): 'who does not see that it is neither appropriate nor advantageous to entrust affairs to one man and make one man master over all the good things that belong to us, even if he is an excellent man? Great honours and excessive commands excite men even of this sort and destroy them.'[19]

The final argument in Catulus' speech, before a lacuna, is one specific to the practicalities of any campaign against the pirates. The area involved, the whole Mediterranean, is too large for one man to handle, as Gabinius' law acknowledges with its provision for legates: would it not then be better to divide the command up among a number of men?[20] Not only would this avoid the problems of a single command, but it would also lead to better results, since the rivalry between

---

[18] τίνος μὲν γὰρ ἕνεκα καὶ τοὺς ἐνιαυσίους ἄρχοντας χειροτονεῖτε, εἴγε μηδὲν αὐτοῖς πρὸς τὰ τοιαῦτα χρήσεσθε; οὐ γάρ που ἵν' ἐν τοῖς περιπορφύροις ἱματίοις περινοστῶσιν, οὐδ' ἵνα τὸ ὄνομα μόνον τῆς ἀρχῆς περιβεβλημένοι τοῦ ἔργου αὐτῆς στέρωνται. πῶς δ'οὐχὶ καὶ τούτοις καὶ τοῖς ἄλλοις ἅπασι τοῖς τι πράττειν τῶν πολιτικῶν προαιρουμένοις ἀπεχθήσεσθε, ἂν τὰς μὲν πατρίους ἀρχὰς καταλύητε καὶ τοῖς ἐκ τῶν νόμων χειροτονουμένοις μηδὲν ἐπιτρέπητε, ξένην δέ τινα καὶ μηπώποτε γεγενημένην ἡγεμονίαν ἰδιώτῃ προστάξητε;

[19] τίς γὰρ οὐκ οἶδεν ὅτι οὔτ' ἄλλως καλῶς ἔχει οὔτε συμφέρει ἑνὶ τινι τὰ πράγματα προστάσσεσθαι καὶ ἕνα τινὰ πάντων τῶν ὑπαρχόντων ἡμῖν ἀγαθῶν κύριον γίγνεσθαι, κἂν τὰ μάλιστα ἄριστός τις ᾖ; αἵ τε γὰρ μεγάλαι τιμαὶ καὶ αἱ ὑπέρογκοι ἐξουσίαι καὶ τοὺς τοιούτους ἐπαίρουσι καὶ διαφθείρουσιν.

[20] Dio 36. 35. 2–36. 4.

individual commanders would lead to greater achievement, and no one would be able to disclaim responsibility for his actions by laying the blame further up the chain of command.

This seems a very weak argument.[21] It was precisely the geographical size of the pirate problem that made a unified response necessary: previous efforts in specific areas had all failed, not least because the pirates could under those circumstances simply move away. Theirs was a threat very different from anything based on land. And even a unified response which depended on a number of commanders of equal status was not necessarily the answer, since it would work only with the co-operation of the various individuals involved, something which the individual thirst for glory, to which Catulus alludes, often made problematic.[22] In fact, Catulus' argument here indicates, in a paradoxical fashion, what was the most difficult issue to get round for any opponent of the Gabinian law: the fact that the pirates had proved so resistant to conventional Roman methods of warfare. It is, however, a proposal that could plausibly have been put forward in 67, embracing the idea of popular control in order to restrict, rather than augment, Pompeius' power.

The unifying feature of the arguments against both laws is a concern for constitutional propriety.[23] However, comparison between Dio and Cicero on Catulus shows how far Cicero has simplified and weakened Catulus' position. His anxiety that this law will reduce the number of commanders is transmuted into a thoughtless caution, and although Cicero retells the anecdote of Catulus' appeal to the people, it appears now simply as a compliment, rather than, as in the version preserved in Xiphilinus, a rhetorical question embodying a serious concern, which went wrong only through the people's

---

[21] It gains an accidental importance in our texts through being the last thing before the manuscripts break off: it is possible that it was originally hidden in the middle of Catulus' speech, where bad arguments belong.

[22] Dio 36. 36. 2. Cf. tension between Crassus and Pompeius while concluding the slave war, and later problems between Pompeius and Metellus Creticus over who should take the lead against the pirates in Crete: see e.g. M. Gelzer, *Pompeius* (Munich: Bruckmann, 1949), 60–1; 85–6.

[23] It is interesting that there is no sign that the opposition to either law attacked Pompeius personally: this seems to be a tribute to his popularity, which would make any *ad hominem* attack backfire.

unexpected response. And the doubts about the wisdom of this specific constitutional innovation found in Dio's version are in Cicero's speech a blunt statement of the foolishness of any sort of innovation. In particular, the fear that the concentration of power in the hands of Pompeius could lead to serious tensions within the state, provoked both by the grievances of those excluded from positions of power and by Pompeius himself, is hard to find in Cicero's summary. Yet this is clearly the implication of Catulus' remarks in Dio 36. 31. 3–32. 1 on the examples of Marius and Sulla, and his saying that no disparagement of Pompeius is meant by his observations hardly reassures. If anything, it brings the possibility that Pompeius might emulate Marius or Sulla in staging a coup even more sharply into focus.

Of course this assessment of Cicero's summary does depend on assuming that Catulus used the same sorts of arguments both years. Otherwise, one might want to believe that Cicero's account of Catulus' opposition is so much more straightforward simply because Catulus' opposition was much less effective in 66 than in 67. But it seems more probable that Cicero simplified to his own advantage, than that Catulus did not try, a second year running, the kinds of analysis that Dio preserves, however far Pompeius' successes had taken away from their credibility.[24]

How did the supporters of the two laws set about refuting these kinds of objections? Cicero's response not only lies in his explicit engagement with Hortensius and Catulus in §§51–63, but can be traced in the structuring, and arguments, of the whole speech. But before returning to the main topic of this chapter, I want to look briefly at the arguments in favour of the Gabinian law which Dio preserves. In 67 the contest was much fiercer: senatorial opposition was formidable, and

---

[24] This position remains tenable even if one concludes that Catulus' speech in Dio is nothing more than an imaginative reconstruction, and perhaps influenced by a reading of the *de imp.* itself. Cicero's account of both Hortensius' and Catulus' position does look so much like a tendentious summary—which is after all hardly surprising—that even in the absence of Dio it would be tempting to speculate as to what might lie behind it. Plutarch, *Life of Pompeius*, 30. 4, records that Catulus made a speech against the *lex Manilia* in which he urged the Senate to withdraw from the city and thus preserve their liberty.

the law's proponents could not, as in 66, cite a successful precedent.

3.1.1. *Arguments in support of Pompeius' commands*

Dio has two speeches which are more or less in favour of the Gabinian law. Pompeius delivers the first, a farcical concoction in which he begs to be allowed to take early retirement, on the grounds of exhaustion and fear of the jealousy which he might face if entrusted with this command.[25] It is a neat and amusing exemplification of the *dissimulatio* for which Pompeius was renowned, but is hardly a reliable guide to the state of the debate. Potentially more useful is Gabinius' speech, which urges the people to set aside Pompeius' reluctance.[26] His general argument is that Pompeius' past record shows him to be the most suitable man to deal with the pirates; and in the course of it he uses two arguments which it is particularly important to set against the *de imperio*. The first is the way he turns Pompeius' reluctance into an argument in his favour (36. 27. 1–3):

Pompeius' behaviour, Quirites, in this matter, neither seeking after command nor accepting it casually when offered, fits his character. In general a good man has no business in seeking to hold office and manage the affairs of the state; and in this particular case, it is fitting that one should agree to undertake the specified command only after careful consideration, so that it can be accomplished with corresponding safety . . . you should choose to hand matters over to the right men, and not to office-seekers.[27]

As well as suggesting that Pompeius' public stance has been carefully stage-managed, Gabinius' observation can neatly be fitted into the sets of arguments about the need for probity in provincial government which had recently been highlighted by a series of criminal prosecutions, above all in the *Verrines*,

---

[25] Dio 36. 25–6. Pompeius was at this point 38.

[26] Dio 36. 27–9.

[27] Πομπήιος μὲν, ὦ Κυιρῖται, καὶ αὐτὸ τοῦτο ἄξιον τῶν ἑαυτοῦ ἠθῶν ποιεῖ, μήτε ἐφιέμενος τῆς ἀρχῆς μήτε διδομένην οἱ αὐτὴν ἐξ ἐπιδρομῆς δεχόμενος. οὔτε γὰρ ἄλλως ἀγαθοῦ ἀνδρός ἐστιν ἄρχειν ἐπιθυμεῖν καὶ τὰ πράγματα ἔχειν ἐθέλειν· κἂν τούτῳ προσήκει πάντα τὰ προστα ττόμενα μετ' ἐπισκέψεως ὑφίστασθαι, ἵν' αὐτὰ καὶ ἀσφαλῶς ὁμοίως πράξῃ . . . οὐ γάρ που τοὺς σπουδαρχοῦντας ἀλλὰ τοὺς ἐπιτηδείους προστάττειν τοῖς πράγμασι προσήκει.

delivered three years earlier. Cicero refers to this problem openly in the *de imp.*, as I shall discuss below, and, as Gabinius does, attempts to portray Pompeius as a commander of exceptional integrity.

The second point of interest is Gabinius' argument that the people should make full use of outstanding military ability when it occurs.[28] The most important element in this, according to Gabinius, is that he should possess good fortune, ἀγαθῇ τύχῃ χρῆσθαι. This is clearly to be taken as a reference to that good luck which Cicero gives as one of the four requirements of a great general. These arguments which Dio gives to Gabinius, then, fit neatly with other evidence: unfortunately, this *may* simply indicate that Dio has used his sources well, rather than that he had access to information now lost about Gabinius' speech. It is impossible to decide between these two possibilities.[29]

Cicero's response to the arguments he gives to Catulus and Hortensius is not particularly helpful as a contribution to a constitutional debate, since he resolutely avoids the points at issue. His response to Hortensius is to go through, for the second time in the speech, the threat which the pirates posed. Since Hortensius opposed the Gabinian law, Cicero can ask (53): 'Well? Good heavens, if your authority had had more weight with the Roman people at that point than their own safety and true interest, would we possess today this glorious world empire?'[30] and the ensuing narrative recapitulates Pompeius' achievements to leave the audience in no doubt as to his fitness for this new command. Cicero also brings in the red herring of Gabinius' right to be a legate of Pompeius (57–8): not only does this allow him to feign *popularis* indignation about an issue where there is no danger that he will be called upon to act, he can also, in what seems to be a logical progression of ideas, sidestep Hortensius' quite serious point

---

[28] Dio 36. 27. 5–6.

[29] Cf. Millar, *Crowd*, 81, on the events surrounding the passage of the *lex Gabinia*: 'As he does so often, Dio manages to use a remarkable range of contemporary detail, without our being able to be sure that all points in his narrative, or the overall sequence, are really authentic.'

[30] 'quid? tum, per deos immortalis! si plus apud populum Romanum auctoritas tua quam ipsius populi Romani salus et uera causa ualuisset, hodie hanc gloriam atque hoc orbis terrae imperium teneremus?'

about the dangers inherent in the concentration of power, to which it would indeed be difficult to frame a satisfactory answer. Catulus' objections are given a similarly short and misleading treatment. His objection was against innovation, and in the bald and uncontextualized form that Cicero gives it (60), 'at enim ne quid noui fiat contra exempla atque instituta maiorum', is easy to knock down, first by a list of innovations in times of military crisis before Pompeius and then with a summary of all the innovations which Pompeius' earlier career contained.

Cicero's overt engagement with the debates surrounding the Manilian law does not, then, provide a convincing resolution of the constitutional anxieties which the law had provoked. But although 51–63 are the only place in the speech where its opponents are named and their arguments displayed, the strategies which Cicero uses only make complete sense if viewed against the arguments which people were using at the time. There are two elements in Cicero's accommodation with these arguments. One is the way in which the speech as a whole shifts the debate away from the constitutional arguments to what might be described as phantom issues, that is whether or not the campaign against Mithradates should be fought, and whether or not Pompeius is the most experienced and competent general the state possesses. The answer to both these questions was a relatively uncontroversial 'yes' (but see below), and this recasting enables Cicero to construct a speech that is both convincing and unthreatening. The second element is the careful way in which Pompeius is presented as a reliable and obedient figure who will not go beyond his commission. In presenting him in this way, Cicero is responding both to anxieties about the probity of provincial governors, and fears specific to this law, that Pompeius would in effect have no checks on his freedom of action.

3.1.2. The response of the de imperio

To consider the debate surrounding the Manilian law is a useful way of determining what was difficult or controversial about Cicero's task. But it is far from being how Cicero himself starts, and the way he sets up the issue gives a very selective and economical account of what was controversial. This is the opening to the argument of the speech (4): 'and so that my speech can start from the same place as this whole debate: a serious war, one which threatens your tax-revenues and your allies, is being conducted by two very powerful kings, Mithradates and Tigranes . . .'.[31] This is an arresting opening and one which plausibly demands attention and action. Yet, right at the start of the speech, it shifts the audience's focus away from the difficult question of extraordinary commands. Cicero continues this distraction throughout the main argument. He constructs this around three issues which he says he must discuss, namely that this war is of such a *kind* that it needs to be fought, of such a *size* that it should be feared and thus taken seriously, and that Pompeius is the only possible *choice as commander*.[32] It is only when these three have been discussed at considerable length, and Cicero has been able to construct a watertight case, that he turns, in 51, over two-thirds of the way through the speech, to the opposition: and, as I discussed above, he does not actually engage with their points.

While it was clear that the campaign against Mithradates needed to be brought to a successful conclusion, and that Pompeius was the state's most successful general, neither position was entirely straightforward to argue. In the case of the war, the difficulty was the fact that much had already been accomplished, and the theatre of operations was now far outside the areas where Rome had hitherto been involved.[33] Moreover, it had already produced one hero, in Lucullus. At this point, in 66, his march right up to the Tigris and meeting with the Parthians were still unparalleled achievements in geographical terms. Admittedly he had faced a revolt among his troops, and his legate Triarius had suffered a serious defeat at Zela; he had already been replaced by Glabrio, and there was still work to be done. However, there was no immediate threat

---

[31] 'atque ut inde oratio mea proficiscatur unde haec omnis causa ducitur, bellum graue et periculosum uestris uectigalibus atque sociis a duobus potentissimis adfertur regibus, Mithridate et Tigrane, . . .'

[32] This is laid out in 5: 'primum mihi uidetur *de genere belli*, deinde *de magnitudine*, tum *de imperatore deligendo* esse dicendum.'

[33] For an account of the Third Mithradatic War, see Sherwin-White, *Foreign Policy*, 159–85.

to the province of Asia itself, and Cicero needs all his persuasive spin to make it seem as though there was.[34]

One way he does this is by his division of his discussion of the war into two parts, those of *genus* and of *magnitudo*. This gives what is basically a two-point argument a satisfying tripartite structure, but it also allows him to increase the threat, since the burden of both sections is that this war is dangerous and alarming and must be fought. The main source of the menace is Mithradates himself, whose actions, particularly the slaughter of the Italians in Asia Minor in 88, can easily be presented in an emotive and pathetic fashion;[35] and Cicero reinforces this by the use of striking figurative language. Mithradates is an indelible stain on the honour of Rome (7); he is a wild beast, who has emerged from his lairs in Pontus and Cappadocia to range through the province of Asia (7); and, most striking of all, he is Medea (22): 'in the first place Mithradates escaped from his kingdom in the same way that once Medea is said to have done from this same Pontus, who, they declare, dropped the limbs of her own brother into the path of her pursuing father as she fled, so that his sorrowful collection of the scattered parts might slow down the speed of his chase'.[36] The ostensible point of comparison is that Mithradates abandoned a large quantity of treasure which the Romans stopped to gather. But the simile has more disturbing resonances, given that Medea is a barbarian and witch whose career consists of unrelieved destruction; Mithradates is dangerous, savage, and not a part of the civilized world. At the same time, by likening him to a female character, Cicero can exploit long-standing Roman prejudices about eastern effeminacy, and suggest that Mithradates is, like Medea, sly and deceitful. It strips him of any heroic characteristics.[37] The simile also suggests that Mithradates is not a conventional

---

[34] Cf. Sherwin-White, *Foreign Policy*, 188–9.

[35] Note particularly 7, with its repetition of *unus*, the choice of *neco* and *trucido* for the act of killing and the misleading description of the victims as *ciues Romani*.

[36] 'primum ex suo regno sic Mithridates profugit ut ex eodem Ponto Medea illa quondam fugisse dicitur, quam praedicant in fuga fratris sui membra in eis locis qua se parens persequeretur dissipauisse, ut eorum conlectio dispersa maerorque patrius celeritatem consequendi retardaret.'

[37] Cf. Sect. 1.2 (Cicero's likening Gabinius to Semiramis).

opponent: he is not static but ranges over a wide geographical area. And since Medea scattered her brother at sea, Cicero may be trying to set up a similarity with the pirates: like Mithradates, they suffered defeats, but managed to escape and continue their activities. This line of argument would suggest that Pompeius is also the solution to Mithradates' capacity to recover from setbacks;[38] it also helps to circumvent the counter-argument that could be used against the *lex Manilia*, that is, that Mithradates was a different sort of enemy from the pirates.

Using the well-established categories of deliberative oratory, Cicero presents the case for fighting Mithradates in terms both of what is honourable and what is useful. His audience's desire for glory (which is presented as an ethnic characteristic, one which they possess in greater measure than any other people) demands that they deal with Mithradates (7): 'and since you have always been seekers of glory and hungry for praise beyond other nations, you must destroy that blot which you acquired in the earlier Mithradatic war and which has now settled deeply and become ingrained in the name of the Roman people.'[39] This statement is immediately followed by the description of the massacre of 88, thus reinforcing patriotism with pathos. Cicero then gives a brief summary of Mithradates' career, and then turns to the four things with which he defined the *genus* of this war, all being things which were threatened by Mithradates: *gloria* heads the list.[40] His discussion marks the emotional high point of the first part of the speech, taking the form of four rhetorical questions which contrast instances of magnificent behaviour by Romans in the past with the consequences of failure to take action against Mithradates now. In each case, a comparatively minor transgression was in the past dealt with severely, whereas failure to act now would allow a much more serious crime of the same kind to go unpunished. So, for example, insults to ambassadors led to the destruction of Corinth, but no action has been taken against Mithradates'

[38] See esp. 8.

[39] 'et quoniam semper appetentes gloriae praeter ceteras gentis atque auidi laudis fuistis, delenda uobis est illa macula Mithridatico bello superiore concepta quae penitus iam insedit ac nimis inueterauit in populi Romani nomine'.

[40] The other three are the well-being of Rome's allies, the taxes of the Roman state, and the possessions of the citizens operating in Asia.

torturing and killing of ambassadors in this war. Cicero concludes this section by warning his listeners (12): 'take care that
it is not as shameful for you to be unable to protect and keep
what you have inherited from your ancestors as it was
magnificent for them to pass on such a glorious empire'.[41]
Rome's glorious history is also used for emotional effect when
Cicero refers, in a brief and emotionally charged *praeteritio*, to
the defeat at Zela (25): 'allow me at this point, Quirites, to do as
the poets who record Rome's history are accustomed to, that is
for me to pass over our disaster, which was so crushing that
news of it was brought to the ears of our general not by a
messenger from the battlefield but rumours passing from
mouth to mouth'.[42] This manoeuvre assimilates the battle with
the glamour and emotional force of the great disasters of the
past; but it also establishes that we are in a story which has not
yet come to an end, since no historical epic of the Roman
people ever ended with defeat. Pompeius is needed to provide
the glorious conclusion.

The arguments from utility are, not surprisingly, much less
elevated in style. They centre on the tax revenues of the
province of Asia. These, on Cicero's telling, are unique in providing a surplus beyond what the province itself absorbs (14):
'the tax revenues of the other provinces, Quirites, are barely
enough to allow us to pay for their defence, but Asia is so rich
and fertile that . . . it easily outdoes all other regions'[43] and as
a result is of key importance not only for funding military
activity, but also for supplying the *pacis dignitas* (14). Here
Cicero is tapping into the *popularis* view that the spoils of
empire should be enjoyed by the people as a whole which can
be traced back to the younger Gracchus' references to *uestra
commoda* (*ORF* 48, fr. 44), but he is careful to avoid alienating
those who might be alarmed by such profligacy by linking it to
military imperatives.

[41] 'uidete ne, ut illis pulcherrimum fuit tantam uobis imperi gloriam tradere,
sic uobis turpissimum sit id quod accepistis tueri et conseruare non posse'.
[42] 'sinite hoc loco, Quirites, sicut poetae solent qui res Romanas scribunt,
praeterire me nostram calamitatem, quae tanta fuit ut eam ad auris imperatoris
non ex proelio nuntius sed ex sermone rumor adferret'.
[43] 'nam ceterarum prouinciarum uectigalia, Quirites, tanta sunt ut eis ad
ipsas prouincias tuendas uix contenti esse possimus, Asia uero tam opima est
ac fertilis ut . . . facile omnibus terris antecellat'.

The reasons why Cicero is so solicitous in this speech towards the *publicani* and those who trade in Asia Minor are explored in the next chapter: what is worth noting here is the care with which the interests of a small group of people are identified with those of the state as a whole. Since the *uectigalia* are the 'sinews of the state' (*neruos rei publicae*) it is right to call that part of society which collects them the 'basis of all other classes' (*firmamentum ceterorum ordinum*, 17); and since Cicero's argument could be challenged by pointing out that no fighting was at that point going on in Asia, the producer of these lovely taxes, he argues that the kinds of wealth which produce this revenue only function if they are protected from the panic which fear of an invasion would produce as well as from actual damage in war.[44]

Even more striking is the integration of the interests of independent businessmen with those of the state, in Cicero's argument that the people ought to take thought for the *bona ciuium* which are currently in Asia. One reason for protecting these people by undertaking a war against Mithradates is the humanity of the people; but wisdom too suggests this course (18. 4–7). Roman economic activity in Asia is so closely linked with what goes on in Rome that disaster abroad could not fail to have serious repercussions at home. This is usually, and rightly, taken to be a fair point, though it is not always observed that the collapse in credit which Cicero uses to justify this point took place in 88, when affairs in Rome itself were also in a state of considerable confusion.

Cicero is thus able to construct this war as one which honour and self-interest and, ultimately, what it is that makes Romans Roman all demand should be fought. This provides the necessary stage onto which he can introduce the hero who will set right everything which has hitherto been wrong.

3.2. THE PRAISE OF POMPEIUS

The third issue that Cicero set up for himself in his *partitio* in 6 was the choice of commander, and he deals with it in 27–48. He starts by lamenting the fact that there is not a huge supply of

---

[44] See the discussion in E. J. Jonkers, *Social and Economic Commentary on Cicero's De Imperio Cn. Pompei* (Leiden: Brill, 1959), 29–34.

men among whom the choice could be made; having established this, he asks (27): 'but since Gnaeus Pompeius is alone in
surpassing in virtue not only the glory of his contemporaries,
but also the memory of past deeds, what grounds can there be
in this case for anyone to feel hesitant?'[45] In stating the answer
to the problem of which general to choose before presenting the
argument in support of that answer Cicero is doing no more
here than he does in the speech as a whole: Pompeius was the
stated beneficiary of the law which Cicero is here advocating.
More impressive is the way in which he presents his supporting
material. He next says (28): 'this is my opinion: four qualities
are to be found in the perfect general, that is knowledge of
military affairs, virtue, reputation, and luck'.[46] The rest of
the section consists in Cicero's demonstration that Pompeius
possesses each of these four qualities. The most striking feature
about this strategy is that it enables Cicero to avoid com-
parisons: while it is clear from 27 that there is no one to rival
Pompeius, he does not have to denigrate any specific individual.[47] The use of the statement of qualities also allows him to
portray Pompeius as an archetype: he is, it becomes clear, the
summus imperator, since he conforms in every respect to the
model which Cicero has set up. The persuasiveness of this
strategy is obvious.

Cicero's precise choice of attributes cannot be paralleled, but
both rhetorical and philosophical precedents are helpful in
general terms. Rhetorically, this section is epideictic: the praise
of an individual.[48] Although the four qualities he chooses to
discuss are very different from the attributes which the hand-
books list, he can still harness the persuasive force of the genre,
which turns his audience into passive spectators of rhetorical

---

[45] 'nunc uero cum sit unus Cn. Pompeius qui non modo eorum hominum
qui nunc sunt gloriam sed etiam antiquitatis memoriam uirtute superarit, quae
res est quae cuiusquam animum in hac causa dubium facere possit?'

[46] 'ego enim sic existimo, in summo imperatore quattuor has res inesse
oportere, scientiam rei militaris, uirtutem, auctoritatem, felicitatem'.

[47] Note particularly 37, where Cicero says explicitly that he will not name
names when it comes to peculation: 'ego autem nomino neminem'.

[48] [Cicero], *Rhetorica ad Herennium* 3. 10–15; Fronto, *On the Parthian
War* 10 (p. 225 in the Teubner edition of van den Hout (Leipzig, 1988)); cf.
L. Pernot, *La Rhétorique de l'éloge dans le monde Gréco-Romain* (Paris: Institut
d'Études Augustiniennes, 1993).

virtuosity rather than citizens considering which course of action their state should take, which is how they ought to be listening to a deliberative speech. Cicero's shift leaves his audience with no opportunity to exercise their critical faculties on the subject of Manilius' law, which is of course what he wants.

The fourfold division also calls to mind philosophical examination of the Cardinal Virtues. These settled down into a canonical form as wisdom, courage, justice, and self-control;[49] more important, perhaps, than the precise choice of virtues is the existence of a tradition of dividing up the behaviour one should aspire to into a number of discrete qualities. Cicero can suggest that Pompeius is in some way an embodiment of moral excellence by accumulating a series of desirable qualities which he can be shown to possess. In this way Cicero increases Pompeius' authority and confirms the impression that he is the obvious choice for this job. The audience may also be supposed to imagine that Cicero is correcting the philosophical tradition. *Virtus* is only one of the four qualities which the *summus imperator* must possess: he must also have a range of more practical skills. The division which Cicero makes in his discussion of *uirtus* itself between what are commonly considered to make up the *uirtutes imperatoriae* and the *ceterae* supports this view. The former are for the most part practical things, such as speed, effort, and energy, though *fortitudo* is also listed here (29); the latter consist of *innocentia, temperantia, fides, facilitas, ingenium*, and *humanitas* (36). While self-control is here in *temperantia*, and wisdom and justice can be seen in *innocentia* and *ingenium*, good faith, approachability, and being a civilized person are outside the canonical prescription. For Cicero, or rather for Pompeius, the standard model of *uirtus* is shown not to be adequate.

A further influence on Cicero's choice of qualities may be the Hellenistic manuals of kingship.[50] The survival of the works

[49] e.g. Plato, *Republic* 4. 427e10–11; cf. Hall, *Barbarian*, 121–2. For Cicero's use of these four qualities in his argument against Cato in the *pro Murena*, see C. P. Craig, 'Cato's Stoicism and the Understanding of Cicero's Speech for Murena', *TAPhA* 116 (1986), 229–39, 236.

[50] For which see W. Schubart, 'Das hellenistische Königsideal nach Inschriften und Papyri', *Archiv für Papyrusforschung und verwandte Gebiete*, 12 (1937), 1–26, repr. in H. Kloft (ed.), *Ideologie und Herrschaft in der Antike*

only in fragments, if at all, means that the inquiry must be tentative, but it does seem that there was an emphasis on intellectual virtues, particularly on ἐγκράτεια (self-control) and φρόνησις (good sense), as essential components of the good king. It has been argued that Cicero was influenced by this when he makes *temperantia*, which is far from self-evident as a military quality, part of his prescription for the ideal general.[51]

None the less, one does not need to invoke either the rhetorical or the philosophical tradition in order to understand what Cicero is saying: there is nothing strikingly odd in his choice of qualities, nor any obvious gaps, and a member of the audience who knew nothing about possible sources would have no reason to feel confused. Knowledge of warfare is, self-evidently, a useful thing for a general to know about, and *uirtus* in its primary sense of 'manliness' and hence 'courage' is similarly obvious. By shifting it towards 'virtue', Cicero is able to invoke a whole range of further qualities, all of which seem to be good things.[52]

So all-inclusive is *uirtus* that it is at first sight not obvious why Cicero makes *auctoritas* into a separate, third category. An answer may be found in the intersection of the particular value which was ascribed to this quality in Roman public life,[53] with what Cicero presents as a striking event in Pompeius' own career, when his appointment to the command against the pirates was on its own enough to lower the price of corn. Cicero also draws a distinction between *auctoritas* and *uirtus* in the sense that *auctoritas* is the means whereby Pompeius has

(Darmstadt: Wissenschaftliche Buchgesellschaft, 1979); O. Murray, '*Peri Basileias*: Studies in the Justification of Monarchic Power' (D.Phil., Univ. of Oxford, 1970).

[51] Schubart, 'Königsideal'; J. Gruber, 'Cicero und das hellenistische Herrscherideal: Überlegungen sur Rede "De imperio Cn. Pompei"', *WS* 101, NS 22 (1988), 243–58.

[52] For the range of qualities which late republican politicians could and did claim, see J. Hellegouarc'h, *Le Vocabulaire latin des relations et des partis politiques sous la république* (Paris: Les Belles Lettres, 1963), 234–94; on the qualities of the *imperator* specifically, R. Combès, *Imperator: Recherches sur l'emploi et la signification du titre d'imperator dans la Rome républicaine* (Paris: Presses universitaires de France, 1966), 189–449.

[53] R. Heinze, 'Auctoritas', *Hermes*, 60 (1925), 348–66, repr. in *Vom Geist des Römertums* (Leipzig: Teubner, 1938); Hellegouarc'h, *Le Vocabulaire latin*, 293–314.

already, at long range, begun to affect events in the East,[54] which indicates how striking will be his achievements when he arrives in person (45): 'and who can doubt what a man who has achieved so much through his reputation will achieve through his virtue?'[55] *Auctoritas* is also a useful quality for Cicero to stress by putting it under a separate heading, since it is not necessarily a military quality. That is, while one of its most important sources is military success, it is an attribute which does not depend for its existence upon the possession of *imperium*, and can most effectively be displayed in a state of peace. In this respect, it may be designed to reassure those in the audience who were suspicious about Pompeius' willingness to abide by constitutional norms.

The final characteristic, *felicitas*, provides an impressive conclusion to the enumeration of Pompeius' qualities.[56] This is a divinely bestowed virtue, and humans must be careful in what they say on the matter (47). Great generals in the past have possessed it, and as a result have been entrusted with military commands (47); in Pompeius' case his luck has been obvious throughout his career, manifested in the obedience to his wishes which men and even the weather have shown (48). That this is tremendously beneficial and useful to the state is clear, and Cicero concludes with a brief prayer that Pompeius may continue to possess *felicitas*.

Luck is naturally an important quality for a general to have, but it is one that is inherently mysterious. By adopting a religious tone, Cicero reinforces the impression he has already given of Pompeius' own quasi-divine nature (cf. 41); he also justifies not giving any concrete examples, and thus avoids the implication that Pompeius' successes were acquired not through his own good qualities, but by chance.[57]

---

[54] 45: 'huius aduentus et Mithridatem insolita inflatum uictoria continuit et Tigranen magnis copiis minitantem Asiae retardauit'.

[55] 'et quisquam dubitabit quid uirtute perfecturus sit qui tantum auctoritate perfecerit . . .'

[56] E. Wistrand, *Felicitas Imperatoria* (Göteborg: Acta Universitatis Gothoburgensis, 1987); J. Champeaux, *Fortuna: Recherches sur le culte de la Fortune à Rome et dans le monde romain des origines à la mort de César* (Rome: École française de Rome, 1987), vol. 2.

[57] The opposition between *uirtus* and *felicitas* or *fortuna* is very common: see Wistrand, *Felicitas*, 35–9.

This discussion of *felicitas* would evoke the memory of Sulla, who ostentatiously took the surname *Felix*,[58] and to whom Pompeius had been closely attached early in his career. When Cicero says that no one can guarantee that he will possess luck himself,[59] he is indicating his disapproval of the arrogance which Sulla displayed in calling himself 'Lucky', and showing that Pompeius is very different from his mentor: he may be notably lucky, and he may be about to fight in the part of the world where Sulla had had his greatest military triumphs, at least of those outside Rome: but he will not emulate Sulla in marching on Rome with an army.[60]

3.2.1. Murena: an ordinary general

Cicero's choice of these four qualities makes perfect persuasive sense, even if one knows nothing further of Pompeius or of the background to the case. Indeed, it can be difficult, in looking at the *de imperio* alone, to see what is distinctive in the presentation of Pompeius as a military leader. However, a useful comparison can be found in Cicero's speech defending Murena on charges of electoral bribery in 63.[61] Cicero's main tactic in this speech is to portray Murena as a soldier and to contrast him with his unsuccessful electoral rival Sulpicius, whom Cicero presents as a pettifogging lawyer. It seems reasonable to treat the characterization of Murena as Cicero's best attempt to make an ordinary general, whose career had been conducted according to the rules and conventions of office-holding, as attractive as is credible.[62]

Many of the qualities which Cicero says Murena possesses

[58] J. P. V. D. Balsdon, 'Sulla Felix', *JRS* 41 (1951), 1–10; H. Ericsson, 'Sulla Felix: Eine Wortstudie', *Eranos*, 41 (1943), 77–89.

[59] 47. 17–18: 'quam [sc. felicitatem] praestare de se ipso nemo potest'.

[60] For anxieties that Pompeius might do this on his return, see Cicero's guarded words in his famous letter to Pompeius of 62 (*Ad Fam.* 5. 7, esp. para. 1: 'tantam enim spem oti ostendisti quantam ego semper omnibus te uno fretus pollicebar').

[61] On Cicero's strategy in general, see the excellent analysis of A. D. Leeman, 'The Technique of Persuasion in Cicero's Pro Murena', in W. Ludwig (ed.), *Rhétorique et éloquence chez Cicéron* (Entretiens Hardt 28, 1982), 149–92. Further bibliography, Loutsch, *L'Exorde*, 301 n. 1.

[62] For Murena's earlier career, see J. Adamietz, *M. Tullius Cicero Pro Murena* (Darmstadt: Wissenschaftliche Buchgesellschaft, 1989), 16–19.

are the same as those which he earlier ascribed to Pompeius. His service in the army of his father is cited as proof of his *uirtus* and his *felicitas*;[63] he is not prone to manifestations of *luxuria*, and lacks the negative qualities of *auaritia, perfidia,* and *crudelitas*;[64] his behaviour as a legate in Lucullus' army demonstrates his courage, his judgement, and his energy;[65] as praetor he demonstrated *aequitas* and *diligentia*.[66] However, there are important differences in the overall tone of the treatment.

In the first place, Murena is not an archetype in the way that Pompeius is constructed as one: he is not a model of the *summus imperator*, simply an effective soldier. Indeed, much of the humour of the speech depends upon there being a stereotype of the soldier (rather than of the general) to set against that of the lawyer: this is particularly obvious in 22 ff., where Cicero compares minute and trivial details of both ways of life for humorous effect in a way that seems to foreshadow some of the elegiac extravagances of the *militia amoris*.

A second and important difference concerns the relations of the two men with their colleagues. Pompeius appears not to have any, existing in splendid isolation (see below), whereas Murena's achievements are always presented in the context of another's campaigns, be it his father, the elder Murena, or Lucullus. What Cicero presents as his most impressive military actions take place in the Mithradatic War, but they appear in an account of that war rather than as accomplishments in their own right. Murena's subordination to others is reflected in the structure of the speech in his defence, with Cicero placing a justification of his own behaviour before that of Murena's, and drawing attention to his so doing (2):

---

[63] *pro Murena* 12: it also demonstrates his *pietas*: I consider below why it is that Cicero does not ascribe this particularly Roman virtue to Pompeius also.

[64] *pro Murena* 13–14; Pompeius' lack of *auaritia* (*de imp.* 37–40), including his not being prone to statue-snatching; *perfidia* and *crudelitas* can be seen as the opposites, respectively, of *fides* and *humanitas*, which are among Pompeius' other virtues (*de imp.* 36).

[65] *pro Murena* 34: 'hoc igitur in bello L. Murenam legatum fortissimi animi, summi consili, maximi laboris cognitum esse defendimus'; cf. *de imp.* 29: 'neque enim solae sunt uirtutes imperatoriae quae uolgo existimantur, *labor* in negotiis, *fortitudo* in periculis, industria in agendo, celeritas in conficiendo, *consilium* in prouidendo'. [66] *pro Murena* 42.

And since in the performance of this duty my enthusiasm for Murena's defence, and even the fact of my taking it on, has been criticized by the prosecution, I shall say a few words on my own behalf before beginning to speak for my client. This is not because I believe that a defence of my own services is more desirable than that of this man's safety, but because I shall be able to counter the attacks of his enemies upon his standing, reputation, and everything that he holds dear with more effectiveness once I have justified my actions to you.[67]

It is not until 11 that Cicero concludes his discussion of his own position, and in particular how he can justify defending a man who is charged under the terms of a law that he himself, as consul, sponsored earlier in the year, and turns to the charges against Murena. Murena has a similarly low profile at the end of the speech. Cicero's concluding argument on Murena's behalf has nothing to do with his guilt or innocence, but concerns the safety of the state: 'It is hugely important, gentlemen of the jury, that there are two consuls in the state on 1 January—something that I have managed to accomplish despite considerable opposition.'[68] When Cicero moves to his peroration (86–90) he sums up his arguments for acquittal under two heads: in the first place, the jury should respond to his, Cicero's, authority as consul by accepting his advice that an acquittal is essential to the safety of the state; and secondly, 'led by the duty of one who is both defence counsel and a friend', he urges them to pity Murena. He moves through the familiar tropes of the pathetic peroration—the reversal of fortune which Murena faces, the suffering he and his family are enduring—before reverting, in the final sentence of the speech, to his own perspective (90):

This man, gentlemen of the jury, I commend to you—if my commendation has any weight and my support any authority—a consul commending a consul; and that he will be passionate in support

---

[67] et quoniam in hoc officio studium meae defensionis ab accusatoribus atque etiam ipsa susceptio causae reprensa est, ante quam pro L. Murena dicere instituo, pro me ipso pauca dicam, non quo mihi potior hoc quidem tempore sit offici mei quam huiusce salutis defensio, sed ut meo facto uobis probato maiore auctoritate ab huius honore fama fortunisque omnibus inimicorum impetus propulsare possim.

[68] 79: 'magni interest, iudices, id quod ego multis repugnantibus egi atque perfeci, esse Kalendis Ianuariis in re publica duo consules.'

of tranquillity, favourable to sound men, fierce against disorder, courageous in war and utterly hostile to this conspiracy which is at this moment undermining the stability of the state, this I guarantee and promise.[69]

At key moments in the speech, Murena exists simply as an essential part of *Cicero's* government of the state, and it is in response to that, rather than to the facts of the case, that the jury are urged to make their decision. Murena's importance is that he will continue the staunch line which Cicero has begun. It is worth noting that there is no reference to Murena's innocence anywhere in the peroration.

In a similar fashion, Cicero's account of his military activities demonstrates Murena's co-operation with, and often subordination to, others. In the account of his first service in Asia (11–12), Cicero repeatedly mentions that this was in his father's army;[70] he describes what Murena did after his quaestorship in such a way as to stress the identity of his commander, Lucullus;[71] and when he returns to this campaign, after a happy digression poking fun at legal science, his defence of its importance (31–4) invokes the names of many great Romans who fought in Asia and Greece, and those of four of the commanders in the war against Mithradates, namely Sulla, the elder Murena, Lucullus, and Pompeius; but only mentions our Murena right at the end, as one who fought well in this campaign.[72] The name of the younger Murena, on its own, does not guarantee the stature of a campaign. Cicero's mention of Murena's praetorian province, Gaul, is notably low-key.[73]

[69] quem ego uobis, si quid habet aut momenti commendatio aut auctoritatis confirmatio mea, consul consulem, iudices, ita commendo ut cupidissimum oti, studiosissimum bonorum, acerrimum contra seditionem, fortissimum in bello, inimicissimum huic coniurationi quae nunc rem publicam labefactat futurum esse promittam et spondeam.

[70] 11: 'qui si adulescens *patre suo* imperatore non meruisset, aut hostem aut *patris* imperium timuisse aut *a parente* repudiatus uideretur'; 11. 21–3: 'huic donis militaribus *patris* triumphum decorare fugiendum fuit, ut rebus communiter gestis paene simul *cum patre* triumpharet?'; 12. 1–2: 'hic uero, iudices, et fuit in Asia et uiro fortissimo, *parenti suo*, magno adiumento'; 12. 3–4: '*patre* imperatore libentissime meruisse pietatis'.

[71] 20: 'quid Murena interea? fortissimo et sapientissimo uiro, summo imperatori legatus, L. Lucullo, fuit'.

[72] 34, quoted above.

[73] The complete description is simply (42): 'sed tamen L. Murenae

Nowhere does Murena appear as a figure of compelling interest in his own right.

There is nothing particularly surprising in Cicero's choice of tactics. Murena's success in the consular elections depended in large part on his connection with Lucullus, so it is not surprising that Cicero draws attention to it; his service in his father's army was indeed an attractive example of *pietas*; and his praetorian command in Gaul was not particularly distinguished.[74] And because Cicero decides to exploit the continuing threat from Catiline, it is also rhetorically effective to imply that Murena is his own subordinate in some sense.

Cicero's placing of Murena within a web of relationships highlights the isolation he imposes on Pompeius. (The only military colleague whom Cicero introduces is Gabinius, in the context of his desire to serve Pompeius as a legate, which hardly detracts from Pompeius' aloofness.) In part, this is a product of genre: a more modest and plangent approach is required in a defence on a capital charge with an upper-class jury than in a speech in front of the people, where the subject is a popular favourite, and one of the most effective ways of rousing emotion in a jury is to point to the effects of a conviction on the family and friends of the accused.[75] But more lies behind the differences than the different styles appropriate to forensic and deliberative oratory. The *lex Manilia* created an extraordinary command, and Cicero needs to show that Pompeius is the right man for it. The capacity of his Pompeius to dominate and stand out from the rest is exactly what is needed.

The danger of this approach is that it might confirm anxieties about the ability of the state to control Pompeius—anxieties which Pompeius' earlier career could only confirm. Interestingly, Cicero does not ignore the past: instead he presses upon his listeners and readers a brilliantly partial account.

prouincia multas bonas gratias cum optima existimatione attulit. habuit proficiscens dilectum in Vmbria; dedit ei facultatem res publica liberalitatis, qua usus multas sibi tribus quae municipiis Vmbriae conficiuntur adiunxit. ipse autem in Gallia ut nostri homines desperatas iam pecunias exigerent aequitate diligentiaque perfecit.'

[74] Adamietz, *Murena*, 16–17.
[75] Cf. Cicero, *de inuentione* 1. 107–9.

3.2.2. *Whitewashing the teenage butcher*

Pompeius' earlier career is the explicit subject of three passages
in the *de imp.*: 28, where his range and amount of experience is
invoked to justify Cicero's claim for him of *scientia militaris*;
30–5, where Pompeius' conduct in the various campaigns that
he has been involved in demonstrates his *uirtutes*; and 61–2, in
which Cicero lists the constitutional innovations that have
already been made in Pompeius' favour, to reduce the strength
of Catulus' alleged objection to the innovations which the *lex
Manilia* would cause. Despite the difference of emphasis in
each passage, there is considerable repetition between these
passages, and this can be seen as a tribute to the genuinely
impressive, and unprecedented, nature of Pompeius' achievements up to this point. He was the most experienced and
successful general available. Concentration on what he had so
far accomplished also had the probable advantage of being a
crowd-pleaser. An anecdote which Plutarch records demonstrates the popular enthusiasm with which Pompeius' unorthodox career was greeted: when he made his declaration to the
censors of 70 of his military service as an *eques*, he stated that he
had served in all the campaigns required, and all under himself
as *imperator*, at which there was huge applause and he was
escorted home by the censors and a large crowd.[76] It is not
simply the scale of his achievements, but that they were accomplished in so precocious a manner, that led to the popular out-
burst in his favour.

None the less, much of what Pompeius had done in his
earlier life was not so straightforwardly admirable, and a careful reading of Cicero's handling of Pompeius' actions as they
are described in 28 and 30–5 brings a number of elisions and
evasions to light.[77]

Cicero's first description of Pompeius' early career is an
impressive piece of writing which deserves to be quoted in full
and in the original (28):

quis igitur hoc homine scientior umquam aut fuit aut esse debuit? qui

[76] Plutarch, *Life of Pompeius* 22. 4–6.

[77] On Pompeius' career up to 66, see e.g. Gelzer, *Pompeius*, 27–86; J. van
Ooteghem, *Pompée le Grand: Bâtisseur d'Empire* (Brussels: Académie Royale
de Belgique, Mémoires 49, 1954), 27–181; Seager, *Pompey*, 16–22.

e ludo atque e pueritiae disciplinis bello maximo atque acerrimis hostibus ad patris exercitum atque in militiae disciplinam profectus est, qui extrema pueritia miles in exercitu summi fuit imperatoris, ineunte adulescentia maximi ipse exercitus imperator, qui saepius cum hoste conflixit quam quisquam cum inimico concertauit, plura bella gessit quam ceteri legerunt, pluris prouincias confecit quam alii concupiuerunt, cuius adulescentia ad scientiam rei militaris non alienis praeceptis sed suis imperiis, non offensionibus belli sed uictoriis, non stipendiis sed triumphis est erudita. quod denique genus esse belli potest in quo illum non exercuerit fortuna rei publicae? ciuile, Africanum, Transalpinum, Hispaniense mixtum ex ciuibus atque ex bellicosissimis nationibus, seruile, nauale bellum, uaria et diuersa genera et bellorum et hostium non solum gesta ab hoc uno sed etiam confecta nullam rem esse declarant in usu positam militari quae huius uiri scientiam fugere possit.[78]

The repeated relative pronouns in the first sentence, and within the third clause the three occurrences of *quam*, provide the framework which supports the sentence's repetitive message: the early start and, consequently, extent of military experience Pompeius has had. So does the repetition of *pueritia*, the elegant balance between what happened at the end of his child-hood (being a soldier in the army of a leading commander) and at the beginning of his grown-up life (being a commander him-self of a great army), and the piling up of examples of activities where Pompeius' military version far outstrips the civil equival-ent, which is of course much easier to accomplish. This set of

[78] Who has ever been more knowledgeable than this man, or ever should have been? He is a man who went from school and childhood pursuits to his father's army and to military discipline during a great war against extremely fierce enemies; who was, at the end of his childhood, a soldier in the army of a leading commander and at the beginning of his youth a general himself of a great army; who came into conflict with the enemy more often than anyone has struggled with his domestic opponents, waged more wars than others have read about, and established more provinces than others have desired to possess; whose youth was educated in the science of war not through the advice of others but in his own commands, not by military setbacks but by victories, and not by terms of service but by triumphs. What kind of war can there be in which the fortune of the state has not employed this man? Civil, African, Transalpine, Spanish (a war compounded of citizens and excep-tionally warlike tribes), slave, and pirate wars: many and various kinds of wars and of enemies have not only been fought by this one man but also brought to their conclusion, and show that there is no aspect of the military craft of which this man is not master.

contrasts is complemented by the three *non . . . sed* clauses,
which indicate the nature of Pompeius' military education.
Again, what one would expect a young soldier to face—advice
from other men, setbacks, and terms of service—are trumped
in Pompeius' case by his own experience as a commander,
victories, and triumphs. With this last, Cicero plays his most
valuable card, since it was extraordinary that Pompeius had
held two triumphs even before he became consul. The
summary of Pompeius' career is followed by an enumeration of
the kinds of wars that he has been involved in. The six kinds are
divided into three by nature of opponent, citizens, slaves, and
pirates, and three geographical, Spain, Transalpine Gaul, and
Africa, and Cicero goes on to make explicit the fact that this is a
wide variety of wars. Pompeius, we are to understand, is ready
for anything that Mithradates might throw at him.

However, this pleasing and innocent picture of Pompeius'
early years does not mention a number of unfavourable, or
at the least problematic, issues. The first is signalled by the
brevity of the mention of Pompeius' father, Pompeius Strabo,
himself a consul and successful general. This is at first sight
surprising, since descent was a standard source of praise in
epideictic oratory, and was particularly useful when the same
qualities could be praised in father as in son. Moreover,
Pompeius' service in his father's army could have been presented as an instance of *pietas*, as Murena's with *his* father is in
the *pro Murena*.[79]

There was, however, a very good reason why Cicero did not
go down this tempting oratorical path. Pompeius Strabo had
been hated in his life, and his funeral in 87 had been marked by
popular disturbances in which the body was dragged off its
bier.[80] Plutarch, indeed, starts his account of Pompeius' life
with the contrast between father and son in the affections of the
Roman people. But Cicero could hardly have used the contrast
between the two men as a way of setting off the younger
Pompeius' virtues.

In this case, Cicero is simply avoiding an awkward subject.

---

[79] *pro Murena* 11–12; see above.

[80] Plutarch, *Life of Pompeius* 1; Seager, *Pompey*, 5 n. 40. It is noticeable that
the younger Pompeius did not inherit his father's *cognomen*: a conscious
decision to dissociate himself from his unpopular parent?

In the case of Pompeius' activities in the 80s, his account is positively misleading. The key phrase is 'qui extrema pueritia miles in exercitu summi fuit imperatoris, ineunte adulescentia maximi ipse exercitus imperator'. This very strongly suggests that there was no interval between his service in his father's army and his own command. *pueritia* is followed by *adulescentia*, and the impression of a seamless progression is confirmed by the adjectives *extrema* and *ineunte*. The natural assumption of any listener or reader is that the 'beginning of youth' follows immediately on the 'end of childhood'. Certainly it is a surprise to realize that, if these phases are lined up with the actual events of Pompeius' life, there is an interval of some four years between the end of Pompeius' *pueritia* and the beginning of his *adulescentia*. His service in his father's army came to an end in 87, when Pompeius Strabo died while laying siege to Rome; he raised his own army in support of Sulla on the latter's return from the East in 83.

One view of this undoubted elision would be that Cicero is massaging the facts a little to provide a simple and memorable formulation of Pompeius' early life. The suggestion of an immediate progression may, in strictly factual terms, be misleading, but the overall impression given is fair, since Pompeius' military successes did come extraordinarily young, both the fact of his military service and his assumption of sole control. Moreover, *adulescentia* referred to such an extended period of a man's life, from adolescence until his early forties, that it is hardly fair to criticize describing the age of 23 as at the beginning of *adulescentia*.[81]

A less charitable view would be that Cicero is trying to conceal the existence of this period of four years, not because Pompeius did not do anything of note during this period and reference to it would simply confuse Cicero's account, but because this was the period of Pompeius' accommodation with the regime of Cinna.[82] The speed and enthusiasm with which he went to support Sulla on the latter's return from the East could give rise to charges of faithlessness, and it is not surprising that Cicero does not want to acknowledge this period.

[81] On the period covered by *adulescentia*, see J. G. F. Powell, *Cicero: Cato Maior de senectute* (Cambridge: Cambridge Univ. Press, 1988), 178.

[82] E. Badian, 'Waiting for Sulla', *JRS* 52 (1962), 47–61, esp. 54, 58.

The third questionable aspect to this first summary of Pompeius' career, in order to demonstrate his *scientia militaris*, is the statement that his successes in the various wars he has been involved in hitherto have all been achieved *on his own*.[83] This is quite patently false. In the campaigns in Spain, Pompeius was working with Metellus Pius, who was undoubtedly his senior, not only in years and position but also in experience, and who was, unlike Pompeius, involved in the campaign for its entirety;[84] in the slave war, Pompeius arrived when Crassus had virtually concluded the operations;[85] and during the pirate war, although in sole naval command, he clashed with Metellus Creticus over jurisdiction in Crete, insisting that he, and not Metellus, should receive the surrender of some of the Cretans on the grounds that they were pirates and therefore his concern.[86] In the cases of Crassus and Creticus, at least, Pompeius' arrival on the scene, and participation in the credit for the military successes, was met with considerable hostility. Cicero's deception here seems unlikely to be simply in order to suggest that Pompeius was a greater general than in fact was the case. He is also trying to avoid the charge that Pompeius was in the habit of appropriating the military achievements of others; which would be one plausible way of viewing Pompeius' taking over of the war against Mithradates which had, until very recently, been fought with a considerable degree of success by Lucullus.[87]

Most of 30–5 deals with the campaign against the pirates, which demonstrates Pompeius' possession of *uirtus*. The concentration on the pirate war is not surprising: it was a very recent campaign, it had with outstanding success dealt with a

---

[83] 28. 2–3: 'uaria et diuersa genera et bellorum et hostium non solum gesta *ab hoc uno* sed etiam confecta'.

[84] R. Seager, 'The Rise of Pompey', *CAH* 9, 2nd edn. (1994), 208–28, 215–23.

[85] See Plutarch, *Life of Pompeius* 21.2.

[86] Kallet-Marx, *Hegemony*, 318–20; *pro Flacco* 30.

[87] Those in the audience whose knowledge of recent history was imperfect would simply have believed Cicero's claim. For those who recalled the various disputes, Cicero's remark puts his authority and credibility as a speaker behind a pro-Pompeian account of events. In 35 and 46 Cicero makes explicit reference to the fact that the Cretans chose to surrender to him; in 46 this is set up as an explicit alternative to surrender to the (unnamed) Roman commander already in Crete. Indeed, he uses this as an example of Pompeius' *auctoritas*!

severe and long-standing problem, and the command was due to a law very similar to one currently under discussion. As a result of all this, it was the best possible argument for the passage of the Manilian law.

However, it is not the only evidence that is adduced for Pompeius' *uirtus*. Cicero also calls as witness Italy, Sicily, Africa, Gaul, and Spain and Italy again (30). The paragraph, with its insistent anaphora of *testis* and its geographical scope, is impressive testimony to the extent of Pompeius' experience. The forensic language also recalls the more common occasion when provinces, or their inhabitants, were witnesses in Rome, that is *repetundae* trials, and thus foreshadows Cicero's ascription to Pompeius later in this speech of the more peaceable virtues appropriate to a provincial governor. It also leads up to the invocation of the entire world and the whole of the Mediterranean as witnesses, which Pompeius' success in the pirate war has made possible.[88]

The campaigns in Italy (the first time around), Sicily, Africa, Gaul, and Spain were all civil wars in one sense or another. Italy refers to his fighting for Sulla in 83–81, as the latter took control of the country on his return from the East; in Sicily and Africa he was mopping up those who continued to resist Sulla once he had been successful in Italy; it was in Spain that Sertorius continued the Marian resistance well into the 70s and Gaul is presumably mentioned as the route Pompeius took to get to Spain. However, the internecine nature of these conflicts is concealed in Cicero's account. Italy is 'liberated' by Sulla; Africa is 'magnis oppressa hostium copiis'; and Spain witnessed 'plurimos *hostis* ab hoc superatos prostratos' (30). These vocabulary choices give the impression that Pompeius has on each occasion been dealing with an external enemy of the state, rather than a faction within it.

This redescription, by the victors, of civil war in terms of foreign conflict is a familiar feature in the ideological manoeuvrings of the late Republic,[89] and the version of events that Cicero gives here is surely the standard account. However, Pompeius' own behaviour during this period was of

---

[88] Vasaly, *Representations*, 25.

[89] See J. G. W. Henderson, *Fighting for Rome: Poets and Caesars, History and Civil War* (Cambridge: Cambridge Univ. Press, 1998).

questionable propriety, and an extremely unfavourable interpretation could be put on it. Such an interpretation survives,
in an extract from an otherwise lost speech by a man called
Helvius Mancia.[90] In 55, Mancia, then a very old man,
denounced Scribonius Libo to the censors. Pompeius counter-
attacked, in particular drawing attention to Mancia's age, and
saying that he must have returned from the underworld in
order to make the charge. Mancia's reply is given as:

That is quite true, Pompeius: I do indeed come from the underworld,
I come to prosecute Lucius Libo. But while I was there, I saw Gnaeus
Domitius Ahenobarbus, bloodied and weeping, because he, the son
of a great house, of unimpeachable habit of life and outstanding
patriotism, had been killed, in the very flower of his youth, on your
orders; I saw a man of equal distinction, Marcus Brutus, cut by
swords and complaining that this was as a result of your treachery, in
the first place, and then your cruelty; I saw Gnaeus Carbo, who had
been a staunch protector of you when a child, and of your father's
property, in chains in his third consulship, chains into which you had
ordered that he be thrown, protesting that against all justice he had
been butchered by you, a Roman knight, while he held the highest
authority. I saw Perpenna, a man of praetorian rank, with the same
appearance and cry of complaint, cursing your brutality; all were
united in their lament, that without trial they had died at your hands,
those of a teenage butcher.[91]

This is of course a highly emotive and rhetorical account;
while it is undoubtedly true that Pompeius had ordered the
executions of the four men mentioned in this passage, there was
presumably considerable room for debate as to whether he was

[90] Valerius Maximus 6. 2. 8 (*ORF* 71, fr. 1). Cf. Cicero, *ad Att.* 9. 14, on the
crimes of Pompeius' early life.

[91] non mentiris, Pompei: uenio enim ab inferis, in L. Libonem accusator
uenio. sed dum illic moror, uidi cruentum Cn. Domitium Ahenobarbum
deflentem, quod summo genere natus, integerrimae uitae, amantissimus
patriae, in ipso iuuentae flore tuo iussu esset occisus; uidi pari claritate con-
spicuum M. Brutum ferro laceratum, querentem id sibi prius perfidia,
deinde etiam crudelitate tua accidisse; uidi Cn. Carbonem acerrimum
pueritiae tuae bonorumque patris tui defensorem in tertio consulatu catenis
quas tu ei inici iusseras uinctum, obtestantem se aduersus omne fas ac nefas,
cum in summo imperio, a te equite Romano trucidatum: uidi eodem habitu
et quiritatu praetorium uirum Perpennam saeuitiam tuam execrantem,
omnesque eos uno uoce indignantes, quod indemnati sub te adulescentulo
carnifice occidissent.

justified in so doing and whether or not these actions were fairly described as cruel. None the less, Mancia's words show that such an account was possible. And while Valerius Maximus says in commenting on this anecdote that Mancia's speech 'opened up again the gaping wounds of civil war which had long been healed over',[92] it seems improbable that eleven years earlier some at least of Cicero's audience at the *contio* would not have been able to supplement his account with bitter reflections of their own about Pompeius' behaviour.[93]

It seems to me that we need to posit an active recollection of the events of the civil war combined with a hostile attitude to Pompeius' actions during it to explain why Cicero should refer to it, even in this guarded fashion. Talking about Pompeius, even if one were to mention only his fighting the pirates, would mean that some of the audience were reminded of what he had done earlier. So it is not entirely accurate to talk of Cicero's account here of the civil war as an evasion: it is only an evasion for that part of the audience who would not by themselves recall Pompeius' bloodstained career at this time. For those who did, it is a corrective. They might think that Pompeius had been a teenage butcher; Cicero is telling them that Pompeius was an invaluable soldier, fighting against the enemies of the state.[94]

Pompeius' early career, despite its many appealing features, posed a number of problems for Cicero, and we can see the results in some rather strained and improbable statements. However, his tactics in dealing with Pompeius in this speech are generally much less defensive. I want to turn now to the extensive contrast he establishes between Pompeius and Lucullus.

[92] 'obducta iam uetustis cicatricibus bellorum ciuilium uastissima uulnera . . . renouare licuit'.

[93] The civil wars and their aftermath were still potentially a live issue at the time: see Cicero's (fragmentary) consular oration, *On the sons of the proscribed* (J. W. Crawford, *M. Tullius Cicero: Fragmentary Orations* (Atlanta: Scholars Press, 1994), 201-7).

[94] It is interesting, in the light of Pompeius' early career, both in his mopping up of the anti-Sullan forces and in his filching other commanders' laurels, that Cicero has *fides* as one of Pompeius' *uirtutes* (36, 42), albeit a very brief reference: he really is honest and straightforward. However, there is a very pleasing, though doubtless wholly unconscious, irony in what Cicero says in 42, since it is Rome's *socii* and *hostes* who can testify to it. It was citizens alone who suffered from his alleged faithlessness.

3.2.3. Not being Lucullus

It is difficult for us to assess how Cicero's audience might have expected him to handle Lucullus, and the relations between Lucullus and Pompeius. This is in part because Lucullus appears to us to be a second-rank figure in the late Republic: important, certainly, but not to be counted with Sulla, Pompeius, Cicero, Caesar, or even Crassus—an attitude compounded by what has come to be seen as his dominant trait, the love of luxury. A second problem is the hostility which is held to have existed between Pompeius and Lucullus, and which can be seen to structure many of the anecdotes about the two men and is a recurrent motif in Plutarch's biographies. Whatever the state of relations between the two men later, it has been convincingly demonstrated that Plutarch's retrojection of the quarrel to the 70s is highly implausible;[95] and it is quite possible that the opposition between the characters and abilities of the two which Cicero uses so effectively in this speech is its first occurrence. Cicero certainly had the choice not to make Lucullus so prominent in this speech.

At first sight, Cicero's references to Lucullus appear very favourable, and one view would be that he is bringing in Lucullus as part of the delicate balancing act of trying to please everybody. That is, despite supporting a very *popularis* measure, he is still giving due credit to the achievements of the representative of oligarchic government: and this is very much in keeping with his apparent politeness towards Catulus and Hortensius. Lucullus is described as 'a brave man, a wise person, and a great commander', mention is made of his *uirtus*, *adsiduitas*, and *consilium* and his achievements against Mithradates are listed at some length (20–1).

However, just as Cicero's treatment of Catulus and Hortensius is not quite as respectful as a cursory reading might suggest, so with Lucullus. The first mention of Lucullus in the speech is in 5, in Cicero's opening summary of events: 'Lucius Lucullus has left the war after great achievements.'[96] As this comes in a passage which appears to be an objective account, it

---

[95] T. P. Hillman, 'The Alleged *Inimicitiae* of Pompeius and Lucullus: 78–74', *CPh* 86 (1991), 315–18.

[96] 5: 'L. Lucullum magnis rebus gestis ab eo bello discedere.'

may be fanciful to think that this should be interpreted as a criticism of Lucullus for leaving what has already (4) been described as a *bellum graue* unfinished. It is easier to see the opening for a critical view of Lucullus in his next appearance, when Cicero describes Mithradates' two-pronged strategy after the departure from Asia of the elder Murena: he began to co-operate with Sertorius so that Rome would find itself fighting on two fronts simultaneously (9). However, Pompeius has already dealt with Sertorius (10); and a start has been made on Mithradates himself (10):

> In the other area, matters have been so dealt with by Lucius Lucullus, an outstanding man, that the greatly distinguished opening to his campaign seems to be owed to his abilities rather than to luck, while the recent events in the closing stages are due to chance and are not his fault. But I shall talk about Lucullus elsewhere, and I shall do this in such a way, Quirites, that it seems that neither have I taken away from him in my speech true praise, nor have I made up false praise.[97]

I shall return below to the specific issue of Lucullus' lack of luck; what is worth attention here is the way that Cicero indicates that the praise due to Lucullus has quite clear boundaries, and that *falsa laus* is conceivable, that is, that exaggeration is possible. The discussion of Lucullus' actions which he promises here occurs in the context of indicating the size of the war (20–6) and in particular explaining that it is still large enough to be dangerous and therefore worth taking very seriously and shows a similar desire to set limits to his achievements and the praise due to them. What Lucullus has done (20–1) is followed by a much longer section on what still needs to be done (22–6): thus the structure of this part of the argument inevitably makes Lucullus look a failure.

This trend in the structure is supported by the ostentatious way that Cicero draws attention to how generous he is being. He introduces his discussion of Lucullus as follows (20): 'and so that everyone understands that I am giving Lucius Lucullus

---

[97] in altera parte ita res ab L. Lucullo, summo uiro, est administrata ut initia illa rerum gestarum magna atque praeclara non felicitati eius sed uirtuti, haec autem extrema quae nuper acciderunt non culpae sed fortunae tribuenda esse uideantur. sed de Lucullo dicam alio loco, et ita dicam, Quirites, ut neque uera laus ei detracta oratione mea neque falsa adficta esse uideatur.

as much praise as is due to a brave man, a wise person and a great commander, I state that . . .'.[98] There follows a list of what he accomplished. At the end of which, he concludes (21): 'I think that this is enough praise for you, Quirites, to understand that Lucius Lucullus has not been praised from this platform in a similar way by any of those who are finding fault with this law and measure'.[99] The achievements mentioned between these two passages are impressive, with references to the benefits that the *populus Romanus* has gained, and plenty of glamorously distant proper names. However, it is difficult to escape from the impression of a list which could have been very much expanded had Cicero so chosen; and the introductory and concluding remarks give a strong impression of setting limits to the praise due to Lucullus. He will get what he deserves, but no more. This in itself is in obvious contrast to the boundlessness of the praise one could devote to Pompeius, according to Cicero's remark earlier in the speech, where he congratulates himself on having a topic which could leave no speaker without something to say (3).

The contrast is maintained when it comes to the qualities the two commanders possess. In each case the contrast is, unsurprisingly, to Pompeius' advantage: taken together, they show that the people were right to replace Lucullus and are right now to appoint in his place a man who in many important respects is his opposite.

Pompeius is exceptional for his *felicitas*, and this is a demonstration of the approval the gods feel for him. Lucullus, on the other hand, is specifically said to lack *felicitas* in the passage which I quote above. In the first part of the sentence Cicero's formulation seems to be positive: Lucullus hasn't just been lucky; it is his good qualities which have led to his success. Similarly, the second part of the sentence can be read in a positive way: when bad things *have* happened, they have been the result of bad luck and not incompetence. But while this is ostensibly polite and favourable, it is clear that the results of

[98] 'atque ut omnes intellegant me L. Lucullo tantum impertire laudis quantum forti uiro et sapienti homini et magno imperatori debeatur, dico . . .'
[99] 'satis opinor hoc esse laudis atque ita, Quirites, ut hoc uos intellegatis, a nullo istorum qui huic obtrectant legi atque causae L. Lucullum similiter ex hoc loco esse laudatum.'

Lucullus' luck have been unfortunate. Moreover, the contrast between *felicitas* and *fortuna* works against him: he does not have that innate quality which makes things turn out right for him, and as a result is vulnerable to the workings of chance.[100] Lucullus' family history must have made Cicero's appropriation of *felicitas* on Pompeius' behalf particularly galling. The first, and at this point the only, temple to *Felicitas* in Rome had been dedicated by Lucullus' grandfather who was consul in 151.[101] Lucullus himself probably commissioned a statue of *Felicitas* from one of the leading sculptors of the day.[102] Moreover, he seems to have cultivated close links with the cult of *Fortuna* at Praeneste.[103] Cicero is challenging these claims to a favoured relationship to luck: what Lucullus has achieved has been due to his own qualities, and not to good fortune. This latter belongs firmly to Pompeius.[104]

Pompeius is fast: *celeritas* was one of the distinguishing features of his campaign against the pirates (34–5), and is also cited in connection with his campaign in Sicily (30). Lucullus' actions against Mithradates were marked, in contrast, by a fatal slowness, in particular on the occasion when, according to Cicero, Mithradates managed to escape from the Roman army by abandoning his treasure, since the soldiers stopped to gather it (22):

While our men stopped to gather the treasure up very carefully, the king himself slipped through their fingers . . . joy *slowed* them down.[105]

---

[100] D. Magie, *Roman Rule in Asia Minor* (Princeton: Princeton Univ. Press, 1950), 1. 343–8; Champeaux, *Fortuna*, 237–8.

[101] E. M. Steinby (ed.), *Lexicon topographicum urbis Romae* (Rome: Quasar, 1993–), 2. 244–5; L. Pietilä-Castrén, *Magnificentia Publica: The Victory Monuments of the Roman Generals in the Era of the Punic Wars* (Helsinki: Societas Scientiarum Fennica, 1987), 124–8.

[102] Pliny, *NH* 35. 155–6. However, the dating is problematic, and it is possible that Lucullus' son is meant: see K. Jex-Blake and E. Sellers, *The Elder Pliny's Chapters on the History of Art* (London: Macmillan, 1896), 179–80.

[103] F. Coarelli, 'Architettura sacra e architettura privata nella tarda Repubblica', in *Architecture et société* (Paris and Rome: Collection de l'École française de Rome 66, 1983), 191–217, 200–6.

[104] C. J. Classen, 'Ciceros Kunst der Ueberredung', in Ludwig (ed.), *Rhétorique*, 149–92, 186.

[105] 'haec dum nostri conligunt omnia diligentius, rex ipse e manibus effugit . . . hos laetitia *tardauit*', and cf. Sect. 3.1.2 above.

Lucullus is also, it is suggested, an incompetent diplomat. Cicero does not make any explicit statement to this effect; but he describes the fear with which the approach of Lucullus was greeted (23):

> After Lucius Lucullus came with his army to Tigranes' kingdom, many of the inhabitants also were stirred up against our commander. This was because these people, whom the Roman people had never thought to make a trial of in war or to provoke, had become frightened. In addition there was another serious and firmly held belief which had taken hold in the minds of the barbarians, to the effect that our army had been brought to those regions in order to plunder a particularly rich and sacred shrine.[106]

Moreover, Cicero, in summing up the position of the war, indicates its seriousness by saying that it is one which (26) 'powerful kings are joining, nations in a state of turmoil are renewing and peoples who had hitherto been at peace are taking up'. In the light of his earlier remarks about shrines, it is not difficult for a listener or reader to supply reasons for this enthusiasm to fight Rome. Pompeius, on the other hand, is hugely popular with the provincials whom he has come into contact with. This popularity is one of the best demonstrations of his *auctoritas* (43–6), and has led to the belief among some provincials that he is a being sent from heaven (41).

Cicero also makes it clear that Lucullus had difficulty in commanding the loyalty of his troops. His description of their mutiny draws attention to itself, through the device of *praeteritio*, without his having to describe what happened in any detail (23. 26–24. 2): 'although our forces had taken a city from Tigranes' kingdom and had been successful in battle they were distressed by being so far from home and were missing their families. *I shall now say no more*: for the end result was that our soldiers preferred an early return from that region rather than further advances.'[107] Cicero does not say much

---

[106] cuius in regnum postea quam L. Lucullus cum exercitu uenit, plures etiam gentes contra imperatorem nostrum concitatae sunt. erat enim metus iniectus eis nationibus quas numquam populus Romanus neque lacessendas bello neque temptandas putauit; erat etiam alia grauis atque uehemens opinio quae per animos gentium barbararum peruaserat, fani locupletissimi et religiosissimi diripiendi causa in eas oras nostrum esse exercitum adductum.

[107] 'noster autem exercitus, tametsi urbem ex Tigrani regno ceperat et

about Pompeius' popularity with his troops, and this is probably to avoid the worrying reflections that might arise from the existence of a commander whose troops' primary loyalty was to him, rather than to the *res publica*. None the less, Pompeius' popularity may be a fact which Cicero is encouraging his audience to compare with Lucullus' lack of success; and it has been argued that Pompeius' whole style of leadership was in sharp and self-conscious contrast with that of more 'old-fashioned' commanders such as Lucullus.[108]

Pompeius and Lucullus also have different habits in relation to the question of money and the extent to which commanders abuse their positions out of greed.[109] One of the most admirable things about Pompeius, in Cicero's account, is his probity. He possesses both *innocentia* and *temperantia*. The former is displayed by the fact that the post of centurion is not for sale in his army, nor does he appropriate for his officials the money he has from the treasury, or leave it at Rome lent out at interest (37). This is, according to Cicero, in stark contrast to the behaviour of other officials. The latter, his ability to resist temptation, is shown in a number of ways: he has not allowed himself to be diverted by the search for booty, or by pleasure, or by sight-seeing, or by the need for a rest, and—most important—did not even go to look at the Greek statues which others have been in the habit of stealing (40). There are strong suggestions, on the other hand, that Lucullus is prone to greed: there was the 'Medea' episode, and the anxiety among some of the inhabitants of Tigranes' kingdom that his purpose in coming was to pillage a shrine.[110] This may be another point at which Cicero is

proeliis usus erat secundis, tamen nimia longinquitate locorum ac desiderio suorum commouebatur. *hic iam plura non dicam*; fuit enim illud extremum ut ex eis locis a militibus nostris reditus magis maturus quam progressio longior quaereretur.'

[108] A. Marcone, 'Il nuovo stile dell'uomo politico: Pompeo "princeps civilis"', *Athenaeum*, 78 (1990), 475–81.

[109] On the perception of greed as a characteristic of the Romans, see A. Erskine, 'Money-Loving Romans', *PLLS* 9 (1996), 1–11. Compare also Plutarch's description, in his life of Lucullus (37. 1–2), of the tribune Memmius' opposition to Lucullus' getting a triumph, 'on the grounds of widespread profiteering and having prolonged the war'.

[110] 22–3. Cicero's remark about Pompeius, 'non auaritia ab instituto cursu ad praedam aliquam deuocauit' (40. 24–5), is a particularly pointed contrast with the Medea episode.

expecting his audience to fill in the gaps in his account with their own knowledge. While Lucullus' reputation for luxury seems to have developed for the most part after his return from the East, there is some evidence for his being known for extravagant living earlier. There is an interesting anecdote in the *pro Sestio*: Cicero is attacking Gabinius for *his* luxurious style of life, and one of his charges is that 'he builds a villa in the sight of everyone which now makes the villa, of which he once displayed a picture in a *contio* when he was tribune of the plebs, look like a little hut'.[111] The point of showing the picture was to arouse the crowd against the owner: clearly this refers to the *lex Gabinia* which replaced Lucullus by Glabrio, and shows that Lucullus' villa was, even in 67, a remarkably lavish building.[112]

The contrast between Pompeius and Lucullus is set up in an extremely skilful way: Cicero suggests that Pompeius has a whole range of desirable qualities which Lucullus lacks, while avoiding any openly hostile remarks about the latter.

3.2.4. Not being Alexander

With Lucullus, and to a lesser extent with Sulla, Cicero needs his audiences to perceive the contrast with Pompeius and to read it in Pompeius' favour. Not being Lucullus is a deliberate strategy. Not being Alexander, on the other hand, refers to a very different phenomenon. In this case there are good reasons for expecting a positive comparison: yet we find no trace of it.

Alexander was a figure of huge fascination for the leading politicians of the late Republic and Triumviral periods.[113] The sheer scale of his conquests, and the glamour which

---

[111] *pro Sestio* 93: 'uillam aedificare in oculis omnium tantam tugurium ut iam uideatur esse illa uilla quam ipse tribunus plebis pictam olim in contionibus explicabat'.

[112] It is worth noting that Cicero does not name Lucullus in the *pro Sestio* passage, presumably because Lucullus' reputation for luxury was so firmly established by 56 that it would have been difficult to argue that Gabinius outstripped him.

[113] For the whole topic, see D. Michel, *Alexander als Vorbild für Pompeius, Caesar und Marcus Antonius. Archäologische Untersuchungen* (Brussels: Latomus, 1967), and O. Weippert, *Alexander-Imitatio und Römische Politik in Republicanischer Zeit* (Inaug. diss. Würzburg: Augsburg, 1972); but cf. P. Green, 'Caesar and Alexander: Aemulatio, Imitatio, Comparatio', *AJAH* 3 (1978), 1–26.

was associated with him as a man of action who also lived a luxurious life, made it very tempting for politicians to try to exploit his name in self-promotion.[114] Pompeius was probably the first of the late Republican figures to do so, and he seems to have sought the comparison at an early stage in his career. According to Plutarch, he modified his appearance to suggest a physical likeness and he liked being called Alexander.[115] His adoption of the *cognomen* Magnus may be supposed to evoke Alexander, since this adjective had been attached to Alexander's name at Rome since at least the early second century.[116] Further, there is an anecdote about Marcius Philippus and Pompeius which suggests that the nickname was well known by the 80s: Philippus, while defending Pompeius in court, possibly on charges of *peculatus* arising from his father's conduct during the Social War, is recorded as having said that there was nothing surprising if he, being Philip, should love Alexander.[117] It has also been suggested that Pompeius' use of elephants at his first triumph was designed to recall Alexander.[118]

Thus, the comparison seems to have been well established by 66, even if its most impressive occurrences are later,[119] and it is

[114] J. Griffin, *Latin Poets and Roman Life* (London: Duckworth, 1985), 39–40.

[115] Sallust, *Historiae* 3. 88 (Maurenbrecher); Plutarch, *Life of Pompeius* 2. 1–2.

[116] Pliny the Elder, *NH* 7. 96; Plutarch, *Life of Pompeius* 13. Apart from possible reminiscences of Alexander, to adopt a *cognomen* of this sort—neither inherited, physically descriptive, nor geographical on the basis of military achievement—was extraordinarily bold: only Sulla, with 'Felix', provided a precedent. See Balsdon, 'Sulla Felix'.

[117] Plutarch, *Life of Pompeius* 2. 2; for the trial, see M. C. Alexander, *Trials in the Late Roman Republic, 149 BC to 50 BC* (Toronto: Univ. of Toronto Press, 1990), 62–3.

[118] See Weippert, *Alexander-Imitatio*, 70–1. This is an interesting suggestion, though I wonder whether elephants and an African connection might not tend instead to recall Hannibal. At any rate, Pompeius' piece of self-promotion went ludicrously wrong, since the gates were too small to let the elephant-drawn chariot through: Plutarch, *Life of Pompeius* 14. 4.

[119] He wore, or is said to have worn, Alexander's *chlamys* at his third triumph in 61 (Appian, *Mith.* 577): by this point his military achievements in the East gave real substance to the comparison (Weippert, *Alexander-Imitatio*, 84–6). See also Cicero, *ad Att.* 2. 19. 3 (from the summer of 59), where he describes how Pompeius' *cognomen* laid him open to a hostile pun at the theatre.

not difficult to see why Pompeius should have been so attracted by it, even at the risk of seeming ridiculous: it emphasized how young he was when he began to do great things, and it suggested that his military successes were huge in scope. In relation to the Manilian law, the promise through the identification of Pompeius with Alexander of invincible conquest, in the East, seems as though it should be irresistible.

It is, however, very difficult to find any reference to Alexander in Cicero's speech. The one possible candidate is in 67, when he says, of the widespread corruption in provincial administration, 'It is as though we did not see that Pompeius is great (*magnus*) both because of his own virtues, and as a result as well of the vices of others'.[120] But Weippert's caution is justified: the choice of *magnus* is pointed, and Cicero could have chosen some other adjective, but it can be explained simply as a reference to the *cognomen*, which had after all received only reluctant acceptance among the elite.[121]

Why does Cicero pass up the chance to evoke this attractive comparison? The answer seems most plausibly to lie in the ambiguity that could be evoked by the figure of Alexander, since he represents not just stunning military success, but also unchecked dictatorial power. It is potentially dangerous to suggest that someone going to Asia Minor and taking charge of a large army resembles Alexander: what, in that case, will stop him from marching all the way to India and never coming back? Given the anxieties about the constitutional propriety of this law, Cicero does not want to risk suggesting that Pompeius may follow his own ambition rather than the needs of the state.

3.3. CAESAR IN THE *DE PROVINCIIS CONSVLARIBUS*

In the *de prouinciis consularibus* Caesar is explicitly given some of the same qualities which Cicero ascribed ten years earlier to Pompeius: *uirtus, felicitas,* and *fides* (35). But his character and

---

[120] 67. 5–6: 'quasi uero Cn. Pompeium non cum suis uirtutibus tum etiam alienis uitiis magnum esse uideamus'. See Weippert, *Alexander-Imitatio*, 67.

[121] On punning references to Pompeius' *cognomen*, see D. C. Feeney, ' "Stat magni nominis umbra." Lucan on the greatness of Pompeius Magnus', *CQ* 36 (1986), 239–43.

abilities are not the focus of an extended and systematic survey such as Cicero devotes to Pompeius in the *de imp*.; instead information about him emerges at various points in a speech whose structure is not dominated by one individual.[122] Cicero is offering, to the Senate, his considered response to a policy issue.

There are other reasons why Caesar does not need to be given as thorough a treatment as Pompeius. He had been in Gaul for two years by this stage, and as a result his accomplishments can take the place of qualities. And while he held his command through a tribunician law, debating the allocation of provinces under the *lex Sempronia* was a standard part of the Senate's activities, and thus the issue need not have seemed quite as innovative and therefore dangerous as the *lex Manilia* clearly did seem to at least some people.

Cicero reinforces in a number of ways the idea that there is nothing untoward or unusual in the situation that the Senate is debating. One way is by his extensive citation of examples from Roman history.[123] In general these illustrate, and thus give precedents for, the triumph of patriotism over private enmities and so are a part of Cicero's wider strategy of reformulating the terms of the debate into a matter of his own likes and dislikes;[124] while the obvious ground for so doing is Cicero's desire to assert his independence while giving an opinion which would seem to make his obedience to the first triumvirate unmistakable, this tactic serves very effectively the argument which he is forced to present. It allows him to suggest that the only thing clouding the debate and preventing Caesar's reappointment is private likes and dislikes, and thus he can trivialize the serious constitutional arguments which were involved.

Another method of reassuring the Senate is making Caesar come across as a good public servant, whose actions are dictated by the needs of the state, rather than by his own desires. This is an attitude which Cicero indicates that he too shares. Nothing has determined his contribution to the debate other than the 'situation of the war' and the 'advantage of the state'.[125] He goes

---

[122] Unless, of course, we count Cicero.

[123] Note in particular the long sequence in 18–22.

[124] See Sect. 4.3.

[125] 29: 'in hac me nihil aliud nisi ratio belli, nisi summa utilitas rei publicae moueat'.

on to ask (29), 'what reason is there for Caesar himself to want to stay longer in his province, except the desire to hand over to the republic in a finished state that which he has begun?'[126] There follows an extraordinary passage in which Cicero sarcastically lists a wide variety of reasons why Caesar might want to stay in Gaul.[127] The first few items, the pleasure and civilization which Gaul affords, seem straightforward, playing on the Roman view of long-haired Gauls as barbarians.[128] The final two involve a shift, since they are 'the desire for victory' and 'advancing the borders of the empire'. This is odd because these seem like two perfectly respectable ambitions for a Roman commander to hold. Yet, as Cicero goes on to explain, Caesar is now beyond these things: his victories so far are such as to be unsurpassable, and he has already reached the edge of the known world. Caesar has accomplished so much that there is nothing that he, personally, can gain from staying in Gaul; all that is keeping him there is the *utilitas rei publicae*. Indeed, the obvious course for his enemies is not to recall him, but to keep him in his province (29). In the face of such devotion to duty Cicero's own duty, as a senator, is clear: he must support Caesar's desire to stay (30).

There follows a brief history of Rome's relations with Gaul, in which Cicero describes the threat which Gaul has always been, the limited nature of its military successes beyond the Alps before Caesar, and the comprehensiveness of what Caesar is accomplishing now (30–4). He concludes this part of his speech by returning to the idea that there is no personal advantage to Caesar in staying in Gaul, and that the needs of the state require that he should. The Senate's duty is therefore clear (35): 'since he has long since done justice to his own glory, but not yet to the state, and since he prefers to come later to his own reward than to leave unfinished the task he is undertaking for the state, we ought not to recall a general who is aflame to serve

---

[126] 'nam ipse Caesar quid est cur in prouincia commorari uelit, nisi ut ea quae per eum adfecta sunt perfecta rei publicae tradat?'

[127] 29: 'amoenitas eum, credo, locorum, urbium pulchritudo, hominum nationumque illarum humanitas et lepos, uictoriae cupiditas, finium imperi propagatio retinet. quid illis terris asperius, quid incultius oppidis, quid nationibus immanius, quid porro tot uictoriis praestabilius, quid Oceano longius inueniri potest?'

[128] Cf. *pro Fonteio*; Woolf, *Becoming Roman*, 74–82.

the state, nor should we throw into confusion and interrupt the whole plan of the Gallic war, now almost complete.'[129] This approach is a very good way of showing how magnificent Caesar's achievements are, and at the same time indicating that it is to the advantage of the state that he should not be recalled. It also enables Cicero to address anxieties about Caesar's personal ambitions, inasmuch as he tries to suggest that such anxieties are completely unfounded. Caesar wants to stay in Gaul, and should be kept there, simply because that is what is best for the state. It is only after he has set up Caesar as this devoted public servant that he turns to the awkward possibility that Caesar may at some point not obey the Senate, and make his own dispositions for the government of Gaul (38–9). Moreover, the danger that this may happen is not due to Caesar but to the Senate, inasmuch as their intransigence may alienate him. Cicero concludes his argument as follows (39): 'it is my duty as a senator to ensure, as far as I can, that no distinguished or powerful man seems to have justifiable grounds for anger against this order.'[130]

Cicero's presentation of Caesar also takes into account the relations between Caesar and Pompeius. One aspect of this is how Cicero handles the unprecedentedly long period of supplication which had been granted in response to Caesar's victories in Gaul: fifteen days, as opposed to the ten which had been granted to Pompeius at the news of Mithradates' death (26–7). Far from allowing this to be a source of rivalry or ill-feeling between the two, he pays tribute to Pompeius' *uirtus* and *animi magnitudo* in desiring a greater honour for another man than he himself had received. And, it appears, Caesar's military achievements complement those of Pompeius. Pompeius has brought peace to all other parts of the world; Caesar is doing the same for the last unconquered part of the world, that is Gaul (31). Just as they are allies in the political sphere, so in the

---

[129] 'cum uero ille suae gloriae iam pridem rei publicae nondum satis fecerit, et malit tamen tardius ad suorum laborum fructus peruenire quam non explere susceptum rei publicae munus, nec imperatorem incensum ad rem publicam bene gerendam reuocare nec totam Gallici belli rationem prope iam explicatam perturbare atque impedire debemus.'

[130] 'praestare hoc senator debeo, quantum possum, ne quis uir clarus aut potens huic ordini iure irasci posse uideatur.'

military: Cicero is quite well aware of his duties to the first triumvirate.

Cicero's presentation of Caesar is designed to show him as a potentially dutiful servant of the Senate and to the state: he acknowledges the possibility of disagreement, while placing the responsibility for provoking a breach, if one were to occur, with the Senate.[131] Cicero manages to acknowledge the unprecedented nature of Caesar's military achievements while avoiding discussion of the unorthodox route by which he came to be in a position to act in this way.

3.4. ILLUSIONS OF CONTROL

Pompeius and Caesar come across in these two speeches as very different figures: Pompeius is an isolated figure whereas Caesar is shown as a self-sacrificing public servant. But the same ideological impulse lies behind these divergent rhetorical strategies. In both cases Cicero is arguing for the creation or continued existence of military commands which were new, extremely powerful, and outside the normal methods of senatorial control. His response is to set up Pompeius and Caesar as men who will not exploit the dangerous potential inherent in their positions. This enables him to suggest that constitutional anxieties are irrelevant. One might even want to argue that the very fact of Cicero's oratory on these subjects offers a reassurance which is groundless. The debates in which he is participating give a specious impression that the centre is in control, yet it is unclear whether there was absolute confidence that Pompeius at the conclusion of the campaign against the pirates, and Caesar in Gaul in 56, would return quietly to private life should their commands *not* be renewed. Cicero's speeches, in these two cases, give a questionable view of the empire not simply in their rhetorical strategies but in their very existence.

Personal probity as the answer to the problems of empire is becoming a familiar ploy in Cicero's oratory. So far I have suggested explanations for this phenomenon in terms of anxieties about empire: that the cases Cicero is dealing with

---

[131] 37–8. Cf. Caesar's self-justifying account of the outbreak of the civil war at the beginning of his *de bello ciuili*.

present problems which were insoluble, and so best avoided by an orator seeking to be persuasive. Hence the emphasis on individuals to create attractive and comprehensible solutions. In the forensic cases I considered in Chapters 1 and 2, Cicero's reasons for wanting to be persuasive are clear: he had clients to defend or attack. But why did he find himself supporting radical initiatives such as the Manilian law or (in effect) the extension of Caesar's command—a decision particularly surprising given his generally conservative stance in political matters? At this point it is necessary to address Cicero's imperial oratory as a facet of his own career as a politician and orator.

4

Portrait of the orator as a great man: Cicero on Cicero

IN the previous three chapters I have looked at the three different kinds of speeches that Cicero delivered about empire and offered interpretations which relate his strategies of persuasion to the attitudes and opinions of his audience. That is, I have considered how the speeches attempt to persuade their audience to do whatever Cicero is advocating: which might seem to be the most important function of a speech. But whenever Cicero speaks he is also engaged in creating or maintaining his own persona as an orator and as a public figure. It is of course impossible to separate these two aims completely. The character which a Roman orator projected was an important factor in his success.[1] Cicero himself laid great emphasis on the importance of *ethos* in his mature rhetorical theory.[2] But for any orator with political ambitions, there are wider implications for his career as a whole, which make his image a matter for continuous attention.

In this chapter I shall turn to the relationship between the speeches I have been looking at and Cicero's own career. His heavy dependence on oratory for his political success means that every time he spoke in public, he could not but draw attention to the basis of his political success and thus justify it or not. To provide a context for his self-presentation in the speeches dealing with empire, I begin by looking at the figure of Cicero in the Catilinarian speeches. The situation from which these speeches arose might seem to have provided an opportunity for Cicero to transcend the civilian bias of his career, because he was defending the state from what turned into an external peril:

[1] May, *Trials of Character*.
[2] J. Wisse, *Ethos and Pathos from Aristotle to Cicero* (Amsterdam: Hakkert, 1989).

but even here, in fact, he does not escape from his reliance on oratory, because he presents his actions in suppressing it as those of an orator, in explicit contrast with military activity. This self-presentation is to be seen as an attempt to justify his lack of military experience, but paradoxically it confirms the civilian and rhetorical foundation of his career and increases his political dependence on his own oratory.

Against this background of Cicero's inevitable self-consciousness every time he speaks in public, the persuasive strategies of the two deliberative speeches relevant to this inquiry gain in effectiveness. In both speeches, it is possible to relate the constraints which his own career places at that point on what he can say to his failure to engage directly with what we might consider to be the fundamental issues in the republican government of its empire.

4.1. FIGHTING WORDS: REACHING THE CONSULSHIP

Although it is not clear what precisely constituted being a new man in Roman politics, there is no doubt as to Cicero's status as such.[3] Not only did he have no consular ancestry; none of his ancestors had ever held office in the city, and he did not come from Rome. As a result, he had no access to what seems to have been one of the most important factors in electoral success, belonging to a family which had already been distinguished at Rome.[4] Moreover, Cicero chose not to use many of the methods of gaining popularity and electoral success which could compensate for the absence of distinguished ancestors. His military experience was extraordinarily limited for a Roman, consisting only of brief service during the Social War before his campaigns while governor of Cilicia; and though he

---

[3] M. Gelzer, *Die Nobilität der römischen Republik* (Leipzig: Teubner, 1912); T. P. Wiseman, *New Men in the Roman Senate 139 B.C.–A.D. 14* (Oxford: Oxford Univ. Press, 1971); P. A. Brunt, '*Nobilitas* and *Novitas*', *JRS* 72 (1982), 1–17; L. Burckhardt, 'The Political Elite of the Roman Republic: Comments on Recent Discussion of the Concepts *nobilitas* and *homo novus*', *Historia*, 39 (1990), 77–99, surveys the progress of the debate.

[4] But see K. Hopkins and G. Burton, 'Political Success in the Late Republic', in K. Hopkins, *Death and Renewal* (Cambridge: Cambridge Univ. Press, 1983), 31–119.

did hold the office of aedile his games were in no way remarkable for their splendour.[5] These gaps may in part have been due to a lack of talent for things military, and the absence of the financial resources necessary for hugely impressive games.[6] But to a certain extent they were the result of *choices*: not to seek further military service after the Social War, not to take a province after his praetorship, not to borrow heavily, as others did, to provide an impressive public spectacle and hope to recoup the costs through an exploitative provincial governorship. It is also interesting to note that Cicero seems not to have made any particular use of his connections, both geographical and through marriage, with Marius.[7] He relied for his electoral success, as well as for the means to maintain his influence after he had reached the consulship, almost exclusively upon his abilities as an orator.[8]

Verres' career provides an interesting contrast with Cicero's, since his family too had little political history at Rome, even if, with a senatorial father, he does not meet the strictest criteria for a new man. Verres built his career on extensive military service followed by an extended period as governor of Sicily, leading, according to Cicero, to his bon mot that he needed a third of his spoils to bribe the jury, a third to pay his lawyers, and a third for himself.[9] In effect, Verres built his career by exploiting the opportunities which the empire presented. Cicero, by contrast, kept his attention firmly on Rome, and his decision not to seek unauthorized profits meant that he regarded the one period outside Italy on official business before Cilicia, when he was a quaestor in Sicily, as wasted

---

[5] For the importance to electoral success both of military achievements and of lavish games, see the speech *pro Murena*; Wiseman, *New Men*, 116–22; for the scale of investment required by the games, see Shatzman, *Wealth*, 84–7. Cf. also Cicero's self-justifying remark on the holding of games in *de off.* 2. 58: 'faciendum est, modo pro facultatibus, nos ipsi ut fecimus'. It is also suggestive, regardless of who was the author, that there is no mention of games as a source of popularity in the *Commentariolum petitionis*.

[6] Shatzman, *Wealth*, 403–25, surveys Cicero's financial position.

[7] E. D. Rawson, 'Lucius Crassus and Cicero: The Formation of a Statesman', *PCPhS*, NS 17 (1971), 75–88, repr. in Rawson, *Culture and Society*, 16–33.

[8] Cf. A. J. E. Bell, 'Cicero and the Spectacle of Power', *JRS* 87 (1997), 1–22.

[9] Cicero, first *actio in Verrem*, 40.

time.[10] Indeed, one of the reasons for the peculiar venom and persistence which Cicero displayed in attacking Verres may be the consciousness of the different sets of values their respective careers embodied.[11]

Cicero was of course not the first Roman to be a good speaker and make use of that skill.[12] The ability to speak effectively in public was a traditional part of the Roman prescription for a good man. In the famous epitaph on L. Metellus, being a good speaker is one of the ten characteristics which are listed, and the elder Cato was well aware of the value of oratory to a politician and had written versions of some at least of his speeches disseminated.[13] And, with changing modern views of the role that the popular assemblies played in Roman politics, there is increasing acknowledgement that oratory was an important skill for a politician to possess.[14] But Cicero is exceptional in the prominence which he gave to oratory in his career. Publication of the *de inuentione* is a particularly interesting case. Its lack of originality has led to its being ignored in favour of its more intellectually challenging successors, the rhetorical treatises of Cicero's maturity: but the composition of the *de inuentione* was, at its time of writing, an innovative and ambitious piece. The writing of *artes* was still in its developing stages at this point, and Cicero's is surely meant, in the light of its reflective prefaces, as a serious contribution to this field.[15] His remarks much later in the *de oratore* about its lack of sophistication should not be taken too seriously as denigration; they remind the reader that Cicero has been contributing to the technical literature since a young man, and his statement that they are

[10] See Introduction, above.

[11] Cf. Sect. 1.1 above.

[12] For a survey of oratory's place in Roman society, see E. Fantham, 'The Contexts and Occasions of Roman Public Rhetoric', in W. J. Dominik (ed.), *Roman Eloquence: Rhetoric in Society and Literature* (London: Routledge, 1997), 111–28.

[13] Metellus: Pliny, *NH* 7, 139–40. Cato: A. E. Astin, *Cato the Censor* (Oxford: Oxford Univ. Press, 1978), 131–56.

[14] Millar, 'The Political Character of the Classical Roman Republic', 1–19, 'Politics, Persuasion and the People before the Social War', 1–11, and *Crowd*; Brunt, 'The Fall of the Roman Republic', 45–9.

[15] On the development of *artes*, see E. D. Rawson, 'The Introduction of Logical Organization in Roman Prose Literature', *PBSR* 46 (1978), 12–34, repr. in Rawson, *Culture and Society*, 324–51.

'hardly worthy of the age I have reached' would suggest that they were perfectly adequate, and indeed more so, as the product of a young man.[16] Cicero seems to have been about 20 when the work was disseminated, and it is worth asking why he did so: unlike Roman politicians who had previously written on the subject, he had no experience or reputation yet as a performer to justify the work. It is plausible to imagine that he was deliberately giving his allegiance to oratory, and signalling his abilities in that area, at a time in his career when it would have been much more natural for someone who was ambitious for a political career, particularly one without resources of birth or outstanding wealth, to be looking for military experience.

Cicero's departure for the East to study rhetoric after his successful defence of Roscius can also be seen as a self-conscious move by someone who wants his ambitions as a speaker to be well known. There is still debate about Cicero's motivations for this trip: were there grounds to fear Sulla's displeasure at the outcome of the Roscius case, or was his concern about his health genuine?[17] It is not necessary to adjudicate between these two accounts to point out that his departure to improve his skills, in the aftermath of a sensational, and successful, case, would indicate that this newcomer Cicero had extremely high standards, which he was making great efforts to meet.

Theoretical as well as practical concern for oratory continued to be a feature of Cicero's career. It is thirty years before he produces another rhetorical treatise, but his publication of written versions of speeches shows how important it was to reach a wide audience, and the *Verrines* and the self-consciously chosen 'consular' orations are an indication of his continuing concern to present himself as an orator as well as be one.[18] What I want to focus on here is the way that Cicero sets up oratory as a rival to military action, or on occasion its substitute.[19] Oratory's importance does not exist in a vacuum: Cicero

[16] *de or.* 1. 5: 'uix sunt hac aetate digna'; Cicero's originality would of course be reduced if his work was written with knowledge of the *rhetorica ad Herennium*. But even if that is the case, Cicero's 'publication' would still be an indication of great intellectual self-confidence and promise of oratorical ability.   [17] See e.g. Rawson, *Cicero*, 25–6.

[18] Consular orations: *ad Att.* 2. 1. 3.

[19] Cf. C. Nicolet, ' "Consul togatus": Remarques sur le vocabulaire

sets up his skill as the necessary complement to the military skill that was of such importance at Rome, both ideologically and practically, and of which he had virtually no experience.

Cicero's use of the word *hostis* in the second *actio* of the *Verrines* is a small example.[20] It can mean simply a personal enemy, but the contrast with *inimicus*, and its use to designate enemies of the state, make it likely that Cicero is using it to imply that Verres has, through his behaviour, put himself outside the Roman state, and, further, is in some sense a danger to it. This is particularly clear in a comment on the Gavius trial in the fifth book, since Verres shows his hostility towards *ciues* (5. 169): 'but why do I say any more about Gavius? As though Gavius were your target during those events, and you were not the enemy of the name and class and rights of Roman citizens as a whole.'[21] Cicero also uses the sense of an 'enemy of the state' in a powerful denunciation of Verres' wickedness in stealing the statue of Ceres from Henna, which showed him to be worse than a *hostis* (4. 112):

During the consulship of Publius Popilius and Publius Rupilius that place [sc. the city of Henna] was in the hands of slaves, runaways, barbarians, public enemies; but those slaves were less in thrall to their masters than you to your lusts, those runaways had not got as far from their masters as you from right and the rule of law, those barbarians were less savage in their language and race than you in character and behaviour, and those public enemies were less hostile to men than you to the immortal gods. What pleas in mitigation are still available for a man who surpasses slaves in baseness, runaways in rashness, barbarians in crime, and public enemies in cruelty?[22]

politique de Cicéron et de Tite-Live', *REL* 38 (1960), 236–63; E. Noè, '*Cedat forum castris*: esercito e ascesa politica nella riflessione ciceroniana', *Athenaeum*, 83 (1995), 67–82. On a more theoretical level, T. N. Habinek, 'Ideology for an Empire in the Prefaces to Cicero's Dialogues', *Ramus*, 23 (1994) 55–67.

[20] 1. 9, 38; 2. 17; 4. 75, 112; 5. 169. On the use of *hostis*, see Achard, *Pratique*, 343–4.

[21] 'sed quid ego plura de Gauio? quasi tu Gauio tum fueris infestus ac non nomini generi iuri ciuium hostis.'

[22] tenuerunt enim P. Popilio P. Rupilio consulibus illum locum serui, fugitiui, barbari, hostes; sed neque tam serui illi dominorum quam tu libidinum, neque tam fugitiui illi ab dominis quam tu ab iure et ab legibus, neque tam barbari lingua et natione illi quam tu natura et moribus, neque tam illi hostes hominibus quam tu dis immortalibus. quae deprecatio est

The main point of this vocabulary is naturally to arouse
hostility towards Verres and suggest that he is a danger to
Rome as well as to the provincials and thus make his condemnation a matter of urgent importance. But the trope adds
to the characterization of Cicero too, as a gallant and quasi-
military figure who is taking up the fight against Verres, quite
literally, in the lawcourts.

That Cicero is the essential civilian counterpart to the
Republic's military commanders is made emphatically clear in
his consular orations dealing with the threat from Catiline. The
declaration of Catiline as a public enemy after his departure for
Etruria helped Cicero to present himself in this way, and the
conspiracy did have to be suppressed by military force:
Cicero's vocabulary of war is not metaphorical in the way that
his invective against Verres is.[23] But the importance of Cicero
the civilian leader, as opposed to the actual military force used
against Catiline, needed to be made clear. By wearing a breast-
plate at the consular elections in 63, Cicero gave a dramatic
indication of the quasi-military role he would claim that he was
forced to adopt to counter Catiline's plotting,[24] and a constant
theme in the Catilinarian orations is the military aspect of
Cicero's oratory.[25] The culmination of this line of persuasion
comes at the end of the fourth Catilinarian (20–4). Cicero starts
by turning explicitly to himself: 'Now, before I ask for your
votes, let me say something about my own position.'[26] He
points out that he has acquired a large number of enemies from
among the conspirators, but dismisses the danger, even of
death, that they threaten, because he has won unparalleled
glory by saving the state. He then gives a list of five great
generals—the two Scipios, Aemilius Paulus, Marius, and
Pompeius—and their achievements, and finishes by saying
(21), 'There will certainly be a place for my glory among the
praise given to these men, unless perhaps it is a greater thing to

igitur ei reliqua qui indignitate seruos, temeritate fugitiuos, scelere barbaros,
crudelitate hostes uicerit?

[23] Even the exhortation to Catiline at the end of the first Catilinarian
speech, to set out 'ad impium bellum ac nefarium' (33), was almost certainly
written after this had proved to be true.
[24] *pro Murena* 52.
[25] See in particular *Cat.* 2. 28; 3. 26.
[26] 'nunc ante quam ad sententiam redeo, de me pauca dicam.'

open up provinces where we may journey than to make sure that even those who are away may have somewhere to return as victors.'[27] Cicero does not simply put his achievement on a par with the greatest military victories of recent history, but elevates it above them, because it has preserved the centre. The special nature of what he has done, because it is a Roman and a civilian action, occurs again later in this passage. It is also remarkable that he feels able to reduce military campaigns overseas to an adjunct of the tourist trade: the empire derives its meaning from the centre. And it is also obvious, by the end of the sentence, that Cicero has in mind not military campaigns in general, but specifically those of Pompeius, since it is he who is about to return in triumph to Rome. Cicero is indicating that even Pompeius' conquest of the East needs his, Cicero's, actions in Rome for its completion.[28]

Cicero returns at this point to the personal danger he is in. Overseas conquerors can turn their enemies into grateful clients (22), but his enemies are beyond any redemption: 'as a result I am aware that I have taken on an unending war against citizens who are utterly depraved'.[29] The threat, however, will be repulsed by the union of senators, knights, and all honest men which he has brought into being. He then moves into the closing emotional appeals, starting with a request that the senators preserve the memory of his consulship as a protection for Cicero himself. This is in return for various services (23): 'the command, the army and the province which I gave up, the triumph and other marks of glory which I rejected in order to protect the city and your safety, the provincial clients and supporters, which I struggle to replace with help from the city, all these services, then, my outstanding vigour on your behalf and my care and attention, which you see, in saving the state'.[30]

---

[27] 'erit profecto inter horum laudes aliquid loci nostrae gloriae, nisi forte maius est patefacere nobis prouincias quo exire possimus quam curare ut etiam illi qui absunt habeant quo uictores revertantur.'

[28] If Cicero's letter to Pompeius containing an account of his suppression of the conspiracy, now lost (*pro Sulla* 67–8), were similar in tone, it is hardly surprising that Pompeius was less than pleased: see Berry, *Pro Sulla*, 267.

[29] 'qua re mihi cum perditis ciuibus aeternum bellum susceptum esse uideo'.

[30] 'pro imperio, pro exercitu, pro prouincia quam neglexi, pro triumpho ceterisque laudis insignibus quae sunt a me propter urbis uestraeque salutis

Cicero's failure to pursue the standard proconsular career becomes the essential factor in saving the state; he relies on the powerful sweep of his oratory here to stop anybody asking why going to a province in the year after holding the consulship should prevent him, while consul, from acting to crush internal enemies. Cicero relies on the city/empire distinction, the one civilian, the other military, to justify his own civilian career as the essential complement to the soldier's and to slide over the fact that the traditional republican career combined both spheres: 'domi militiae*que*'.

In the *pro Murena*, delivered during the conspiracy, and with its arguments dominated by the coming threat, Cicero is not as dismissive of overseas activity as he is at the end of the fourth Catilinarian: he cannot afford to be, since military competence in effect constitutes Murena's claim to office. I have discussed above in Chapter 3 the particular spin which Cicero places on Murena's military abilities, the way that he is presented as a bland team-player whose importance is that he is an essential part of *Cicero's* plan for the salvation of the state. I want to look here at the explicit comments about oratory which Cicero makes.

The speech is usually admired and studied for its brilliant and witty demolition of a parody of the Stoicism which was espoused by the younger Cato, one of the prosecutors. The humour of the speech has perhaps concealed quite how unexpected Cicero's strategy is and how useful for him personally. Though it is a bribery trial, the most prominent argument is the extended use of *ethos* in the comparison of the lives of Sulpicius and Murena. This in turn depends heavily on the contrast between their two professions, soldiering and legal science, to which is added a third, oratory. In the *pro Murena*, military activity regains its common-sense place as the necessary condition for all other activity (22):

And indeed—for I must say what I believe—ability in military matters is more important than all other kinds. This is what has won a

custodiam repudiata, pro clientelis hospitiisque prouincialibus quae tamen urbanis opibus non minore labore tueor quam comparo, pro his igitur omnibus rebus, pro meis in uos singularibus studiis proque hac quam perspicitis ad conseruandam rem publicam diligentia . . .'

name for the Roman people and everlasting glory for this city, this has
forced the whole world to obey our commands; all the affairs of the
city, all our splendid studies and our rewarding efforts here in court,
these are all in the protection and guard of the courage shown in war.
As soon as the whisper of a military alarm sounds, our skills here fall
silent.[31]

But the apparent equality in position in this passage between
ceterae omnes does not last. Oratory joins military skill as one of
the *artes* which please the Roman people and lead to electoral
success: both have *admirabilis dignitas* and *pergrata utilitas* (23).
Oratory has these qualities because the orator can persuade the
Senate, people, and jurors, he can control tribunician disturbances, guide the people, resist bribery, and even enable
those who are not of noble birth to reach the consulship
because oratory creates obligations and friendships and
enthusiastic support (24). He then turns bluntly to Sulpicius:
'None of these belongs to that trade of yours.'[32]

It is of course obvious that Cicero is not describing the
power of oratory in abstract terms. This is a description of his
own achievements as consul, in particular blocking the agrarian
law of Rullus and another tribunician proposal to restore the
sons of the proscribed, persuading the people to observe distinctions of rank in seating in the theatre and defending
Rabirius on the antique charge of high treason.[33] The introduction of bribery into the list is particularly neat. Cicero must
have spoken in favour of his bribery law when it was passed,
but as far as we know he did not publish his remarks. It belongs
here because it shows that Cicero is anti-bribery, and this in
turn implies that his client Murena cannot be guilty of bribery.
Cicero's anxiety on this score is shown by his dealing with
Cato's charge against him of inconsistency, that he is defending
someone prosecuted under his own law, as the first topic in the
speech (3–5), and the mention of bribery here reinforces his

[31] ac nimirum—dicendum est enim quod sentio—rei militaris uirtus
praestat ceteris omnibus. haec nomen populo Romano, haec huic urbi
aeternam gloriam peperit, haec orbem terrarum parere huic imperio coegit;
omnes urbanae res, omnia haec nostra praeclara studia et haec forensis
laus et industria latet in tutela ac praesidio bellicae uirtutis. simul atque
increpuit suspicio tumultus, artes ilico nostrae conticiscunt.
[32] 'quorum in isto uestro artificio, Sulpici, nihil est.'
[33] For these events, see e.g. Rawson, *Cicero*, 63–8.

argument there, that he can be doing no wrong in defending someone who is innocent of the charge.

Sulpicius' legal knowledge cannot compete with oratory in terms of usefulness or capacity to impress the people. Cicero expands on its ludicrous nature at some length, concluding with the observation that, just as among Greek musicians, those who can't manage the lyre take up the pipes, so at Rome anyone who cannot make the grade as an orator turns instead to the study of law (29). There are two professions which can take a man to the top of the political tree: one is that of the commander, the other that of the good speaker (30). Cicero does not need to spell out that Murena embodies one and he the other, and that if the jury wish to take advantage of their skills, they must acquit Murena the soldier on the advice of Cicero the orator.

Effective as this strategy is in making Murena seem indispensable to the state, it is not clear that Cicero needed to place quite as much emphasis on the orator as he does in order to accomplish that end, even given the importance of the speaker's *auctoritas*. Securing Murena's acquittal is only one of the objects that this speech is pursuing. The trial came during the unfolding of the conspiracy, when it was still unclear whether Cicero would be able to persuade the Senate to take decisive action. It is Cicero's insight, and the capacity to lead which his oratory gives him, that are essential to the state's survival; as I discussed in Chapter 3, Murena's military skill is to be deployed as part of Cicero's plan, which he is expounding by means of his oratory. The emphasis on oratory gains immensely from the self-reflexive context: Cicero is not simply asserting that he possesses oratorical skills which are of immense value to the state, he is showing that it is so by doing it, and by preserving the man who will continue the success the following year. In a sense, then, it is wrong to say that the speech is not wholly about Murena's acquittal; it is, insofar as that acquittal is an essential part of Cicero's own successful consulship.

In the *pro Murena*, then, oratory and fighting are complements of one another, and while Cicero in deference to his client gives first place to soldiering (22), the overall strategy of the speech indicates the prior claim of oratory, since it is oratory, particularly Cicero's, that in this case will allow the soldier Murena to perform his vital task. In his poem on his consulship Cicero seems to have returned to the unconcealed triumphalism of the fourth Catilinarian. In the long fragment preserved in *de diuinatione* 1. 17, his vocabulary makes it clear that the Catilinarian conspiracy is to be viewed as a war (ll. 20, 27) and that its consequences which he averted are those of a war (50, *cladem*; 53, *stragem*). More emphatic is the single line of fragment 12, 'cedant arma togae, concedat laurea linguae'. On one level, the civilian virtues of oratory have defeated an armed conspiracy; more generally, Cicero the peaceful orator has saved the state, in place of generals such as Pompeius.[34]

It is worth noting at this point that Caesar, much later, acknowledged and paid tribute to Cicero's attempts to place his oratory on the same level as military activity. Somewhere in his writing, possibly in the dedication to Cicero of his *de analogia*, he said to Cicero 'You have won greater laurels than the triumphal wreath, for it is a greater achievement to have extended the frontiers of the Roman genius than those of Rome's empire.'[35]

4.2. THE *DE IMPERIO CN. POMPEI*

A good place to start looking at how Cicero presents himself as a potential leader of the state is the *de imperio Cn. Pompei*, his first public speech and, of the speeches relevant to this study, the one most important to his bid for the consulship. The prime usefulness of the speech would be in allying Cicero to Pompeius, at that point by far the most important politician at Rome: even though Pompeius was unlikely to have returned to Rome in time for the consular elections in 64, the ones that

---

[34] Or as Rose, 'Rhetoric of Imperialism', 369–70, puts it: 'One of the few surviving fragments from the epic poem which Cicero, with characteristic modesty, composed to celebrate his victory over Catiline in 63 BC, can easily be taken as the motto of his whole career: cedant arma togae—literally, "Let weapons yield to the toga", or more loosely, "To hell with the generals, it's rhetoric that really makes the world go round."'

[35] From Pliny's laudation of Cicero, *NH* 7. 117: 'salue primus omnium parens patriae appellate, primus in toga triumphum linguaeque laurea merite et facundiae Latinarumque litterarum parens aeque *(ut dictator Caesar, hostis quondam tuus, de te scripsit)* omnium triumphorum laurea maiorem, quanto plus est ingenii Romani terminos in tantum promouisse quam imperi.'

Cicero had his eye on, his influence, exerted indirectly, could be essential to Cicero's success. One assumes that as soon as the written version was available he arranged for a copy to be sent to Pompeius in the East. But, as has often been observed, the speech is also notable for its *popularis* colouring, and it is clear that Cicero was seeking to conciliate as wide a range of his listeners as possible.[36] I want here to analyse how Cicero sets up this persona, and to suggest that he is very careful indeed to limit his *popularis* pronouncements.

The speech's exordium, 1–3, seeks to explain why it is that this is the first occasion that Cicero is addressing the people. His opening words make clear, even before the drift of the argument is apparent, that this was not because of any disrespect for this type of oratory: 'although I have always found the sight of a crowd of you, citizens, extremely pleasant, and this place has seemed to be the most dignified to do something in and the most honourable to speak from . . .'.[37] He goes on to explain that it was not his inclinations which kept him away but the plan of life he had adopted: he had decided not to address the people unless his skills as a speaker were at their highest pitch, and instead devoted his attentions to his friends. He then indicates that the people did not suffer from his absence, since there were other men available to look after their interests. What has allowed Cicero to change his habits has been his success in the praetorian elections: fortified by the *auctoritas* he has gained from the people through their choice of him, and with oratorical skills honed by constant forensic activity, he now has both the confidence and the duty to address them (1–2). He concludes the exordium by congratulating himself on having, in the character of Pompeius, such a fruitful topic.

This opening combines the two things for which Cicero would at this point be best known: his brilliance as a forensic orator and his recent striking success in heading the poll in the elections for the praetorship. But while he states explicitly that the two are linked, that his election was a reward for his tireless efforts in the courts, oratory and politics are presented as

[36] Rawson, *Cicero*, 53.

[37] 1: 'quamquam mihi semper frequens conspectus uester multo iucundissimus, hic autem locus ad agendum amplissimus, ad dicendum ornatissimus est uisus . . .'.

distinct operations. His skill at speaking, which we are to assume has now reached the standard necessary for addressing the people, has been acquired and polished simply in the courts.

It may seem unnecessary to labour this point: there is no deceit in this passage, since Cicero had only delivered speeches in the courts before this occasion. Indeed, it would have been most unusual if he had addressed the people as a quaestor or aedile, since mounting the *rostra* was a privilege restricted to senior political figures. What surely lies behind it is the fact that Cicero had not held the tribunate: that was the only likely way that he could hitherto have given a speech in front of the people. And it is interesting to observe that Cicero's opening remarks can be read in both *popularis* and non-*popularis* ways. This is his first speech to the people: that can be taken as a reminder to conservative elements in the audience that while he is supporting, on this occasion, a radical law, this is not his regular behaviour. On the other hand, his earnest justification for not having so done in the past can be read in the light of an exculpation: this speech will make up for his earlier silence. Cicero reaches the end of his exordium with all his options still open to him.

Cicero's finely balanced position on his past career is matched by a similarly ambivalent approach to the institution of popular legislation. As we would expect, he begins with flattery, praise for the speaker's platform as the most distinguished arena for the orator, and reluctance on his part to present to them anything which is less than perfect. However, while the people are praised, it is made clear that their role is simply to bestow approval on those who speak to them from a position of metaphorical as well as physical superiority.[38] Addressing the people is an *aditus laudis* for 'all the best men', and Cicero indicates that his behaviour has been in accord with the principles of hierarchy through his use of the word *auctoritas*. At first he seems to suggest that the people possess *auctoritas*, since he refers to the 'standing of this place' (1), that is, of the *rostra*, which he has not previously been in a position to aspire to. But a little later (2) he refers to the *auctoritas* which he has got by

---

[38] The speakers' platform was probably some 12 feet high: Vasaly, *Representations*, 62–3.

being elected. One of the effects of a speaker's possessing *auctoritas* is of course to have his advice followed, and so the overall impression is that the people have power, but only to choose whose advice they will follow.[39] This is strengthened by Cicero's description of what a speaker does when addressing the people as *uestram causam defendere* (2), since this suggests that the people are in the position of a *cliens*, being protected, in court, by his *patronus*. Cicero is here adopting the conservative model of popular participation. It is striking to compare his tone with that of Gaius Gracchus, most notably in his speech opposing a *lex Aufeia*, in which he urges the people to distrust everyone who addresses them, since all, including him, have their self-interested motives.[40]

Describing the speaker's task as *uestram causam defendere* also has implications for what Cicero himself is doing in this case. By using the language of forensic rhetoric Cicero perhaps tries to suggest that he is more experienced in this kind of speaking than in fact he is. It also implies that Pompeius' getting the command against Mithradates *is* the people's *causa*. The people are not faced with a choice between two courses of action: they are identified with one of them, and any opposition to Manilius' proposed law is also, Cicero suggests, opposition to them. And this vocabulary also enables Cicero to sidestep the question of the law's novelty. It becomes the natural and current state of affairs, which just happens, at this moment, to be under attack, and Cicero is just one of a large number who have stood up to protect it.[41]

Cicero, then, uses unashamedly *popularis* language in his opening, but combines this with a conservative view of what the people can and ought to do. The peroration (69–71) shows similar care in positioning. For the first time in the speech, Cicero acknowledges the existence of Manilius, the proposer of

[39] Cicero makes use of *auctoritas* later in the speech, when discussing Hortensius' and Catulus' opposition to the law (51): he acknowledges their standing, but draws attention to the standing of those who support the law, concluding that this deadlock should be resolved by the people acknowledging the need for Pompeius *omissis auctoritatibus* (51. 8). Cicero's ability to make this judgement confirms, of course, his own *auctoritas*.

[40] *ORF* 48, fr. 44.

[41] Cicero continues to use the word *causa* throughout the speech: 3. 6, 4. 12, 6. 29, 53. 23, 68. 10.

the law. This delay is striking: even though there are no other speeches where Cicero speaks in favour of a popular law to provide a control, it would surely be natural for him to have spoken approvingly of the proposer in the opening paragraph, or soon after. That he does not can best be interpreted as a sign of his reluctance to align himself with so disreputable a figure.[42] Moreover, the address to Manilius comes immediately *after* a list of the distinguished consulars who have thrown their *auctoritates* behind the measure (68). Manilius is, quite literally, put in his place. While the consulars are full of *auctoritas*, as well as qualities such as *ingenium, prudentia, grauitas*, and *integritas, ueritas*, and *constantia*, Manilius has only *animus* and *perseuerantia* (69).

Cicero refers to Manilius' spirit and perseverance in support of the advice that he is giving Manilius, which is to hold on to his opinion whatever threats or violence he might face. He then adds another argument to encourage him (69): 'when we see the size of the crowd gathered here and their enthusiasm to confer a command on Pompeius a second time, how can we have any doubts about the rightness of the position or about achieving it?'[43] This allows him to make explicit what ignoring Manilius up to this point has strongly implied: Pompeius is so obviously the right man for the job that Manilius' proposal is in some sense otiose. At this point, Cicero does grant the people decisive powers of choice: *auctore populo Romano*, Manilius should persist. What is involved is the people's judgement directly on Pompeius. Of course it is very effective in terms of the prime aim of the speech, getting the law passed, to assume that Pompeius is the inevitable choice; but it also fits with Cicero's not wanting to come out in too *popularis* a fashion, by making the *popularis* proposer of the law unnecessary to its passage. And this argument also allows Cicero to suggest to the audience that Manilius is unreliable: there is a chance that he might falter. Of course, there is no indication anywhere else that

[42] On Manilius, see Crawford, *Cicero: The Fragmentary Orations*, 36–7.
[43] 'cum tantam multitudinem tanto cum studio adesse uideamus quantam iterum nunc in eodem homine praeficiendo uidemus, quid est quod aut de re aut de perficiendi facultate dubitemus?' It is not clear from the first person plural whether Cicero is speaking for himself and Manilius, generalizing, or simply using the orator's plural.

Manilius' commitment was in doubt, or that there was any chance that he might withdraw the law.

Cicero turns from the potentially unreliable Manilius to himself: *ego autem* (69). He offers his services to the Roman people: these are his *studium, consilium, labor*, and *ingenium*, and *auctoritas, fides*, and *constantia*, though with becoming modesty he does not claim any of these absolutely, but instead dedicates whatever amount of them that he may possess. He then goes on to disclaim any personal interest in the case, whether to win over Pompeius or from more general desire for honour and position (70): he has acted *rei publicae causa*. This leads him to contradict the exordium, inasmuch as he now denies that he is looking for *honos* 'from this place', that is, the *rostra* (70; cf. 1). Provided that the people agree, the *laboriosissima ratio uitae* will be enough. This provides a neat echo of the opening, where it was *uitae meae rationes* (1) which had stopped Cicero from addressing the people earlier; now his way of life will lead him to public success. The dichotomy also, on reflection, confirms that Cicero will not be engaging in *popularis* politics, since he is not expecting to achieve office through Pompeius (*ab uno*, 70) or from addressing the people. So disinterested, in fact, is Cicero that he has allowed himself to become embroiled in various hostilities by taking on the case, and he concludes the speech by dismissing his own comfort in favour of more worthy ends (71): 'but I decided, citizens, that since I had been the recipient of this honour and had been granted so many favours by you, I should put your wishes, and the reputation of the state and the safety of the provinces and of the allies, above all my private interests and advantage'.[44] The speech ends with Cicero having ousted Manilius from position of the defender of the people, and taking that place himself, and assuming, as though this were not a matter for contest, that the people are entirely passive. His willingness to face dangers on the part of the people also looks back to the discussion of Gabinius' legateship in 57–8, where Cicero asserts that he will face any *iniquitas* in order to defend the *ius* and *beneficium* of the people. This is a

---

[44] 'sed ego me hoc honore praeditum, tantis uestris beneficiis adfectum statui, Quirites, uestram uoluntatem et rei publicae dignitatem et salutem prouinciarum atque sociorum meis omnibus commodis et rationibus praeferre oportere'.

passage of emotive and popular language: but closer consideration indicates that Cicero is being much less radical than at first
appears.

Gabinius had been tribune the previous year and had been
the proposer of the law giving Pompeius the command against
the pirates. According to Cicero, he was not being allowed to be
a legate to Pompeius, despite Pompeius' wishes that this should
happen. Cicero says that he will bring up the matter in the
Senate if there is any further opposition to Gabinius' being a
legate, and the only thing that will stop him will be a veto. He
concludes this section with an ominous remark to those who are
standing in Gabinius' way (58): 'those who are making threats
will themselves think more and more about what is permitted
to them'.[45]

The anonymity of the opposition is rhetorically effective,
since the absence of definition allows scope for all sorts of
alarming possibilities to be imagined; it also distracts attention
from what was surely the real reason that Gabinius could not be
a legate, that is, that the proposer of a law should not benefit
personally from it.[46] If that was the case, then, once the *lex
Gabinia* was superseded by the *lex Manilia*, there would be no
obstacle to Gabinius' being a legate. And in fact Gabinius did
go off to the East almost immediately. Cicero is able, in this
passage, to work himself up into a fine state of *popularis* indignation about an abuse of the people's rights, and commit himself to defending them come what may, at least up to a veto,
while running absolutely no risk, in reality, of having to fulfil
his promises.

Cicero maintains a consistent persona in the *de imperio* with
regard to his political stance. He adopts *popularis* language:
such was necessary in a man seeking election to the consulship
two years later. But, at the same time, he operates with a very
conservative model of how the people and those addressing
them relate; and draws back from what were, from a conservative point of view, the worst excesses of popular legislation.

The value of this strategy of ambivalence to a potential
candidate is clear. But it also provides a framework in which to
interpret Cicero's attitude to the constitutional implications of

---

[45] 'isti ipsi qui minitantur etiam atque etiam quid liceat considerabunt'.
[46] Cf. Cicero, *de leg. ag.* 2. 21.

the law. As I discussed in Chapter 3, it is possible to reconstruct at least part of the debate surrounding the proposal to
give an extraordinary command to Pompeius, and see that
much of it was cast in terms of objections to the constitutional
impropriety of the law. Yet Cicero sidesteps such objections,
even when countering the objections of Catulus and Hortensius. It would have been difficult for him to do otherwise if he
were to maintain the ambivalent position which I have explored
above, of adopting a *popularis* style without committing himself
to its substance. To have given a serious and convincing refutation of the constitutional objections to the law, while supporting its passage, would have involved asserting the primacy of
popular legislation in matters of foreign policy and considering
why the old pattern of year-long proconsulships was no longer
effective. It is also worth noting that the one principle that
Cicero does employ in 51–68 is that the Romans have always
innovated (60–3), refuting the argument ascribed to Catulus,
that nothing should happen 'in contravention of the examples
and customs of our ancestors'.[47] This position, of course, neatly
and seamlessly combines the *popularis* willingness to disregard
precedent with the conservative appeal to the past: *popularis*
tactics are justified in true optimate fashion.

Cicero's tactics in the *de imperio* are in fact just what we
would expect from an ambitious politician seeking election,
whose circumstances mean that he cannot afford to disregard or
alienate any group of people who could provide him with votes.
What has not always been observed, however, is the extent to
which his carefully studied political ambivalence shapes his
approach to the constitutional implications of the Manilian
law.[48] It would have been difficult to engage thoroughly with
the objections to the law without using lines of argument that
were distinctly *popularis*: committing himself to the fundamental principles of popular sovereignty, for example, or claiming
that the Senate had failed to deal adequately with Mithradates
and so the people needed to take the initiative directly. Cicero
could not have done this and maintained his character as a man

---

[47] 60: 'at enim ne quid noui fiat contra exempla atque instituta maiorum'.
See Sect. 3.1 above.

[48] But cf. Rawson, *Cicero*, 53, who draws attention to the links between
Cicero's stance in this speech and his political theory.

who offered something to everyone: far better to project an air
of sympathy for the people while drawing attention away from
the measure's most serious implications.

4.3. THE *DE PROVINCIIS CONSVLARIBUS*

The importance of the *prou. cons.* in Cicero's own career as a
politician has always been recognized. Invariably, however, the
speech has been seen simply as a sign of his decision to drop his
opposition to the first triumvirate, often accompanied by the
commentator's disapproval at his change of policy.[49] And, on
one level, this interpretation is valid: he is doing what Caesar
wanted, in arguing that his command in Gaul should not be
ended, and as my discussion of the speech in Chapter 3 showed,
his praise of Caesar is lavish, and he also draws his audience's
attention to the excellent relations which exist between
Pompeius and Caesar, a key point since it was dissension
between Pompeius and Caesar which had led many to believe
that the alliance was about to break up. However, the *prou. cons.*
is a much more complex speech than this interpretation allows.

The clue to unravelling what Cicero is trying to achieve is
the passage of savage invective against Piso and Gabinius in
3–12, the consuls of 58 who had failed to stop Clodius' campaign against Cicero which had culminated in Cicero's being
forced to go into exile. Piso was at this point governor of
Macedonia, Gabinius of Syria. Cicero brings them into his
argument as follows (3):

There are four provinces, gentlemen, about which, I understand,
opinions have been expressed: the two Gauls, which we see are combined in a single command at this time, and Syria and Macedonia,
which those doom-laden consuls have taken possession of, in defiance
of your wishes and as rewards for their part in overturning the state.
We, under the terms of the Sempronian law, must designate two.
What possible reason is there to hesitate in naming Syria and
Macedonia?[50]

---

[49] e.g. Stockton, *Cicero*, 213: 'Henceforth, the egotism and the impetuosity
were to be restrained, the pride humbled, the oratorical genius exercised at the
instruction of his masters'.

[50] quattuor sunt prouinciae, patres conscripti, de quibus adhuc intellego
sententias esse dictas, Galliae duae, quas hoc tempore uno imperio uidemus

He then proceeds to substantiate his hostile description of Piso and Gabinius. Piso is militarily incompetent: he lost his troops to famine and disease as well as defeat and by harassing peaceable Thracian tribes has provoked a war;[51] his unbridled lust has led to an outbreak of suicide attempts among upper-class young women;[52] and he has indulged in that prevalent vice among provincial governors, statue-snatching (6–7). Gabinius too has presided over military reverses (9); through a variety of unjust measures, he has driven the tax-farming companies in Syria to the brink of financial disaster (10–12); and Cicero hints at more lurid vices by calling Gabinius by the contemptuous nickname 'Semiramis'. He sums up the pair as 'this twofold plague on the allies, disaster for the troops, destruction for the tax-farmers, devastation of the provinces, and stain on our empire'.[53]

This is stirring and enjoyable invective; but it is hardly essential to Cicero's argument. Even if we accept that there are only four possible provinces, Cicero could have indicated his support for the choice of Syria and Macedonia without such hostility: he could have argued, for example, that Piso and Gabinius would deserve to be relieved of their burdens after three years' continuous service, and combined a call for their supersession with lavish praise of their achievements up to this point. But it is also clear that Cicero need not have restricted himself to these four provinces. The result of the debate was to designate as consular Macedonia and another province, whose identity is not clear but which was neither one of the Gauls nor Syria; and when the whole debate was rendered pointless the

esse coniunctas, et Syria et Macedonia, quas uobis inuitis et oppressis pestiferi illi consules pro peruersae rei publicae praemiis occupauerunt. decernendae nobis sunt lege Sempronia duae. quid est quod possimus de Syria Macedoniaque dubitare?

[51] 4–5. For the truth behind Cicero's charges, see Nisbet, *In Pisonem*, 172–80.

[52] 6; cf. Syme's ironically enthusiastic recapitulation (R. Syme, *The Roman Revolution* (Oxford: Oxford Univ. Press, 1939), 149), 'Virgins of the best families at Byzantium cast themselves down wells to escape the vile proconsul.'

[53] 13: 'has duplicis pestis sociorum, militum cladis, publicanorum ruinas, prouinciarum uastitates, imperio maculas'. For a fuller analysis of the invective against Piso and Gabinius in this speech, see Sect. 1.2 above.

following year by the *lex Trebonia*, the provinces in which the consuls Pompeius and Crassus were given five-year commands were Syria and Spain. It was a choice on Cicero's part to construct his argument in this way, despite its apparent inevitability.

Why should he have done so? The most obvious answer is that it allowed him to pursue his vendetta against Piso and Gabinius. Cicero's grounds for so doing are usually seen simply in terms of bitterness about his exile. But, whatever personal resentment may have been involved, the invective against the two men (which is not of course restricted to this speech) served an important political function. Cicero's exile marked the nadir of his political career: the fact that he had been forced away from Rome indicates quite how powerless he was at that point. And while his recall, through legislation in the centuriate assembly, did reverse this to a certain extent, he was still faced on his return with the need, somehow, to rebuild his authority despite the fact that none of the individuals who had sought his exile, or acquiesced in it, had suffered any ill consequences as a result. This lies behind his oratorical productivity in the months immediately after his return: *post reditum in Senatu*, *post reditum ad Quirites*, *de domo sua*, *de haruspicum responso*, *pro Sestio*, and *in Vatinio* as well as the consular provinces speech, and his decision to publish his words. By saying the most outrageous things about the people whom he set up as responsible for his exile he demonstrated that the power relations which had existed in the early months of 58 existed no longer: he was now in a position to engage in hostilities. The invective is an essential part of the recreation of Marcus Tullius Cicero as a political force.[54]

The invective takes on particular meaning in the *prou. cons.* given Cicero's accommodation, in the speech, with the reformed first triumvirate. The fact that Cicero had had to give way to Pompeius' veiled threats and abandon his opposition to Caesar's land law showed that he was not nearly as powerful as

---

[54] The speech about his house, which Clodius had had pulled down and replaced with a shrine to Libertas, was concerned with repairing the physical damage which exile had caused. It is of course significant that Cicero uses oratory to rebuild his position, which was due largely in the first place to his skill as a speaker.

he might have hoped, and as his actions since his return from exile had pretended. His own career, and more importantly that of his brother Quintus, needed help: Pompeius and Caesar seemed to be the only people who might provide it.[55] His abuse of Piso and Gabinius in the same speech is an attempt to set limits to his weakness: he may have had to give way to the leading players, but that does not mean that he has to abandon his opposition to other important figures.[56]

This becomes even more striking when one considers the links between Caesar and Pompeius on the one hand, and Piso and Gabinius on the other. Piso's daughter Calpurnia had married Caesar in 59; Gabinius had been, throughout his career, a faithful adherent of Pompeius: the proposer of the law giving Pompeius the command against the pirates and a legate during the campaign against Mithradates.[57] It is unlikely that he would have reached the consulship without the support of Pompeius; although Piso could well have been elected on his own merits, in view of his distinguished ancestry (as well as recent consular relations), the marriage connection with Caesar, whether it took place before or after his election, was an obvious indication of readiness to co-operate with Caesar politically.[58] That is, their links with two of the three triumvirs were closely connected with their obtaining the consulships which had allowed the pair to wrong Cicero. What are the effects of abusing close supporters of the first triumvirate in a speech which is supposed to mark a reconciliation with this grouping?

In the first place, it makes Cicero's placing of himself in relation to the current political hierarchy even more precise than I suggested above. He has had to make his peace with Caesar and Pompeius: but it goes no further than that.[59] Supporting an

---

[55] *ad Att.* 4. 5.

[56] Cf. the interpretation of T. P. Wiseman, 'The Ambitions of Quintus Cicero', *JRS* 45 (1966), 114–15, who sees permission to attack Piso as a part of the deal which Cicero made with the triumvirs. I would prefer to see a rather less cosy situation.

[57] It is (according to one's view of Cicero) either amusing or depressing to read the abuse of Gabinius in the speeches of 57–55 in comparison with his effusive remarks in the *de imp.*, discussed earlier in this chapter.

[58] C. Calpurnius Piso, cos. 67; M. Pupius Piso, cos. 61.

[59] There is no mention at all of Crassus in the speech.

extension of Caesar's command does not mean being nice to Caesar's friends, at least not when they are also enemies of Cicero. He is showing that he still has considerable independence.[60]

This, on its own, would be sufficient to detract from the value of Cicero's praise as far as Caesar and Pompeius were concerned. But there are still further barbs. By restricting his discussion to four provinces, Cicero has suggested that Caesar's continuing command in Gaul is directly dependent upon Piso and Gabinius being replaced: it is either them, or Caesar. Cicero's presentation of the case in effect makes Caesar's success depend on the public humiliation of his father-in-law. The structure of the speech emphasizes this, since Cicero begins with the shortcomings of Piso and Gabinius and sums up this first section by saying (17): 'whoever assigns the two Gauls to the two consuls, leaves this pair in charge; and if you assign one of the Gauls and either Syria or Macedonia, you still keep one of them, and reward crimes of equal gravity with a different outcome'.[61] All this before there has been a word about Caesar's achievements in Gaul, or he has even been named: on Cicero's ordering, his brilliance is in one sense irrelevant, since Piso and Gabinius must go, regardless of events elsewhere. This is neatly indicated when Cicero does turn to Caesar, with the words (18): 'But even if these [sc. Piso and Gabinius] were excellent men, none the less, in my view, I would not yet think that Gaius Caesar should be replaced.'[62] The implications of an unreal conditional are clear.

Cicero gives the Senate the impression that they are faced with a very clear choice between two diametrically opposed ways of being a provincial governor, which Caesar and Piso represent.[63] Piso, as we have seen, is a military disaster, who is

---

[60] That this was, for Cicero, an untenable position did not fully emerge until the humiliating events of the autumn of 54, when Cicero gave evidence against Gabinius and saw him acquitted, and then had to defend him at the trial at which he was condemned.

[61] 'atqui duas Gallias qui decernit consulibus duobus, hos retinet ambo; qui autem alteram Galliam et aut Syriam aut Macedoniam, tamen alterum retinet et in utriusque pari scelere disparem condicionem facit.'

[62] 'quod si essent illi optimi uiri, tamen ego mea sententia C. Caesari succedendum nondum putarem.'

[63] The relationship between Caesar and Piso is not the only reason for

enriching himself at his province's expense. Caesar, by contrast, is a highly successful military commander, whose campaigns in Gaul are solving a long-standing security problem by
pacifying those who had hitherto been Rome's implacable
enemies and thus ending the traditional threat from the North.
'We have always put up resistance when provoked: but now
we have made the end of our empire and the end of their territory the same point.'[64] And there is no advantage to Caesar
personally in staying on in Gaul: quite the reverse. His
province is deeply unattractive, remote and uncivilized.[65] They
also face different fates when they return to Rome. Cicero
implies strongly that Piso will face a prosecution under the
repetundae laws: this is surely what he means when he says,
while explaining why he is not dwelling on Piso's assaults on
young women (6), 'I don't skate over these matters because
they're not serious, but because at this moment I am speaking
without witnesses'.[66] It is inconceivable that Cicero would
admit that he had no evidence for this charge; *sine teste* must be
taken as a reference to the Senate's not being a legal court, as
well as suggesting that there will be an occasion when he will be
able to call upon witnesses.[67] No such fate will greet Caesar,
since he is already in a position to return to celebrate a triumph
(35).

Among the other reasons why Caesar might desire to return
home is his wish to see his 'darling child' and 'distinguished
son-in-law'.[68] This description of Caesar's family ignores

Cicero to say much more about Piso than Gabinius (who had no such link) in
this speech: the failure to help in 58 was much more galling from Piso, a man
from whom good could have been expected and to whom Cicero appealed in
person, than from the obviously partisan Gabinius.

[64] 33: 'restitimus semper lacessiti: nunc denique est perfectum ut imperi
nostri terrarumque illarum idem esset extremum.'

[65] See Sect. 3.3.

[66] 'nec haec idcirco omitto quod non grauissima sint, sed quia nunc sine
teste dico'.

[67] Cicero did not, of course, prosecute Piso for extortion (and neither did
anyone else). Part of Piso's attack on Cicero after he returned from Macedonia
was to ask why Cicero didn't prosecute him: so one can deduce from the *in
Pisonem* (82, 94), where Cicero is reduced to saying that he hasn't instituted a
prosecution because he doesn't want to cause Caesar any worries.

[68] 'si ad iucundissimos liberos, si ad clarissimum generum redire
properaret'. H. E. Butler and M. Cary, *De prouinciis consularibus* (Oxford:

completely his links with Piso. Where is the mention of Caesar's dear wife and distinguished father-in-law? One would never guess, from the *prou. cons.*, that Caesar was married to Piso's daughter.[69]

This silence enables Cicero to maintain an unblemished surface of praise for Caesar: there is nothing in the speech that Caesar, or Pompeius, could find fault with. However, it is tempting to see Cicero's silence also as part of a wider programme of giving Caesar advice on his political behaviour which is drawn from Cicero's habits and behaviour. A recurrent theme in the speech is Cicero's own relationship with Caesar. Cicero has apparently been criticized for attacking Gabinius and not Caesar, when he has just as strong grounds for complaint against the latter as the former (18): 'an excellent man says that I should not be more hostile towards Gabinius than towards Caesar: that the whole of that storm to which I gave way was stirred up at Caesar's instigation and with his help'.[70] In 18–28 he admits that he has in the past been at odds with Caesar (25), but has now been reconciled with him, as his recent actions show. He justifies his change of attitude by citing a large number of instances from the past century at Rome where notorious enemies have allowed themselves to abandon their enmities when this has been in the interests of the state (18–22). It is Cicero's patriotism which has led to the reconciliation (23), and he sums up with the words, 'I am not able not to be a friend of anyone who has deserved well of the state.'[71]

Cicero, then, is someone who moderates his personal

Oxford Univ. Press, 1924), 68, suggest that the plural *liberos* is a 'rhetorical exaggeration', Caesar having only one child. But there seems to be no singular form of *liberi* in use at this period, and the plural is used regardless of numbers of children. See Gellius, *NA* 2. 13; J. D. Denniston, *Orationes Philippicae prima et secunda* (Oxford: Oxford Univ. Press, 1926), 65–6.

[69] In 7, Cicero does refer to Piso's actions as having been committed in breach of the law of his son-in-law (*contra legem generi tui*), but does not include Caesar's name and thus preserves the illusion that there are no links between the two. The use of *gener* alerts his audience to the fact of this silence, as well as showing that Piso's illegalities are particulary heinous because they breach family connections as well.

[70] 'negat me uir optimus inimiciorem Gabinio debere esse quam Caesari: omnem illam tempestatem cui cesserim Caesare impulsore atque adiutore esse excitatam'.

[71] 24: 'nemini ego possum esse bene merenti de re publica non amicus.'

relationships in accordance with the good of the state. Is this true also of Caesar? It seems not. He is married to the daughter of a man who is causing havoc to Rome's empire. His own advantage in securing a consular supporter has led to disaster, by putting Piso in a position of authority.[72] In a metaphorical sense, Cicero is setting up a choice for Caesar: does he follow Cicero's salutary example and put country above family and friendship, a path indicated by Cicero's silence over his links with Piso, or does he persist in his connection with this dangerous monster? I do not mean to imply that there is a real choice here or that Caesar would be moved to act once he received his presentation copy of the speech. The point is to show Pompeius, Caesar, and indeed the whole of Rome, that Cicero is still a brilliantly clever orator who can pose embarrassing questions and assert his own independence even while being forced to comply with distasteful orders.[73]

Cicero's concern with his own position in this speech makes it much less effective as an argument in favour of retaining Caesar in the Gauls and designating Syria and Macedonia as consular. His decision to support Caesar and the first triumvirate was itself a U-turn, and as such the result of Cicero's calculations about his own position, rather than a decision as to what might in general terms be advantageous to the state; and the abuse of Piso and Gabinius would already be familiar to the Senate. A reasonable response from anyone listening to the debate would be to think that Cicero *would* make this kind of argument: as a result Cicero's effectiveness as an advocate of a particular line of action would be undermined. In effect, Cicero has subordinated the task placed on him by Pompey and Caesar to his continuing campaign of post-exile recovery, very much to the former's disadvantage. He was giving his apparent superiors an elegant and skilful lesson in the problems of hired eloquence.

[72] Some listeners and readers may have recalled Caesar's earlier opportunistic marriage history with his divorce of Pompeia in the aftermath of the Bona Dea scandal.

[73] On the strength of Cicero's political position in the spring of 56, see D. L. Stockton, 'Cicero and the *Ager Campanus*', *TAPhA* 93 (1962), 471–89, esp. 487–8; though I would not agree entirely with his statement (488) that '[t]he dynasts were very anxious to have him [sc. Cicero] defend men like Gabinius or deliver speeches like the *De provinciis consularibus*'.

It is of course in no way surprising that we can relate Cicero's speeches and his own career: since he was a politician, and the speeches I have been considering political, that is a truism. More interesting is the scale of Cicero's dependence on oratory and the consequent limits on the advice he, as an orator, can offer. We are so used to the image of Cicero as the pre-eminent orator of the Roman world, if not antiquity, whose phenomenal skill enabled him to pull off miracles of eloquence, that it is startling to realize that in some respects Cicero is a slave to his skill. One might want to argue that he relied too heavily on oratory to take risks with it, and that, as a result, there were strict limits on the issues he discusses. In the *de imp.* he is trying to appeal to as wide an audience as possible in the run-up to his attempt on the consulship; in the *prou. cons.* he is concerned to assert his authority in an extremely difficult personal situation. In both cases, the demands of his own persona forced him away from uncomfortable issues and towards the simpler demands of personalities.

5
Imperial contexts

CICERO'S speeches on imperial matters have, despite their range and flexibility, two unifying features. One is that they are adapted, where possible or necessary, to the demands of Cicero's own activities as a politician; and the second is that they share a model of Rome's relationship to the areas under its control. In his speeches, Cicero sees Roman imperialism in terms of individual magistrates: what is at issue is what specific men have done or will do, and when things go wrong they go wrong because of individual misbehaviour and immorality.[1]

As an analysis of the Roman empire during the Republic, this is not as absurd as at first sight might appear, because it does fit in with the peculiarities of imperial government. Roman provincial administration did involve an astonishingly small number of people, whose relationship to the governor was central to their employment, whether through direct patronage, as was the case for his *cohors*, or because custom decreed that there should be a close relationship, as in the case of the *quaestor*.[2] These links were reinforced by the informal but none the less considerable influence a governor could wield over his staff's financial opportunities in the province and subsequent careers.[3] Nor was a governor constrained by any general rules coming from the centre or by the conduct of his predecessor. A *prouincia*, was, in its original sense, a magistrate's sphere of operations, and the only check on his freedom

---

[1] C. Edwards, *The Politics of Immorality in Ancient Rome* (Cambridge: Cambridge Univ. Press, 1993), argues that a moralizing view of politics was a feature of Roman culture more generally (4): 'It was the weakness or perversity of individuals, their lack of self-control . . . which caused undesirable events. Problems can be solved only if individuals embraced virtue.'

[2] See in general J. S. Richardson, 'The Administration of the Empire', *CAH* 9, 2nd edn. (1994), 564–98.

[3] As Catullus found to his rage: see poems 10 and 28, and cf. the intriguing interpretation in Braund, 'The Politics of Catullus'.

of action within his province was the possibility of punishment on his return to Rome.[4] The Roman governor was, in his province, a figure of virtually unlimited power, standing out from a very small official community: as a result, the character and behaviour of individual governors were the most important factors in determining how a province was governed during his period in office; and personal relations between provincials and governors did matter. Moreover, the *repetundae* speeches are all forensic speeches, and so it is unsurprising that they focus on personal behaviour.

None the less, the limitations of Cicero's analysis are profound, as becomes apparent if his oratorical view of empire is considered in relation to any attempt to explain the collapse of republican government. It is generally agreed that the possession of an empire was an essential factor in this transformation: competition for its resources fatally destabilized the ruling oligarchy and concentrated uncontrollable power in the hands of a few super-oligarchs, while the reluctance of the elite to distribute wealth more widely also created the discontented manpower which made up the armies of the civil wars. The *repetundae* speeches and those concerning provincial commands deal with crucial aspects of the imperial problem: on the one hand, exploitation of the provinces in order to guarantee electoral success, and on the other, the emergence of warlords as a result of special commands designed to deal with imperial emergencies. But, as I have shown, Cicero does not deal with the broader context in these speeches.

The remainder of this study is an attempt to explain *why* Cicero's imperial analysis in the speeches is so unsatisfactory and unilluminating. I shall suggest that it is much more helpful to see the problem in terms of the functions of oratory rather than the limitations of Cicero's intellect: there are things which it is not useful to say. But before turning to the limits of Cicero's oratory, it may be valuable to set the speeches against contemporary analyses of Rome and its empire. Cicero's political philosophy and letters are one important source; so too are

---

[4] Richardson, 'Administration of Empire', 575. In Polybius' analysis, the consuls' powers made them the regal element in the mixed constitution (6.12.5–9): see F. W. Walbank, *A Historical Commentary on Polybius*, vol. I (Oxford: Oxford Univ. Press, 1957), 675–8.

the actions of other major political figures at the time. This chapter is not intended as a comprehensive treatment of imperialism in the late Republic, and I consider as alternatives only Cato the Younger, Caesar, and Pompeius; but even a brief and selective survey will indicate the extent to which the proper running of empire was a contentious issue during the last twenty years of the Republic, and give an indication of the intellectual context within which Cicero was operating when he spoke on imperial issues.

5.1. CICERO ON EMPIRE: *DE OFFICIIS* AND THE LETTERS FROM CILICIA

The point of turning to the treatises and letters is not to pull the rabbit of sincerity out of the hat and to correct Cicero's unreliable rhetoric with his real beliefs. These works, just as much as the speeches, were written with specific audiences in mind, and the treatises, at least, were designed to be disseminated openly.[5] Neither genre gives us access to Cicero's unselfconscious musings. Their value lies in the contingent fact that for this inquiry they contain discussions of imperial matters which complement the speeches by indicating the extent of Cicero's knowledge and assessment of the problems of the day.

Cicero's most extended survey of Roman imperialism, in the *de officiis*, was written in 44, when it was becoming clear that republican government had not been revived by the assassination of Caesar. One of Cicero's concerns in this work is to address the transformation in republican ideology and behaviour which had made the pursuit of glory so dangerously destabilizing to the political system.[6] The possession of empire is presented as one of the factors which provoked the unrestrained pursuit of glory; and despite the change in political circumstances, the *de officiis* is essential background for the speeches I am looking at: Cicero naturally used his imperial

[5] See G. O. Hutchinson, *Cicero's Correspondence: A Literary Study* (Oxford: Oxford Univ. Press, 1998), and the observations of Rose, 'Rhetoric of Imperialism', 372–3.

[6] A. A. Long, 'Cicero's Politics in *De officiis*', in A. Laks and M. Schofield (eds.), *Justice and Generosity: Studies in Hellenistic Social and Political Theory* (Cambridge: Cambridge Univ. Press, 1995), 213–40.

experiences under the Republic to analyse the role of empire in the recent political disasters.

The key passage comes from book 2, during the course of a discussion on how one can encourage others to do what is advantageous to us.[7] He considers various tyrants and then turns reluctantly to the case of Rome. He divides the history of Rome's empire into two stages. The first was when Rome held its empire through the services it rendered, rather than through the harm it did, and its magistrates acted in the best interests of the provinces and the allies (2. 26). As a result, 'that government could more accurately be called a protectorate of the world rather than an empire'.[8] However, these habits have been lost; they had begun to deteriorate even before Sulla, and the cruelty and greed which marked the actions of Sulla and his followers at Rome removed what barriers there might have been to this sort of behaviour in the provinces. Cicero links the proscriptions in Rome to the outbreak of civil war: 'when such rewards are on offer, it should be easy to understand that civil war will always occur'.[9] He then brings the argument back to his starting point: 'we have fallen into this disaster (for I need to return to the point) by preferring to be feared than held in affectionate regard'.[10]

Dyck is surely right to state the importance of these remarks within Cicero's works.[11] But whereas he emphasizes the quality of their theoretical analysis, I would want to stress how this passage combines theoretical insight with an interest in personal behaviour which recalls the speeches.[12] Cicero's ideal of government, the model that existed but has now been lost, is

---

[7] *de off.* 2. 20: 'hoc igitur cognito dicendum est quonam modo hominum studia ad utilitates nostras adlicere atque excitare possimus.'

[8] 2. 27: 'illud patrocinium orbis terrae uerius quam imperium poterat nominari'.

[9] 2. 29: 'ex quo debet intellegi talibus praemiis propositis numquam defutura bella ciuilia'.

[10] 2. 29: 'atque in has clades incidimus (redeundum est enim ad propositum) dum metui quam cari esse et diligi malumus'.

[11] A. R. Dyck, *A Commentary on Cicero, De Officiis* (Ann Arbor: Univ. of Michigan Press, 1996), 400: 'The observations Cicero here offers are the most thoughtful reflections on imperialism that have come down to us from a Roman pen; though written hastily rather than systematically, they challenge comparison with Thucydides' analysis of Athenian imperialism . . .'.

[12] Cf. Perelli, *Il pensiero politico di Cicerone*, 168.

patrocinium, which originally describes the relationship between a patron and a client. And the concept that it is contrasted with, *imperium*, is also, in its primary sense, something which an individual possesses, that is the right, given by the people to a magistrate whom it has elected, to be obeyed. The chief motor for change has been greed: that is, the aspirations of individuals have been the decisive factor. Cicero sums this up epigrammatically: 'only a few men have inherited Caesar's possessions, but to his desires many wicked men are heir'.[13] The moralizing thrust of his argument also accounts for the strained logic of this passage, inasmuch as fleecing the provincials, although an excellent example of personal depravity, could not be said to have led directly to the fall of the Republic.

As I discussed above, there are good reasons for Cicero's inclination to concentrate on personal behaviour when using the empire in historical explanation. When Cicero describes earlier provincial government as a *patrocinium orbis terrae* he is barely being metaphorical, since individual Romans had set themselves up as patrons of provincial communities from the beginning of Rome's overseas expansion.[14] His stress on individual behaviour in the *de officiis*, and in the speeches on empire, on one level merely represents the reality of republican provincial administration: the political was the personal. What Cicero is doing here in *On duties* is to transfer to the state the relationship which really did exist between individuals and provincial communities.

None the less, even if personalities were of particular importance in the Roman system, to concentrate on them to the exclusion of other factors is to accept the inevitability of the situation. The achievement of *de officiis* is to establish a link between the actions of individuals and the problems of empire in a way that explains *why* personal behaviour had such potentially devastating effects on the state. We may wish to challenge the moralizing thrust of his argument; but the key point here is that he offers an analysis of the role of the empire in leading to Caesar's dictatorship which ranges more widely than the faults of individuals.

[13] 28: 'a quo [sc. Caesare] quidem rei familiaris ad paucos, cupiditatum ad multos improbos uenit hereditas'.
[14] See Gruen, *Coming of Rome*, 162–72; Badian, *Foreign Clientelae*.

Cicero's long letter to Quintus concerning his behaviour as governor of Asia provides an interesting comparison with the *de officiis* (*ad Q. fr.* 1. 1). It is a highly self-conscious piece of writing, which refers to Plato's *Republic* and invites comparison between itself and Xenophon's *Cyropaedia*.[15] It is also extremely artificial, since it is difficult to believe that Quintus, during his third year as governor, would gain much from the platitudes of one comparatively inexperienced in provincial affairs.[16] A much more plausible reason for writing is Cicero's desire to protect himself from any adverse consequences of Quintus' governorship. It is clear that Quintus' political successes depended heavily on his older brother's achievements,[17] and as a result, any failure on his part would reflect back very strongly on Cicero himself. If Quintus were to face a prosecution and conviction on *repetundae* charges on his return, the damage to Cicero would be considerable, particularly given his rise to prominence as the prosecutor of Verres. By having a letter of sage advice to the errant Quintus disseminated, Cicero could at least argue that he had not connived in his brother's faults, and had tried to remedy them.[18] It is reasonable, then, to expect this letter to contain Cicero's considered reflections on provincial government, or rather, what he felt it appropriate that his considered responses should be for a wider audience.

Cicero gives a lucid statement of a governor's duty: 'To me, at least, it seems that those who are in positions of authority over others should direct their actions according to this principle, namely, that those who will be in their power should be as happy as possible'.[19] And he acknowledges the main

---

[15] Plato: 29; *Cyropaedia*: 22–3.

[16] Cicero acknowledges this potential criticism of his letter at 18. 5–7: 'what shall I be able to teach someone whom I know to be no inferior of mine in good sense, particularly in this area, and who is much more experienced?' Cf. D. R. Shackleton Bailey, *Epistulae ad Quintum Fratrem et M. Brutum* (Cambridge: Cambridge Univ. Press, 1980), 147.

[17] Wiseman, 'The Ambitions of Quintus Cicero'.

[18] This is most obvious in Cicero's discussion of Quintus' proneness to anger (37–9); and his remarks on the need for caution in entrusting business to slaves (17) can also be read as a veiled warning in the light of Quintus' deplorable intimacy with his slave (and later freedman) Statius (on whom see D. R. Shackleton Bailey, *Cicero's Letters to Atticus*, vol. 1 (Cambridge: Cambridge Univ. Press, 1965), 388).

[19] 24.11–13: 'ac mihi quidem uidentur huc omnia esse referenda iis qui

reason that Quintus may have difficulty in fulfilling this is the aspirations of the *publicani* (32):

> To this painstaking desire of yours the *publicani* are a great obstacle. If we oppose them, we estrange ourselves and our country from an order to which we personally are greatly in debt, and which has been brought into harmony with the government through our efforts. If, however, we toady to them in everything, we shall allow others to perish entirely, people whose advantage as well as simply their safety we ought to take thought for. If we consider matters honestly, this is the one problem you have in the exercise of your office.[20]

A successful solution will need Quintus to satisfy the *publicani* while preserving the allies (33); but it becomes clear that the solution will not be equitable. After listing the reasons why the provincials should not feel resentful at having to pay taxes to Rome, he ends by suggesting that Quintus use his personal influence with the provincials to make them put up with the demands of the *publicani* without fuss (35):

> you too can assist, as you have done splendidly and are doing, by list-ing the high standing of the tax-farmers and the extent of our debt to their order, so that you can reconcile the Greeks with the tax-farmers without bringing to bear the irresistible force of your official position, but through the influence you have from people's gratitude, and so that you can ask people whom you have treated very well and who owe you everything to allow us to use their complaisance to maintain and preserve our good relations with the tax-farmers.[21]

praesunt aliis, ut ii qui erunt in eorum imperio sint quam beatissimi'. See further S. Mitchell, 'The Administration of Roman Asia from 133 BC to AD 250', in W. Eck, *Lokale Autonomie und römische Ordnungsmacht in den kaiserzeitlichen Provinzen vom 1. bis 3. Jahrhundert* (Munich: Oldenbourg, 1999), 17–46, 25–6.

[20] atque huic tuae uoluntati ac diligentiae difficultatem magnam adferunt publicani: quibus si aduersamur, ordinem de nobis optime meritum et per nos cum re publica coniunctum et a nobis et a re publica diiungemus; sin autem omnibus in rebus obsequemur, funditus eos perire patiemur quorum non modo saluti sed etiam commodis consulere debemus. haec est una, si uere cogitare uolumus, in toto imperio tuo difficultas.

[21] potes etiam tu id facere, quod et fecisti egregie et facis, ut commemores quanta sit in publicanis dignitas, quantum nos illi ordini debeamus, ut remoto imperio ac ui potestatis et fascium publicanos cum Graecis gratia atque auctoritate coniungas et ab iis de quibus optime tu meritus es et qui tibi omnia debent hoc petas, ut facilitate sua nos eam necessitudinem quae est nobis cum publicanis obtinere et conseruare patiantur.

While rational argument has some place, the ultimate solution is to come from the governor's using his own influence and negotiating skills. The importance of individual behaviour is constantly emphasized throughout the letter. When Cicero first considers the problems which Quintus has to deal with, he encourages him by asking, 'What difficulty is there is controlling those you are in charge of if you can control yourself?'[22] Difficulties in government can be controlled by personal virtue. Similarly, the increase in provincial corruption at this time is ascribed to a change in *mores* (11; 19). Cicero here is not just accepting the decline in morals thesis; he is also reducing complex questions of provincial administration to a question of individual morality. It is also striking that it is the provincials who are to make the concessions in disputes: Cicero maintains a veneer of probity and concern for the provincials in keeping with his earlier stand, but there is nothing in the letter seriously to alarm any *publicanus* who might read it.

The letter to Quintus shows a more sophisticated awareness of the reasons why provincial government is difficult than, say, the *Verrines*, as the nature of the writing would lead us to expect: but, for Cicero, the resolutions of these problems are still dependent on the chosen behaviour of individuals. Sailing between the Scylla of angry *publicani* and the Charybdis of destitute provincials is to depend on the tact and good sense of a particular governor, unsupported by any institutional framework.

Cicero's own period as a governor shows a similar preoccupation with the personal. A constant theme in the letters to Atticus from this period is Cicero's own personal probity and that which he is insisting on for his officers and companions. Long before he has reached his province, he writes that he is keeping Atticus' parting exhortation in mind all the time, that he and his entourage should behave 'with the utmost decency and restraint'.[23] Throughout the letters he gives examples of his probity: he has not even taken advantage of the allowances under the *lex Iulia*,[24] he has stopped spending by communities on honours for him (*ad Att.* 5. 21. 7), he has established a

---

[22] 7: 'quid est enim negoti continere eos quibus praesis, si te ipse contineas?'
[23] *ad Att.* 5. 9. 1: 'summa modestia et summa abstinentia'.
[24] *ad Att.* 5. 10. 2; 5. 14. 2; 5. 16. 2; 5. 21. 5.

mutually acceptable arrangement between the communities and the *publicani* (*ad Att.* 6. 1. 16). It is also clear that these acts are not isolated expressions of Cicero's benevolence. They are part of a thought-out scheme of behaviour, one that is in obvious contrast with that of Cicero's predecessor in Cilicia, Appius Claudius Pulcher.[25] Cicero indicates that his stance in the past has committed him to this line of behaviour;[26] he also implies that the reputation he has gained by his restrained behaviour is a substitute or alternative for the conventional signs of favour, such as statues or temples.[27] The letters to Atticus from Cilicia form, in effect, a self-conscious description of the wise man as governor, and presumably Atticus was to do his bit in Rome in spreading this picture.[28]

This care for the provincials' welfare is combined with an assumption that they cannot look after themselves, and, as Richardson points out, Cicero's interference in public expenditure cannot have been welcome to all the provincials.[29] In effect, Cicero is putting into practice the ideal of provincial government as a *patrocinium* which he discusses later in the *de officiis*. But although there is a thought-out plan behind Cicero's conduct as governor, the elements of the plan itself are, on the one hand, an insistence on the need for personal probity from the Romans in positions of authority and, on the other, a search for ad hoc solutions to disagreements that will satisfy both parties within existing frameworks. This is apparent if one looks at the

[25] *ad Att.* 6. 1. 2: ; 'Could the difference be greater? Under his command the province has been drained dry by expenses and charges, under mine not a penny has been demanded, either privately or publicly' (quid enim potest esse tam dissimile quam illo imperante exhaustam esse sumptibus et iacturis prouinciam, nobis eam obtinentibus nummum nullum esse erogatum nec priuatim nec publice?).

[26] *ad Att.* 5. 13. 1: 'From this I'm sure you'll understand that the pronouncements I've made over many years are now being demonstrated in practice' (ex quo te intellegere certo scio multorum annorum ostentationes meas nunc in discrimen esse adductas).

[27] *ad Att.* 5. 21. 7; cf. 5. 17. 5.

[28] An impression strengthened by Cicero's references to himself as the author of the *Republic* (6. 1. 8, 6. 3. 3): in the latter passage he says explicitly that his conduct in the province befits the author of that work. It is also significant that he suggests that probity in provincial government is an issue at this point, and that Cato is involved in this (6. 1. 13): see below, Sect. 5.2.1.

[29] Richardson, 'Administration of Empire', 596–7.

solutions which Cicero formulated to various problems which faced him.

When Cicero remarks that his earlier behaviour is now being put to the test (5. 13. 1, referred to above), he expresses confidence in his ability to act as he should, 'particularly since the tax-agreements for my province have already been worked out'.[30] Cicero gives no indication as to whether the terms of the agreements are consistent with the standards he sets up for himself; his concern is simply that he will not find himself personally embroiled in disputes between tax-collectors and provincials. In fact, the strategy that he did adopt for disputes was eminently sensible, that is, if the provincials paid by a certain date fixed by Cicero, the sum that they were liable to pay in interest was capped (*ad Att.* 6. 1. 16). But it is a solution dependent on the restraint and good sense of a particular governor.

Restraint and good sense are qualities that seem to have been signally lacking in the previous governor Appius: in addition to the passage referred to above which highlights the differences between Cicero's regime and Appius', he talks of the *uulnera* which the latter has left in the province (5. 15. 2; 5. 17. 6) and refers to the *iniuria* that Appius does Cicero in holding assizes after his successor has entered the province (5. 17. 6). Appius also took a very different line in the affair of Brutus' loan to Cyprus, which I discuss below. Yet despite all these indications that Appius was what Cicero must have considered to be an appallingly irresponsible governor, Cicero is desperately anxious to avoid incurring any hostility. This caution is apparent not only in the series of letters to Appius himself (*ad fam.* 3. 1–13), but also in Cicero's letters to Atticus, where we *might* expect a degree more frankness. Atticus would know the extent of Appius' misbehaviour from Cicero's letters: but, in the same passage as he talks of Appius' *rapinae*, *libidines*, and *contumeliae*, Cicero explains that none of his remarks are accompanied by hostility towards Appius, and explicitly denies a charge which Appius' friends are making, namely that Cicero's only aim in being upright is to cast opprobrium on Appius.[31] This latter protestation is surely sincere: Cicero must

---

[30] *ad Att.* 5. 13. 1: 'et eo facilius quod in nostra prouincia confectae sunt pactiones'.

[31] *ad Att.* 6. 1. 2: 'nihil enim a me fit cum ulla illius contumelia . . . haec non

have found it extremely embarrassing to be throwing Appius'
actions into stark relief, given the grounds for tension between
the two men due to the recent murder of Clodius, and Cicero's
almost paranoid disinclination to give offence to any important
politician.[32] The contrast in their behaviour is regrettable, but
there is no indication from Cicero that he thinks anything can
be done about it.

Another illustration of how Cicero set about handling problems in his province comes with the famous episode of Brutus'
loan at 48 per cent interest per annum to the people of Salamis,
and his attempt to get the money back.[33] Most of the interest
has centred on its being Brutus, the heroic tyrannicide and
nephew of Cato, who is grinding the faces of the provincials
into the dust and using his influence in the Senate to safe-
guard his position. But there is fascination too in watching
Cicero stuck on the horns of a dilemma. On the one hand, he is
horrified at the methods which were used, with the blessing of
Appius, to extract the money, which included the deployment
of Roman troops and the death from starvation of a number of
members of the Salaminian senate; and he attempted to broker
an agreement which would have left the Salaminians paying no
more than the 12 per cent per annum which he had laid down
in his edict. But, at the same time, Cicero drew back from
imposing this solution against the wishes of Brutus' agent, even
though the Salaminians were keen to pay on these terms; and
expresses considerable anxiety that *he* may have offended
Brutus by his decisions in this affair.

These are of course letters concerning practical problems,
where Cicero is justifying a particular course of action that he
has taken. We should not expect him to justify his behaviour in
theoretical terms. On the other hand, I hope that I have shown
that Cicero is setting himself up as a paradigm for the governor:
his approach to this correspondence is self-conscious, and it is
therefore not unreasonable to look for the principles which,
overtly or otherwise, seem to structure his ideal.

nulli amici Appi ridicule interpretantur, qui me idcirco putent bene audire
uelle ut ille male audiat'.

[32] Cf. Cicero's awkward letter to Appius (*ad fam.* 3. 12. 2–3) on finding out
that Dolabella, who was prosecuting Appius, had become engaged to Cicero's
daughter Tullia.   [33] *ad Att.* 5. 21. 10–12; 6. 1. 2–8.

The letter to Quintus, and the sequence from Cilicia, demonstrate an awareness of the problems that a provincial governor faced which we do not find in the *repetundae* speeches, above all in the difficulties of adjudicating the conflict between the legitimate claims of the provincials to good treatment, which Cicero states with absolute clarity, and the demands of Roman tax-collectors and business to make a profit, which prudence dictates the governor cannot ignore or reject. The idea that Cicero simply did not realize that provincial government was problematic is shown to be untenable. But, on the other hand, Cicero is very reluctant to spell out the nature of this particular problem: that is, that unrestrained profiteering and the well-being of the provincials are ultimately incompatible. He gives us the evidence, and his uneasiness with what is going on in the case of the Salaminians is palpable; but he does not state the conclusion.

One reason for his silence may be a reluctance to state a problem when he is not prepared to do anything about it. But I suspect too that his expectation of who would read his letters also acted as a check on ruthless analysis. As I indicated above, the letter to Quintus does seem to have been aimed at a wide audience, and in that case Cicero could have expected it to be read by men who had business interests in Asia and would not appreciate Cicero's exhorting the governor of the province to favour the provincials instead. And while the letters to Atticus may have had no other *readers* than Atticus, it would be a mistake to assume that Atticus was someone to whom Cicero could pour out his heart without restraint. Atticus made money out of the provinces: he would not welcome news of an assault on the freedom of the *publicani*.[34] Atticus' friendship and approval on their own were very valuable to Cicero; Cicero's restraint becomes even more understandable if he was also hoping that Atticus would disseminate a favourable account of Cicero's governorship.

The letters, therefore, present a situation similar to that in the speeches. The analysis of problems is sharper, certainly,

[34] Cf. Cicero's fulsome explanations for why he was unable to oppose a senatorial measure which seems to have made it impossible for Atticus to recover money which he had lent to the town of Sicyon: *ad Att.* 1. 19. 9; 1. 20. 4; 2. 1. 10.

because Cicero is dealing with actual situations and trying either to offer useful advice or to explain his own position. But there is reluctance to take the discussion to its logical conclusion, and, I would argue, for the same basic reason as in the speeches: it would alienate his audience. Before bringing this discussion to *its* logical conclusion, I shall turn aside to sketch the attitudes of some of Cicero's prominent contemporaries to Rome's empire.

5.2. ALTERNATIVE STRATEGIES: CATO, CAESAR, AND POMPEIUS

5.2.1. Cato's blueprint

The extensive biographical tradition on Cato the Younger which developed as a response to his manner of death makes it possible to assess his stance on empire, despite the fact that he was never a provincial governor in a straightforward sense (I consider his time in Cyprus below); moreover, a letter survives from him to Cicero on the subject of the latter's triumph, which, though short, is highly suggestive.[35] His attitude to empire can most usefully be seen in connection with his views on government generally, and these can be summarized as a belief in the efficacy of rules.[36] The first and most striking demonstration is his quaestorship, of which Plutarch gives a detailed description in his *Life of the younger Cato* 16–18. He prepared carefully for office, not becoming a candidate until 'he had read the laws relating to the quaestorship and found out the details from those who had held the office and formed an idea of the nature of the responsibility';[37] he worked long hours; he took personal charge of his work instead of leaving it to the clerks, which was the practice of his colleagues; he fulfilled the state's obligations as a debtor as well as collecting in full the money owed to it; he took scrupulous account of the validity of senatorial decrees presented at the Treasury for registration. Moreover, he continued his scrutiny of the Treasury, at

[35] On Cato, see R. Fehrle, *Cato Uticensis* (Darmstadt: Wissenschaftliche Buchgesellschaft, 1983); M. Gelzer, 'Cato Uticensis', in his *Kleine Schriften*, vol. 2 (Wiesbaden: Steiner, 1963).

[36] Cf. Gruen, *Last Generation*, 254–5; Gelzer, 'Cato Uticensis', 265–6, 268–9.   [37] Plutarch, *Life of the younger Cato* 16.1.

considerable personal expense, after he had left office (18. 5). Cato's vigour and efficiency were not popular with the permanent staff, and he was not prepared to accept compromises. In the case of one clerk prosecuted, and acquitted, of fraud, he refused to accept the court's verdict, and did not employ, or pay, the offender (16. 4–6).

This adherence to a framework of rules can be seen in other episodes: his refusal to accept any gifts while travelling through Asia Minor as a young man;[38] the threat to prosecute on bribery charges whoever was successful in the consular elections in 63;[39] his attack, as tribune, on the false statements made by returning *imperatores* and his enacting that they swear an oath as to the number of the enemy slain;[40] his campaign to deny official sanction to debt incurred by provincial cities to Roman citizens;[41] his opposition to the rebate that the tax-farmers wanted in 61–60.[42] Two episodes in particular deserve closer attention. One is Cato's special command in Cyprus between 58 and 56, and the other is his demand that Caesar be surrendered to the Germans for treaty-breaking.

Cyprus was annexed to Rome through a law of Clodius in 58.[43] At first it was to be assigned as part of the consular province of Cilicia for the year 57; subsequently it was entrusted specifically to Cato as a quaestor pro praetore. By deciding to accept the command Cato legitimized Clodius' actions as tribune more generally, and greatly weakened senatorial opposition, with disastrous effects for Cicero; and yet, one could argue that a good public servant, such as Cato, was bound to do what the people ordered him.[44] Plutarch's *Life*

---

[38] Plutarch, *Cato* 12–15.

[39] Plutarch, *Cato* 21. 2–3.

[40] Valerius Maximus 2. 8. 1.

[41] So it seems from Cicero, *ad Att.* 2. 1. 10.

[42] Cicero, *ad Att.* 1. 17. 9; 1. 18. 7; 2. 1. 8.

[43] W. J. Tatum, *The Patrician Tribune: Publius Clodius Pulcher* (Chapel Hill: Univ. of North Carolina Press, 1999), 150–6.

[44] *MRR* 2. 198; S. I. Oost, 'Cato Uticensis and the Annexation of Cyprus', *CPh* 50 (1955), 98–109; E. Badian, 'M. Porcius Cato and the Annexation and Early Administration of Cyprus', *JRS* 55 (1965), 110–21. Cicero, keen to absolve Cato at least publicly from any blame for his exile, argues that he would have faced violence, had he refused the command, and since the decision to annex Ptolemy's kingdom had already been made Cato could judge it better that this be done in a conscientious and honest manner (*Sest.* 62).

of Cato the younger (34–40) provides the most detailed account of his command, and despite its insistent moralizing is plausible in its picture of Cato's punctiliousness in realizing Ptolemy's estate and transporting it to Rome. This was the task imposed on him by the state and for the state's benefit, and he sought to accomplish it by talking up the value of the king's chattels before auction, restraining his friends in their desire for a slice of profit, keeping detailed accounts and even, according to Plutarch, putting in place improbable devices to protect the money raised from the danger of shipwreck on its journey to Rome.[45] Cato's command in Cyprus can be seen as an affirmation of the principle that the profits of empire should belong to the people as a whole, and that private profiteering is unacceptable; he was, moreover, remarkably efficient in raising revenue.[46]

His stance on Caesar as a breaker of treaties illuminates a different range of issues: how far the autonomy of a commander in the field should extend. In this case, the question was whether Caesar had attacked the Germans during a truce; and Cato, claiming that he had, demanded that he be handed over to the Germans in expiation for the offence against the gods his action had caused.[47] The seriousness of this charge is well illustrated by Caesar's own account of events in the *Bellum Gallicum* (4. 12–15), which is composed to show that the Germans are the treaty breakers; and it is suggestive that Cato, according to Plutarch (51. 3), links Caesar's transgression, whose implications are primarily religious, with the threat that Caesar poses, he claims, to the citizens of Rome. A commander who ignores the good of the state in a specific issue is likely to become its attacker.

This summary of Cato's career would suggest that the problems of empire can always be solved by acting in accor-

[45] Plutarch, *Cato* 36, 38.

[46] That this is usually seen as a *popularis* trait merely indicates the dangers of over-simplification: Cato in particular used popular methods in order to promote senatorial authority. He claimed to have raised 7,000 talents from the sale of the king's property (Plutarch, *Cato* 38.1): that is, more than a quarter of the sum which Pompeius is said to have brought home from his conquests in the East (Plutarch, *Pomp.* 45.4).

[47] Plutarch, *Cato* 51. 1–5; cf. Gelzer, 'Cato', 131; Fehrle, *Cato*, 176–80 and 317–19.

dance with legislation and the state's interests; and if individuals such as Caesar do not do so, then the Senate must intervene. Probity is all; indeed, in 51 Cicero suggests, in a chance remark in a letter to Atticus, that Cato's views on provincial government could be seen as a prescription for others: 'What you hear in praise of Thermus and Silius is true; they are behaving very well. You can add Marcus Nonius, Bibulus, me if you like. I could wish that Scrofa had an adequate outlet for his talents—he's an excellent fellow. The rest are disregarding Cato's blueprint.'[48] Cato's reputation is such that he can stand for a certain approach to provincial government: strict adherence to the laws of the Republic and the policing and control of the behaviour of members of the elite.

It might seem, therefore, that unlike Cicero, Cato does not acknowledge that there were some areas, particularly the exploitation of empire, where there was no obvious and straightforward right course of action. His inflexibility could certainly appear to some unrealistic; there is the famous observation of Cicero, in relation to Cato's opposition to the claims of the *publicani* in 60, that 'for all his fine intentions and integrity, he sometimes harms the state; he gives his opinion in the Senate as though he were in Plato's Republic, rather than, as he is, in Romulus' cesspit.'[49] And he was not notably popular with the electorate.[50]

---

[48] *ad Att.* 6. 1. 13: 'Thermum, Silium uere audis laudari; ualde se honeste gerunt. adde M. Nonium, Bibulum, me si uoles. iam Scrofa uellem haberet ubi posset; est enim lautum negotium. ceteri infirmant πολίτευμα Catonis.' Shackleton Bailey reads *firmant* in place of *infirmant*: since Cicero has named all the governors in the East, there are no *ceteri* who could be misbehaving; '*ceteri* = all those mentioned except Scrofa, whose post was too unimportant for him to count one way or the other' (D. R. Shackleton Bailey, *Cicero's Letters to Atticus*, vol. 3 (Cambridge: Cambridge Univ. Press, 246)). This is persuasive; but on either reading Cicero is referring to a distinctive Catonian take on imperial administration.

[49] *ad Att.* 2. 1. 8: 'sed tamen ille optimo animo utens et summa fide nocet interdum rei publicae; dicit enim tamquam in Platonis πολιτεία, non tamquam in Romuli faece sententiam.'

[50] He failed in his first attempt to become praetor (*MRR* 2. 216), securing election only for 54, and was defeated in the contest for the consulship of 51. His defeat in 56 is ascribed to the hostility of Pompeius, Crassus, and Caesar; but in the consular elections of 52 he simply lost to more popular candidates (see Wiseman, *CAH* 9, 2nd edn. (1994), 413).

However, there are some interesting episodes which reveal cracks in Cato's integrity, particularly the occasions when Cato gave way to the pressures of family attachment. In 63 his threats of prosecution against the victorious candidates for the consulship specifically excluded his brother-in-law Silanus, not in deference to Silanus' superior standard of behaviour, but because of the marriage connection between the two men. In 50 he was involved in the Senate's decisions on granting honours to its commanders. There is a letter from him to Cicero, proconsul in Cilicia (*ad fam.* 15. 5), explaining why he voted against the proposal to grant Cicero a supplication. The measure passed, and Cato expresses his pleasure at this, if it is what Cicero really wants and if he prefers that the congratulations should be directed at the immortal gods rather than to Cicero, and then goes on to point out that a *supplicatio* is by no means an automatic prelude to a triumph.[51] His explanation for his act, however awkward and ungracious, and indeed his writing to Cicero to explain at all, would suggest that he is trying to prevent his stand from alienating Cicero, and thus is conscious that there is a conflict here between a belief that awarding honours to commanders on inadequate grounds is unsatisfactory and a desire to remain on good terms with Cicero, in many ways a natural political ally and an influential political figure.[52] Even better evidence that Cato found it difficult sometimes to reconcile principle and personal obligations comes a few months later, when he supported a thanksgiving of twenty days for his son-in-law Bibulus, for his actions as proconsul in Syria. Cicero was, unsurprisingly, furious (*ad Att.* 7. 2. 7).

Cato's responses to the problems of empire and their incon-

---

[51] *ad fam.* 15. 5. 2: 'supplicationem decretam, si tu, qua in re nihil fortuito sed summa tua ratione et continentia rei publicae prouisum est, dis immortalibus gratulari nos quam tibi referre acceptum mauis, gaudeo; quod si triumphi praerogatiuam putas supplicationem et idcirco casum potius quam te laudari mauis, neque supplicationem sequitur semper triumphus . . .'.

[52] Cf. D. R. Shackleton Bailey, *Cicero: Epistulae ad Familiares*, vol. 1 (Cambridge: Cambridge Univ. Press, 1977), 449: 'It would have been more in keeping with the accredited character of the writer if he had defended his opposition as a matter of principle instead of resorting to the humbug of §2'; and see the discussion in W. C. Schneider, *Vom Handeln der Römer* (Zurich and New York: Olms, 1998), 533–50.

sistencies indicate, as one would expect, that political life in the late Republic demanded compromise, and that even the rigid Cato had on occasion to bend.[53] But Cato's deviations also illustrate how the norms of political behaviour meant that it was impossible to find solutions to all imperial issues: the web of personal connections and the exchange of services are incompatible with equitable administration (even if it could be agreed what was a 'fair' level of provincial exploitation). And yet there is no hint that Cato saw that there were problems which his rules-based approach might not be able to solve. Which is not to say that the solutions implicit in his behaviour were without merit. He tried to set limits to the profiteering of those who made money from the provincials, and he tried to restrain the governing class by restricting the opportunities to acquire personal *gloria* by making it more difficult to get a thanksgiving or triumph; and the reasons why neither initiative was very successful was not so much that the means adopted were inadequate, but that Cato was unable to persuade the Senate to implement the controls. Cato's failure brings us right back to the central issues: he lost out throughout his public career to men such as Pompeius and Caesar who were prepared to exploit the empire more ruthlessly than he, and the measures which he wished to have adopted, though reasonable in themselves, were all concerned with limiting an individual's opportunities for bad behaviour, and did not address the wider and more intractable problem of finding a system of imperial government which was not so vulnerable to individual abuses.

5.2.2. *Caesar's propaganda and practice*

Caesar might at first sight seem to be the prime example of a self-conscious thinker on imperial issues. Largely as a result of the *Bellum Gallicum* he is the dominant imperial figure of the late Republic, indeed of Rome generally; his conquests may not be without parallel but his propaganda is unsurpassed.[54]

[53] The question of Cato's consistency is further complicated by his character as Stoic; on the peculiarities of the biographical tradition concerning Cato, see Fehrle, *Cato Uticensis*, esp. 1–48, 279–316.

[54] Cf. K. Welch and A. Powell (eds.), *Julius Caesar as Artful Reporter: The War Commentaries as Political Instruments* (London: Duckworth/Classical Press of Wales, 1998).

None the less, Caesar's interventions in imperial questions before the civil war look oddly old-fashioned. His major contribution was the *lex Iulia* on provincial government. Despite the paucity of our evidence concerning its contents, it seems to have been a comprehensive measure, not simply covering extortion by provincial governors but dealing with financial irregularities in general as well as with offences which hitherto had been covered by *maiestas* legislation.[55] Much discussion of this law concentrates on the facts that alone among Caesar's measures as consul it provoked no opposition, and that it was in use well into the imperial period: these are usually interpreted as an indication of the quality of the legislation, and of its comprehensiveness. Yet it is clear, too, that Cato would, and did, approve of this law, and it works on the assumption that what goes wrong in provincial government is the result of the misbehaviour of individuals, and primarily of the governor. There was little point in tightening up *repetundae* legislation while tolerating, and indeed seeking, extended and extraordinary commands. And Caesar's account of Caesar as *imperium*-holder in the *BG* operates absolutely within republican traditions of what makes a great commander and what constitutes imperial success.[56]

The citizenship is perhaps an area where Caesar did show a greater tendency to innovate. Certainly, an interest in extending the franchise to the Transpadanes is a recurrent feature of his career. In 69 or 68 he agitated for citizen rights for Latin colonies,[57] which would have affected those living beyond the Po, since they had been given Latin rights at the end of the Social War.[58] In 63 he prosecuted C. Piso, alleging that he had illegally executed a Transpadane (Sall. *Cat.* 49. 2), and he founded a colony of citizens at Novum Comum under the provisions of the *lex Vatinia* (Suet. *Iul.* 28.3). Rumours were rife in 51 that Caesar was intending to make Transpadanes citizens,[59] and when Marcellus, one of the consuls of the year,

[55] For its provisions, see Gruen, *Last Generation*, 239–43.

[56] A. Goldsworthy, ' "Instinctive Genius": The Depiction of Caesar as General', in Welch and Powell, *Julius Caesar*, 193–219.

[57] Suetonius, *Iul.* 8.

[58] Sherwin-White, *Citizenship*, 157–9.

[59] *ad fam.* 8. 1. 2.; *ad Att.* 5. 2. 3.

had a man from Comum flogged, Cicero assumed that this was to be taken as a specific insult to Caesar.[60] How far, though, these actions presuppose a conceptual framework other than that of individual Romans having entire provinces as their clients is not clear, and the political advantages both of links with Cisalpine Gaul and of extending the franchise to it—the province closest to Rome, and one for whose elite attendance at annual elections would be feasible—may mean that a pragmatic explanation for Caesar's interest is sufficient.

As dictator Caesar adopted a more radical line to the granting of citizenship: not simply to Transpadane Gaul in 49 BC (Dio 41. 36. 3), but also to the city of Gades.[61] He also settled huge numbers of citizens outside Italy, in colonies in Gaul, Spain, and the East; Suetonius gives 80,000 as the figure of citizens moved out Italy.[62] Moreover, he increased the geographical range of the Senate, with a much higher proportion of senators coming from Italy, as opposed to Rome, than hitherto as well as a few from Narbonese Gaul and Spain.[63] This line of policy involved a radical change in the concept of citizenship and of Rome's relations with its empire. With significant numbers of Romans now living outside the Italian peninsula, the idea (which was already, since the Social War, very strained) that citizenship involved direct participation in government through the assemblies was no longer tenable. But, equally, it undermined the model of a Rome which ruled the Mediterranean and a Mediterranean which was ruled from

[60] *ad Att.* 5. 11. 2: 'Marcellus foede de Comensi; etsi ille magistratum non gesserat, erat tamen Transpadanus.' The fact that Cicero mentions that the victim had not held a magistracy makes sense, I would argue, only if this incident involved a man from a community with Latin rights (since having held a magistracy would have given him citizenship), i.e. that Cicero's *Comensi* refers to the original settlement at Comum and not (as in Plutarch, *Life of Caesar* 29. 2) to Caesar's own colony of Novum Comum (though, if we believe Suetonius (*Iulius* 28.3), Marcellus also challenged the legitimacy of this foundation). That Caesar had been cultivating links with the Transpadanes in general would be sufficient to explain the insult. Contra, see Gruen, *Last Generation*, 460–1.

[61] Dio 41. 24. 1; *Periochae* of Livy, 110.

[62] Suet. *Iul.* 42. 1; see Z. Yavetz, *Julius Caesar and his Public Image* (London: Thames and Hudson, 1983), 143–50.

[63] M. Gelzer, *Caesar*, trans. P. Needham (Oxford: Blackwell, 1968), 291; of the senators from outside Rome, some were descendants of Roman settlers, others enfranchised natives: see Syme, *Roman Revolution*, 78–96.

Rome. The logical end of these steps, not at this point reached, was an integration of Rome's possessions through the citizenship, and as a concomitant result the transformation of the relationship between centre and periphery, since the empire would no longer be run solely for the benefit of those at Rome. And it is against this background, of uncertainty about the position of Rome within its empire, that the fantastic rumours that Caesar was intending to transfer the capital from Rome to Alexandria, or Ilium, which circulated at Rome during the last months of his life make sense.[64] And yet these measures were not carried further; Caesar did not persist in the task of reconstruction and was, at the moment of his death, about to abandon Rome and its problems for further conquest. Apart from the extension of the franchise and the founding of colonies, the only significant modification that he made as dictator to imperial administration was to limit the length of time which governors spent in their provinces: a maximum of one year for propraetors and two for proconsuls.[65]

5.2.3. *Pompeius: structures and paradoxes*

The strategies of Cato, and of Caesar as consul, in dealing with the problems of empire indicate a much greater awareness, or at least expressed awareness, that there were indeed problems than we find in Cicero's speeches. But from their behaviour and legislation it seems as though the actions of individuals were still seen as the major factor in misgovernment; and that if individuals could be controlled, then the problems would go away. In this respect, then, their thinking resembles Cicero's, and indeed Cicero's analysis in the letters and treatises shows a much more sophisticated awareness of the *origins* of imperial misgovernment and tension than do the actions of either Cato or Caesar.

[64] Suet. *Iul.* 79. 4; Nicolaus of Damascus, fr. 130.

[65] *MRR* 2. 294. Gelzer rates Caesar more highly as an imperial reformer, and regards Caesar's perception of the failure of the Republic to deal with the problems of empire as one of the impulses driving him towards monarchy (*Caesar*, 278: 'Thus Caesar's personal leaning towards monarchy grew ever stronger: it was reinforced by the failure of the optimate oligarchy and the Republican constitution to cope with the problems of Empire'). But it is difficult to see how centralization in one man, if not accompanied by an overhaul of administrative structures, could have provided a lasting solution.

Pompeius' reputation as an imperial figure is obscured by Caesar; not only did the latter win the civil war to emerge as the ultimate imperial figure in control of everything, but he also left the *Gallic Wars* to become the enduring description of the Roman commander in action. In comparison Pompeius appears, inevitably, as second-best; and even the most extensive account of his campaigns, Plutarch's *Life*, implicitly evaluates their respective achievements by pairing Pompeius with Agesilaus while Caesar is matched with Alexander.

However, Pompeius' actions as a military commander show him to be a much more important figure in terms of the development of the Roman empire than the comparison with Caesar allows; indeed, Pompeius' lasting effect on the ground was in many ways much more substantial than Caesar's own. Moreover, in his settlement of the East and in his legislation during his third consulship one can see efforts to make the empire work which do seem to move beyond the thinking of Caesar and Cato with their continued concentration on the figure of the *imperator* alone.

A good starting point on this question is what Pliny the Elder says about Pompeius and Caesar in his survey of human achievements in book seven of the *Natural History* (91–9). Caesar he treats first, as the outstanding example of *animi uigor*, *clementia*, and *magnanimitas*, the latter shown particularly by his decision to burn Pompeius' papers unread after Pharsalia. Pliny then turns to Pompeius: 'but it concerns the glory of the Roman Empire, and not that of one man, to mention in this place all the records of the victories of Pompey the Great and all his triumphs, which equal the brilliance of the exploits not only of Alexander the Great but even almost of Hercules and Father Liber'.[66] Pliny exemplifies this claim through a survey of Pompeius' triumphs. He concentrates particularly on the third triumph: he quotes the *praefatio*, with its list of thirteen areas and tribes conquered and the two kings Mithradates and Tigranes (compare the list in Diodorus 40. 4), and refers to a remark Pompeius is said to have made in a *contio*, to the effect

[66] Pliny, *NH* 7. 95: 'uerum ad decus imperii Romani, non solum ad uiri unius pertinet, uictoriarum Pompei Magni titulos omnes triumphosque hoc in loco nuncupari, aequato non modo Alexandri Magni rerum fulgore, sed etiam Herculis prope ac Liberi patris'.

that 'he found Asia the most distant of provinces and left it in the middle of his homeland'.[67] He concludes the section with a somewhat cryptic remark: 'If anybody on the other side desires to review in similar manner the achievements of Caesar, who showed himself greater than Pompey, he must assuredly roll off the entire world, and this it will be agreed is a task without limit.'[68] Pliny appears to be saying that although Caesar is the superior human being he does not match Pompeius' achievements as an empire builder.

The idea that Pompeius' imperial achievement is distinctive because of its scale and comprehensiveness occurs in Plutarch's *Life* as well, and again in relation to the third triumph: 'what contributed most to his reputation—and had never been the case for any previous Roman—was that he held his third triumph over the third continent. Other men had had three triumphs, even before this; but Pompeius, with his first triumph over Libya, his second over Europe, and the final one over Asia seemed in some way to have included the whole world in his three triumphs.'[69] The rest of the chapter before the passage quoted gives the areas over which Pompeius triumphed, and the wealth which he displayed; the extent of these is fabulous, but the description itself is of a standard kind and can indeed be seen in terms of an inflationary rhetoric of conquest.[70] What is new is the way that Pompeius' conquests have become coterminous with the world itself; Dio (37. 21. 2) says that in addition to the τρόπαια representing his individual

[67] 'summa summarum in illa gloria fuit (ut ipse in contione dixit cum de rebus suis dissereret) Asiam ultimam prouinciarum accepisse eandemque mediam patriae reddidisse' (*NH* 7. 99).

[68] 'si quis e contrario simili modo uelit percensere Caesaris res, qui maior illo apparuit, totum profecto terrarum orbem enumeret, quod infinitum esse conueniet' (*NH* 7. 99).

[69] Plutarch, *Life of Pompeius* 45. 5: μέγιστον δὲ ὑπῆρχε πρὸς δόξαν καὶ μηδενὶ τῶν πώποτε ʽΡωμαίων γεγονός, ὅτι τὸν τρίτον θρίαμβον ἀπὸ τῆς τρίτης ἠπείρου κατήγαγεν. ἐπεὶ τρίς γε καὶ πρότερον ἦσαν ἕτεροι τεθριαμβευκότες· ἐκεῖνος δὲ τὸν μὲν πρῶτον ἐκ Λιβύης, τὸν δὲ δεύτερον ἐξ Εὐρώπης, τοῦτον δὲ τὸν τελευταῖον ἀπὸ τῆς Ἀσίας εἰσαγαγὼν τρόπον τινὰ τὴν οἰκουμένην ἐδόκει τοῖς τρισὶν ὑπῆχθαι θριάμβος.

[70] On the institution of the triumph, see H. S. Versnel, *Triumphus: An Inquiry into the Origin, Development and Meaning of the Roman Triumph* (Leiden: Brill, 1970); E. Künzl, *Der Römische Triumph. Siegesfeiern im antiken Rom* (Munich: Beck, 1988).

conquests he had one big one with an inscription claiming to be the whole of the inhabited world, ἡ οἰκουμένη, and Diodorus refers to an inscribed dedication in which Pompeius claimed to have 'extended the frontiers of the Empire to the limits of the earth'.[71] In this context, Pompeius' use of the word *patria* in talking about Asia to the people in the passage referred to above is worth further consideration. He has put Asia, he says, 'in the middle of the fatherland', *media patriae*; he is using *patria*, then, to refer to all territory under Roman control. This breadth of reference is unparalleled at this date;[72] even without more evidence for the context of Pompeius' speech, it seems reasonable to think that he was self-consciously redefining Roman possessions and also the nature of being a Roman citizen. The whole of the area under Roman control is also the *patria* of Pompeius and other Romans: there is a suggestion of proprietorship and of geographic unity which goes far beyond the exercise of power.[73] It is perhaps unwise to attempt to pin down the implications of Pompeius' remark too tightly, but there is a sense that not only did the unprecedented scale of Pompeius' conquests in the East allow him to present himself as a world conqueror, but in the context of an address to the people he was able to use this territorial expansion in order to flatter his audience's sense of imperial involvement: it is their empire. It is also worth noting the importance of Asia in Pompeius' remark, in contrast to the *titulus* quoted by Pliny immediately before, where Asia comes first in the list of con-quered or reconquered territories which seems to be ordered in terms of increasing exoticism. Of course, Pompeius' argument

---

[71] Diodorus 40. 4: τὰ ὅρια τῆς ἡγεμονίας τοῖς ὅροις τῆς γῆς προσβιβάσας. Cf. K. Clarke, *Between Geography and History: Hellenistic Constructions of the Roman World* (Oxford: Oxford Univ. Press, 1999), 308–11.

[72] Linguistic arguments from silence are particularly dangerous, but note e.g. Cicero, *Cat.* 1. 27: 'si mecum patria, quae mihi uita mea multo est carior, si cuncta Italia, si omnis res publica loquatur'; *Tusc.* 5. 106: 'sin abesse patria miserum est, plenae miserorum prouinciae sunt'; apart from this passage, the earliest example of *patria* referring to the whole empire which *TLL* (*patrius* (*patria*) IA1aγIV) cites is from Ovid's *Fasti* (1. 531), and there *patria* may refer simply to Italy.

[73] Contrast Cicero's remarks about his two *patriae* in the opening of the second book of *de legibus* (2. 5), Arpinum and Rome: the concept is legally problematic, but in both cases *patria* seems to be conceptualized in terms of a city state.

depends on a perception of the existence of new and extended
province and client kingdoms further east, which has shifted
the empire eastwards so that Asia becomes its centre; but
the remark also shows the emotional force of 'Asia' as a geographical concept, a province of such richness that its loss
would be catastrophic.[74] And what his remark reveals above all
is that his conquests were so extraordinary in extent that he
could claim to have transformed the nature of the entire
empire.

But was there anything else distinctive about Pompeius'
settlement of the East apart from its scale? This is perhaps a
foolish question, since the amount of territory and the increase
in revenues meant that the transformation was qualitative as
well as quantitative.[75] But one can also point to the structures of
government that Pompeius left in place, as indeed the reference
to revenues indicates: his achievement was not simply a one-off
pile of booty, but organized exploitation designed to last. So,
what exactly did Pompeius do?

He substantially extended the province of Bithynia by
attaching to it the area of Mithradates' kingdom on the south
coast of the Black Sea. This territory was given the name of
Pontus and divided into eleven areas each under the control of a
city. Some of these cities were well-established settlements, as
in the cases of the Greek cities of Amastris, Sinope, and Amasis
and Mithradates' capital inland at Amaseia; but to complete the
network Pompeius founded or completed new cities, leaving in
the process a personal memorial in the names of Magnopolis
and Pompeiopolis. To the south and east he confirmed the
position of rulers who had proved friendly to Rome, dividing
Paphlagonia between two dynasts and Galatia between the
three tetrarchs who had survived Mithradates and acknowledging Ariobarzanes as king of Cappadocia and extending his
kingdom.[76] He extended the province of Cilicia eastwards to

[74] See Cicero, *de imp.* 14–15.

[75] According to Plutarch (*Life of Pompeius* 45. 3), Pompeius' conquests
raised the state's tax revenues from 50 million drachmae to 85 million
drachmae: an increase of 70%.

[76] S. Mitchell, *Anatolia: Land, Men and Gods in Asia Minor* (Oxford:
Oxford Univ. Press, 1993), i. 31–4; Magie, *Roman Rule*, 351–78; A. H. M.
Jones, *The Cities of the Eastern Roman Provinces* (Oxford: Oxford Univ. Press,
2nd edn., 1971), 156–62. On Pliny and the *lex Pompeia* in Bithynia, see A. N.

include the Cilician plain and resettled defeated pirates in cities
which had been depopulated by Tigranes.[77] He transformed the
bulk of the Seleucid kingdom into the new province of Syria,
although he also granted autonomy to a group of cities in Coele
Syria known as the Decapolis, and confirmed the position of a
number of local rulers; further south, he intervened in the confusion in Jerusalem with eventual support for Hyrcanus, and
the Nabataean ruler Aretas acknowledged the authority of his
lieutenant Scaurus with a payment of 300 talents.[78]

Many of the components in this were not new; the mixture of
direct rule and client kings is a hallmark of Roman imperialism
in the East during the Republic, and the foundation of cities
was already familiar as a way of establishing provincial government in 'uncivilized' areas in the West.[79] But there are two
wider aspects to what Pompeius did which are novel and distinctive. One is the scale and systematic nature of his territorial
settlement, covering a huge area (and one, of course, that
extended well beyond his original commission under the
Manilian law to deal with Mithradates) but at the same
time showing the attention to detail necessary for a lasting
arrangement. No other province was the target of a comparable
strategy of urbanization. Second, and perhaps more important,
is the fact that Pompeius made these arrangements himself: he
did not wait for a senatorial commission to come out and over-
see the administration of newly captured territory.[80] Although

Sherwin-White, *The Letters of Pliny* (Oxford: Oxford Univ. Press, 1966),
669–70; A. J. Marshall, 'Pompey's Organization of Bithynia-Pontus: Two
Neglected Texts', *JRS* 58 (1968), 103–9.

[77] Appian, *Mith.* 96, 115; Strabo 14. 3. 3, 14. 5. 8.

[78] G. W. Bowersock, *Roman Arabia* (Cambridge, Mass.: Harvard Univ.
Press, 1983), 28–44; Jones, *Cities*, 255–60.

[79] D. C. Braund, *Rome and the Friendly King* (London: Croom Helm,
1984); J. Reynolds, 'Cities', in D. C. Braund (ed.), *The Administration of the
Roman Empire* (Exeter: Univ. of Exeter, 1988), 15–51. On city foundation in
the western provinces, see Woolf, *Becoming Roman*, 24–47; A. Fear, *Rome and
Baetica: Urbanization in Southern Spain c.50 B.C–A.D. 150* (Oxford: Oxford
Univ. Press, 1996), 36–47.

[80] Under the terms of the Manilian law Pompeius had the power to make
peace and war and to form alliances (Appian, *Mith.* 97), an innovation in
formal terms, although in practice this happened regularly; but there is no
indication that he was also entrusted with the capacity to organize any territorial gains.

the institution of the commission of ten men was in principle simply advisory, its use had become standard practice by this period: one has to go back to the early second century to find examples of generals bringing substantial amounts of territory under Roman rule on their own.[81] Pompeius may or may not have had precedent in mind when he acted, and his motive may simply have been to protect himself and his achievements from his opponents in Rome. The effect, however, was to break down the distinction which had developed during the second century between the conquering commander, whose efforts are military, and the subsequent establishment of peace, which had been the task of the Senate. The model of a Roman commander, who not only defeats Rome's enemies but also determines the territorial shape of the victory, which Pompeius' actions establish, may not technically have been without precedent, but in practice must have appeared as a worrying extension of his power. His settlement, not surprisingly, met with fierce opposition in Rome from the Senate, which refused to ratify Pompeius' arrangements, and getting this ratification was Pompeius' motive for joining the electoral compact of 60.[82] It had always been difficult for the Senate to control commanders while on campaign; Pompeius' settlement had the potential to increase the autonomy of *imperium*-holders even more by bringing what happened after the fighting under their control as well.

There is, however, no evidence that Pompeius intended his own actions to justify greater powers generally for *imperium*-holders. Indeed, another facet of Pompeius as a commander is the way in which he established himself as the sole holder of *imperium* in the very large areas in which he operated, maintaining control through a system of legates, who had no formal

[81] Tiberius Gracchus the Elder organized Hispania Citerior in 178 without recourse to advisers.

[82] Securing ratification of his settlement was the chief task of Pompeius' candidates for the consulship in both 61 (M. Pupius Piso) and 60 (L. Afranius), neither of whom had any success: see T. P. Wiseman, 'Caesar, Pompey and Rome, 59–50 B.C.', *CAH* 9, 2nd edn. (1994), 358–67. They faced vigorous opposition from Cato and Lucullus; in addition the Senate was preoccupied in this period with other matters, including the Bona Dea affair and attempts by *publicani* to renegotiate the Asian tax contracts. Unfortunately there is little evidence to show the sorts of arguments which were used to block ratification.

authority independent of Pompeius' and yet were allowed to operate with considerable autonomy. Under the terms of the *lex Gabinia* for the campaign against the pirates he was given fifteen legates, and later twenty, each with praetorian *imperium*, and by dividing up the Mediterranean between them he was able to exploit delegation within a unified command in order to deal with the pirates with what seemed to his contemporaries extraordinary speed;[83] by so doing he demonstrated the merit of one big command in dealing with a Mediterranean-wide problem which had notoriously resisted solution by holders of more limited *imperium*.[84] Although the campaign against Mithradates did not pose similar logistical problems, Pompeius retained the same number of legates under the terms of the Manilian law and this in practice transformed the scope of his activities. In particular, legates began the intervention in Syria and Judaea in 65 or possibly as early as 66, well before Pompeius' own arrival on the scene and while he was still occupied much further north.[85]

In the case of Pompeius' command to deal with the corn supply in the years following 57, which again gave him fifteen legates, the evidence is too scanty to determine to what extent he was adopting an integrated approach;[86] but in 55 he took the use of legates to what his earlier strategy made seem the logical conclusion, that is as a substitute for the *imperium*-holder instead of a supplement. Under the terms of the *lex Trebonia*, Pompeius received both Spanish provinces, but did not go out to them himself and immediately sent Afranius and Petreius as his legates.[87]

The final area in which Pompeius' actions suggest a distinctive view of Rome's empire and its administration is the actual

---

[83] The most detailed description of the division of the Mediterranean into areas under separate legates is in Florus (3. 6), though erratic: see further Ormerod, *Piracy*, 233–41.

[84] Cf. the argument Dio ascribes to Catulus (36. 35. 2–36. 4): the Mediterranean is too large for a single commander, so the campaign against the pirates should be divided up between a number of commanders. See further, Sect. 3.1 above.

[85] Josephus, *BJ* 1. 125–32; E. Badian, 'The Early Career of A. Gabinius (cos. 58 B.C.)', *Philologus*, 103 (1959), 87–99.

[86] Rickman, *Corn Supply*, 55–8; Garnsey, *Famine and Food Supply*, 201.

[87] *MRR* 2. 220.

holding of *imperium*. This is most obvious in the legislation which he initiated as consul in 55 and 52, but an important context is provided by his own career: he was notable for holding *imperium* without being a magistrate, and thus provides a new model of how the military commander might relate to the organs of government.

Although the holding of *imperium* did not depend formally on office-holding, but followed from a *lex curiata* and the taking of auspices,[88] *imperium* in the middle Republic was almost always preceded by a magistracy. Exceptions were fairly rare, authorized by a popular assembly or by the Senate, and the men who received *imperium* had already held a magistracy, usually the consulship: the appointment of Scipio Africanus to proconsular *imperium* in 210, having held only the aedileship, is remarkable.[89]

However, in 83 Pompeius raised an army on his own authority in Picenum, relying on his father's connections in that area, and marched with it to join Sulla. He was at this point not only a *priuatus*, and only 22 or 23, but also had never held any elected office. His meeting with Sulla was the occasion for the anecdote in Plutarch (*Pomp.* 8. 2–4) describing how Sulla replied to Pompeius' salutation of him as Imperator by calling Pompeius himself *imperator*. An *imperator* must have *imperium*; but was Sulla bestowing *imperium* or recognizing that it already existed? No *lex curiata* had been passed on Pompeius' behalf;

[88] See Richardson, '*Imperium Romanum*', 1–9, esp. 2–4; 'Although closely associated with the elected magistrates, it was not election by the *comitia centuriata* which gave the consul or the praetor his *imperium*. Election had to be followed by the curious formality of the *lex curiata*, passed in the late republic by a vestigial assembly consisting of thirty lictors, as a result of which the magistrate was given the right to take the auspices.'

[89] The case of Scipio was repeated in 206, when L. Cornelius Lentulus, who had not even held the aedileship, was appointed as proconsul in Spain, where he remained until 200; his successors, Cn. Cornelius Blasio and Lucius Stertinius, were appointed by plebiscite and similarly inexperienced. It was not until 197 that the Spains became regular praetorian provinces: see Richardson, *Hispaniae*. The only subsequent comparable case is L. Oppius Salinator, who received *imperium* by decree of the Senate, in 192, to command the fleet in Sicily: he had been plebeian aedile the previous year. See Livy 35. 23. 6–7; 24. 6; W. F. Jashemski, *The Origins and History of the Proconsular and Propraetorian Imperium to 27 B.C.* (Chicago: Univ. of Chicago Press, 1950), 40–1.

he might have asserted his own authority over his army by taking the auspices at the beginning of the campaign, or he might only have done so once Sulla had recognized his independent command. At any rate, Pompeius could not be said to hold *imperium* in any constitutional sense until Sulla took control of Rome late in 82; yet he was exercising all the functions of a commander with *imperium* during the campaign.

This is the most striking anomaly in Pompeius' career, because there could be absolutely no grounds for someone to assume *imperium* for themselves. Even with Sulla's authorization Pompeius' position was extremely questionable, and until the meeting with Sulla Pompeius was in effect a *hostis*.[90] Subsequent grants of *imperium* to Pompeius were authorized by assembly or Senate, though his commands continue to be independent of his office-holding until 55. Thus, he chose not to take a provincial command after his consulship in 70,[91] but was granted *imperium* in 67 under the *lex Gabinia* to deal with the pirates and again in 66 under the *lex Manilia* to attack Mithradates[92] and in 57 *imperium* for five years in order to sort out the corn supply. Even in 55, when he was consul, the command he received in Spain was innovative: not by this stage through being the result of a popular law (though it was, as was Crassus' command, allotted through the *lex Trebonia*), but because he operated the command through legates and remained himself in Italy. The justification he offered for this was, according to Dio, that his continuing responsibility for the corn supply meant that he needed to be in touch with events in Rome (Dio. 39. 39. 4). Finally, in 52 he was appointed to the position of sole consul, and held it for some five months before overseeing the appointment of a colleague.[93]

---

[90] Dio (fr. 107) says that he planned at first to use his army 'to do something notable on his own' (ἐλλόγιμον τι πρᾶξαι καθ' ἑαυτόν) before setting off to join Sulla. Crassus also raised troops on his own account without holding *imperium* when Sulla arrived in Italy; the difference between the two is not in their actions, but in Sulla's response: Sulla did not recognize Crassus as an independent commander (cf. Plut. *Crassus* 6. 5–6).

[91] Gelzer, *Pompeius*, 64; cf. Velleius 2. 31.

[92] See Sect. 3.1 above.

[93] Asconius 34–6, esp. end of 35–6: 'Meanwhile word was spreading that Gnaeus Pompeius should be appointed dictator and that that was the only way that the country's problems could be settled; and so it seemed safer to the opti-

Up to this point, Pompeius had benefited from increasing flexibility in how *imperium* could be conferred and held. Others—Caesar and Crassus above all—had also benefited; what is distinctive about Pompeius is the way in which he sidestepped the pattern of office followed by provincial command so completely. It is noticeable that the one time he did not take up a command was after his first consulship. Velleius approves;[94] but the reason was surely not laudable self-restraint, but the absence of a suitable challenge. Pompeius did not want to blot his record by an undistinguished command (and presumably this was also Crassus' motive in returning to private life at the same time). The military commands which he did hold were one-off posts, designed specifically to a particular job; it is noticeable that even in the case of the command against Mithradates, where the creation of a special post was, arguably, unnecessary, Cicero works hard to create the impression that there is a crisis and that Pompeius uniquely embodies the qualities necessary to resolve it. All this is well known, and the intepretative pattern which can be developed from it: Pompeius' aspiration to a special place within the republican constitution helping to create, through the precedent he created of special commands, the conditions in which Caesar could destroy the Republic.[95] But what is important for this inquiry is not simply that Pompeius' career reinforced the sense that annual or biennial governorships of limited areas were not the most effective way to administer the Republic's territory,

mates to appoint him as consul without a colleague. When the matter was discussed in the Senate, a senatorial decree was passed on the motion of Marcus Bibulus and Pompeius was made consul by the *interrex* Servius Sulpicius, four days before 1 March in the intercalary month, and immediately took up office' (inter haec cum crebresceret rumor Cn. Pompeium creari dictatorem oportere neque aliter mala ciuitatis sedari posse, uisum est optimatibus tutius esse eum consulem sine collega creari, et cum tractata ea res esset in senatu, facto in M. Bibuli sententiam S.C. Pompeius ab interrege Seruio Sulpicio V. Kal. Mart. mense intercalario consul creatus est statimque consulatum iniit).

[94] Vell. 2. 31: 'qui [sc. Pompeius] cum consul perquam laudabiliter iurasset se in nullam prouinciam ex eo magistratu iturum idque seruasset'.

[95] E. Meyer, *Caesars Monarchie und das Principat des Pompejus: innere Geschichte Roms von 66 bis 44 v. Chr.* (Stuttgart: Cotta, 1918); A. E. R. Boak, 'The Extraordinary Commands from 80 to 48 B.C.', *American Historical Review*, 24 (1918), 1–25. Pompeius' famous *dissimulatio* is more usefully seen as a strategy developed to obscure his ambition than as a trait of character.

but also that he innovated in more ways than the holding of commands extended in terms of space and time.

One of the innovations was his legislation in 52, during his third consulship, which radically altered how *imperium* was held.[96] This was a law which laid down that an interval of five years must elapse between holding a magistracy and being a provincial governor— which sent Cicero to Cilicia, Bibulus to Syria, and various nonentities to other destinations.[97] The legislation was not Pompeius' idea, but had originated as a senatorial decree the previous year, passed as an attempt to reduce the corruption and disorder surrounding elections by postponing the serious financial rewards of office-holding (Dio 40. 56. 1). And yet the implications were potentially much wider than that. The disjunction between office-holding in the domestic sphere and military operations abroad, between magistracy and *imperium*, which was always a formal possibility, and was a reality in the case above all of Pompeius, would now become a rule. Moreover, whereas Pompeius had received *imperium* without holding a magistracy—and in addition to the normal magistrates of a particular year who wished to take a province—now it would be a matter of magistrates not receiving immediate *imperium*. Indeed, holding of a magistracy in Rome would now become a prerequisite for, but not a guarantee of, a provincial command.

How this new dispensation would in practice have worked never fully became clear, because of the outbreak of the civil

[96] This law has often been seen as a move specifically against Caesar, making it much easier for the Senate to supersede him: for a discussion of earlier scholarship, see Gruen, *Last Generation*, 457–60 with 458 n. 34, for references; see also A. J. Marshall, 'The *Lex Pompeia de prouinciis* (52 B.C.) and Cicero's Imperium in 51–50 B.C.: Constitutional Aspects', *ANRW* i. 1 (1972), 887–921. I agree with Gruen's conclusion that the law should rather be seen as an attempt to reduce or eliminate electoral corruption and improve provincial government; but he seems to me to underestimate how radical the proposal was in its temporal divorce of office-holding and provincial government.

[97] Cicero, *ad Att.* 6. 1. 13; his claims to be surprised that the legislation affects him personally (*ad fam.* 3. 2. 1) should be taken with a pinch of salt, since his correspondent in this letter was the governor he was replacing, Appius Claudius Pulcher; since Appius presumably had hoped for a third profitable year in post, Cicero would be keen to avoid appearing complicit in his supersession.

war; but it could have had a transformative effect, far beyond
reducing the incentive for electoral corruption. As Caesar
argues in his *Civil War* (1. 85. 9), during a speech which he
presents himself as giving to the surrendering Pompeian commanders in Spain, the change would place power in different
hands; and he puts the law of 52 into the context of a sustained
campaign by Pompeius to weaken his, Caesar's, position:

There was no other reason [than to attack him] for sending six legions
to Spain or for raising a seventh there, or for preparing so many large
fleets and sending out experienced military commanders. None of this
was intended for the conquest of Spain or for the benefit of the
province: it has been at peace for a long time and needs no assistance.
All had been done to attack him; new kinds of command had been set
up against him, so that the same man could sit at the city gates and
control affairs in Rome and hold two extremely militarized provinces,
in absentia, for extended periods; the rights of magistrates had been
changed in an attack on him, so that men would be sent to provinces
not directly after their praetorship or consulship, as always was the
case earlier, but when chosen and approved by a small group; in the
assault on him the excuse of age did not work, and men who had been
tested in earlier wars were called out to command armies; in his case
alone the rule which always obtained for all generals was not observed,
that after successful campaigns they might return home and dismiss
their army, with a degree of honour or at least without disgrace.[98]

Caesar's 'small group', *pauci*, who would, he claims, be in
charge of the distribution of provinces is clearly to be understood as a reference to Pompeius. Is this plausible? I refer
above to the scholarly discussions which would indeed see
the law of 52 as a direct attack on Caesar, and while I would

---

[98] Caesar, *BC* 1. 85. 6–10: neque enim VI legiones alia de causa missas in
Hispaniam septimamque ibi conscriptam neque tot tantasque classis paratas
neque summissos duces rei militaris peritos. nihil horum ad pacandas
Hispanias, nihil ad usum prouinciae prouisum quae propter diuturnitatem
pacis nullum auxilium desiderarit. omnia haec iam pridem contra se parari;
in se noui generis imperia constitui, ut idem ad portas urbanis praesideat
rebus et duas bellicosissimas prouincias absens tot annos obtineat; in se iura
magistratuum commutari, ne ex praetura et consulatu, ut semper, sed per
paucos probati et electi in prouincia mittantur; in se aetatis excusationem
nihil ualere, quod superioribus bellis probati ad obtinendos exercitus
euocentur; in se uno non seruari quod sit omnibus datum semper imperatoribus, ut rebus feliciter gestis aut cum honore aliquo aut certe sine
ignominia domum reuertantur exercitumque dimittant.

be sceptical about this degree of *ad hominem* attack, it is
undoubtedly true that the law, in changing the whole process of
distributing provincial commands, might have advantaged
prominent figures within the Senate. Consuls and praetors
could no longer use the position they had as magistrates in
order to ensure a provincial command, even a specific command, but would be dependent on the Senate of five years later.
Individual ambition and imperial management would presumably have begun to interact in a different way; this law
would certainly have left room for the Senate to make strategic
decisions about the jobs which needed doing and then choose
specific individuals to do them. However unlikely in practice it
would have been for the frenzied competition of the 50s to have
dissipated into an environment of measured decision-making,
Pompeius' law certainly left open the possibility of provincial
governors being subordinate to the Senate and becoming military and administrative agents whom the Senate could deploy
as it judged best; and, should Pompeius have achieved his
ambition of pre-eminence within a senatorial system, then he
would have had influence over this aspect of senatorial government too.[99]

So, from one point of view the law of 52 would seem to allow
the whole system of provincial government to be flexible as it
had been at various points in Pompeius' career: potentially
opening the way to a system of provincial government in which
the military and administrative concerns of the *res publica* as a
whole could come before individual careers. And yet there is a
paradox embedded in the law: on the one hand, trying to make
general the ad hoc approach of Pompeius, but on the other, and
much more openly, trying to curb the pursuit of individual
ambition of which Pompeius was still in 52 the most striking
example. The paradox is in theory to be resolved by the Senate:
it would control the distribution of posts, and so while
Pompeius-like careers might be possible, they would become so
as a result of the deliberations of the Senate. In practice, of
course, one might doubt whether the new dispensation would
have worked so smoothly.

None the less, the legislation of 52 seems to address one of

[99] The similarities between the system abortively set up in 52 and
Augustus' provincial management are striking.

the two major problems of the late republican empire: how to manage such a large amount of territory without making room for dangerously destabilizing personal ambition. It is clear, too, that at some level it also had implications for the other big problem, how to control imperial administrators and stop misgovernment in the pursuit of private profit. The legislation's ostensible motive was to reduce electoral corruption, by removing the prospect of immediate reward to pay off the costs of electoral success; it would become more difficult to borrow, with no prospect of a return for five years, and with the risk that the potential governor would either die in the intervening period or not receive a particularly lucrative province. A possible consequence would be that the motives for profiteering while governor would, at least in theory, be reduced.[100]

Pompeius was, therefore, a thorough and competent administrator who produced in the East a lasting model of government. Both his military and administrative success derive in part from his ability, in practice, to remove the destabilizing factor of personal ambition from imperial administration: instead of a multitude of independent and autonomous commanders pursuing their own interests, legates subordinated to one command and one commander. But was there more to Pompeius' dealing with empire than a sure grasp of what was practically effective? Is it misleading to talk about a *conception* of empire, rather than an ability to exploit specific situations? The series of big commands—the pirates, Mithradates, the corn supply, Spain—could all be seen as attempts to accumulate power, in which the greater efficiency of the model of a supreme commander with legates came about not from any disinterested desire on Pompeius' part to improve the running of the empire but in order to improve his own position.[101] And the law of 52 was not originally Pompeius' idea, nor was its aim to alter the management of empire, but rather to control rampant corruption in elections: by sponsoring it Pompeius was indicating deference to the Senate and his intention of bringing

[100] Cf. Gelzer, *Caesar*, 232, who suggests that Cato may have made a specific appeal in relation to the *lex Pompeia* for probity.

[101] A recurrent feature of Pompeius' early career is the difficulties he had in co-operating with other commanders: note his strained relations with Crassus in the campaign against Spartacus, and with Metellus Creticus over the subjection of Crete. See above, Sect. 3.2.2.

order back to domestic politics, not engaging in a deliberate overhaul of how the empire was run.

All this does not, however, mean that Pompeius' actions were instinctive or the consequences unforeseen. While it is unconvincing to argue that his prime motivation was an altruistic desire to improve provincial government,[102] it is not improbable that Pompeius undertook a conscious pursuit of efficiency in the belief that efficient provincial government was the best way to improve his own position. And while the original intentions of the decree of the Senate in 53 on holding provinces may have been domestic, it is unlikely that the wider implications of the measure did not occur to Pompeius, and even that, as Caesar implied, he saw in it the possibility of extending his indirect control over all facets of imperial government.

Cato, Caesar, and Pompeius seem to have had such a variety of approaches to the problems of empire that it is not possible to produce a neat summary: indeed, one conclusion to be drawn is that very basic questions about how to run the empire were a source of intense debate at this period: Cicero's cautious, moralizing, and at times obtuse approach was not universal. And while he was not alone in thinking that a solution to the problems might be found in controlling and improving the behaviour of individuals, Pompeius also tried to build a system of imperial government which did not leave everything to the dubious probity of individual governors, or at least placed their freedom to act within much stricter limits.

---

[102] Pompeius did, of course, make large personal profits from exploiting the provincials: Shatzman, *Senatorial Wealth*, 389–93; cf. Cicero, *ad Att.* 6. 1. 3, on Pompeius' loan to Ariobarzanes, which was producing 33 talents (HS 792,000) *a month*, and that did not cover the monthly interest completely.

Epilogue: the limits of oratory?

CICERO'S imperial oratory provides just one of a number of competing approaches to empire that were being proposed or acted out in the late Republic: Caesar, Pompeius, Cato, and even Cicero himself in his more esoteric writing provided different assessments and solutions. The essential points about Cicero's *rhetorical* view of empire are its avoidance of problems and its 'great man' presentation of events. Morally upright Romans are the answer, and the whole answer.

It is easy to criticize Cicero's myopia, which, as I argued in Chapter 5, is at least in part deliberate. His reluctance to challenge the status quo concerning the position of governors in their provinces (despite his personal probity) can be regarded as regrettable; he is even more vulnerable to attack on the basis of his participation in the development and extension of special commands, the consequences of which, in terms of the end of republican government, were much more striking. Whatever one's view of the desirability or otherwise of the progression from oligarchy to monarchy, it is quite clear that Cicero was unwittingly colluding in the destruction of the system under which he had flourished and which he prized so highly. (And it is worth noting that Cicero also took the wrong side, as it were, over the land distributions, a highly pertinent matter inasmuch as the weakening of soldiers' loyalty to the state is as important a factor in the civil wars as is the accumulation of power of their leaders.)

This conclusion is valid, even if the precise importance of the two relevant speeches, *de imperio Cn. Pompei* and *de prouinciis consularibus*, is debatable. As I argued, the former was by no means a decisive contribution to the debate on the Manilian law: the outcome of the vote was probably already clear, and Cicero is giving his support largely so that he can be seen to give his support. Pompeius had more to offer Cicero, in 66, than

Cicero did Pompeius. The effect of *de prouinciis consularibus* is more difficult to determine; Cicero was only half successful in terms of which provinces the Senate nominated as consular, and while his intervention on Caesar's behalf was unexpected and startling, there is no sign that Caesar's position in Gaul would have been in the slightest danger had Cicero remained silent.[1] And yet, Cicero did deliver these speeches and produce written versions of both: as the considered public pronouncements of a senior politician (and highly persuasive speaker and writer) and one, moreover, of conservative inclinations, one should not underestimate their importance in legitimating and rendering safe extraordinary commands among the elite. One must trace a careful path between treating Cicero's speeches too seriously, because little else survives, and dismissing them if their immediate practical importance seems limited.

One can pursue the question of how successful Cicero was as an orator further. The general assumption is that he was extremely successful: a conclusion based on the quality of his surviving speeches, his self-presentation as an orator (above all through his rhetorical treatises), and, perhaps most importantly, the success of his career as a politician: as he had no other political capital, his speaking *must* have been good. The unsuccessful patches of his career are the result, so the consensus goes, of inept political judgements rather than a failure at speaking (with the exception of the *pro Milone*). I do not want to challenge that judgement on the oratory directly here (though I do wonder whether we are seduced by Cicero, particularly in the *Brutus*, into ignoring other speakers unduly, particularly his younger contemporaries such as Calvus); but some rather different conclusions can be drawn.

I would suggest that Cicero's reliance on oratory actually *restricts* what he can say: that his brilliance is not accompanied by freedom. On each occasion that Cicero spoke in public, he put his position into jeopardy. In general terms, a bad performance would dent his reputation, and consequently his influence and power; more specifically, he might say things that could alienate parts of his audience. Stalwart resistance, for example, to the tax farmers' demands for a recalculation of their payments to the Treasury in 60 would have led to a rapid

[1] Cf. *ad fam.* 1. 7. 10.

diminution of Cicero's popularity with them. Cicero expresses the view that their demands are pretty shameless, *impudentius* (*ad Att.* 2. 1. 8), but he deplores Cato's resistance; he does so on the grounds that he is threatening the *concordia ordinum*, but it would have been foolish for Cicero to emulate Cato on personal grounds too. Indeed, one can speculate how far Cicero's policy of *concordia ordinum* and *otium cum dignitate* can be linked with his own career as an oratorical statesman, a strategy that required the widest possible coalition to be successful.

Cicero is constrained, then, by the exigencies of relying so heavily on oratory to create the agreeably unproblematic parallel universe that we find in the speeches on empire, where the only thing necessary for good provincial government is the probity of the governor, where Roman citizenship is extended only to individuals who have deserved it (such as Greek poets who participate wholeheartedly in spreading the praise of imperial Rome), and where it is safe to grant *imperium* for extended periods and accompanied by substantial resources because the return in imperial expansion is high and the commanders themselves are dutiful servants of the *res publica*. Inhabiting this universe allows Cicero to steer a course between the demands of his public reputation (and open approval of provincial extortion was not acceptable) and his need for good relations with the *publicani*; to fulfil obligations to powerful men by protecting their protégés while not approving of extending the franchise; and, above all, to make convincing to his audiences the positions of Pompeius and then of Caesar, since only thereby could he maintain his position as Cicero. This latter is of course the key point; Cicero did indeed try to resist the coalition of Pompeius and Caesar, and failed.

Cicero's rhetoric of empire reveals, then, his weaknesses; not weaknesses of judgement, but weaknesses of tools. But this statement needs to be refined a bit more. As it stands, it simply reaffirms the familiar point that the sword overpowered the word; that Cicero could try his hardest, but in the end men in command of soldiers won. I would contend that Cicero's career, on its own, does not quite prove this: that we need to take into account the limitations that Cicero himself put on what he said, because of a belief that if he did otherwise he would not have a political career. It would be valuable to have a systematic study of the ways in which other politicians used oratory in the late Republic: what they could say, the extent to which they could rely on public speaking alone, and their effectiveness. Was the experience of Cato, who caused wide offence and, ultimately, failed at the polls, the only alternative? How far did Clodius complement his inspired recourse to violence with a capacity to mobilize the people at the *contio*? In short, was Cicero's caution justified, and oratory, despite its prominent formal position within the workings of the Roman republican constitution, ultimately a broken reed?

These are not questions I propose to address here; but light may indirectly be thrown on them by a final example of Cicero the imperial politician, in relation to that cause célèbre of the 50s, the restoration of Ptolemy Auletes to his Egyptian throne.[2] Cicero was involved in the complex series of events in two ways. He participated in the debates in the Senate about how Ptolemy should be restored and who should do it, and he also spoke in a number of trials that arose from the situation.

The evidence for Cicero's contribution to senatorial debates comes primarily from the series of letters to Lentulus Spinther (*ad fam.* 1. 1–9), then governor of Cilicia, who had been instructed by senatorial decree to restore Ptolemy in the autumn of 57. The situation was, however, becoming more complicated: Ptolemy and various of Pompeius' supporters wanted Pompeius to have the command, even though he maintained, publicly at least, his support for Spinther; and the tribune Gaius Cato had complicated matters by publicizing a passage of the Sibylline oracles which seemed to forbid any intervention with a multitude, πλήθει (Dio 39. 15. 2). Spinther had been prominent in securing Cicero's return from exile, and Cicero, in these letters, presents his continuing support for Spinther over the Egyptian command as an act of gratitude: this involved, however, resisting a number of other scenarios. The Senate accepted overwhelmingly Gaius Cato's interpretation of the oracle, and there was intense debate in January 56 concerning what course of action which did not involve an army should be followed. Cicero, with Hortensius and Terentius Varro, proposed that the responsibility should still

---

[2] For a summary of the background, see Wiseman, 'Caesar, Pompey and Rome', 391–2.

lie with Spinther, though he was not to use his army, and Cicero spoke at length (*ad fam.* 1. 2. 1, *multa uerba fecimus*) in the Senate on 13 January, and contributed to the meeting on the 14th and possibly to the one on the 15th as well. None the less, the grouping to which he belonged did not succeed; the debates were talked out, a period of comitial days followed, the tribune Cato put forward in February a law to have Spinther recalled, and when eventually the Senate did vote on the matter it supported the motion of Servilius Isauricus, which was to do nothing—and this in turn was immediately vetoed.

As far as Cicero is concerned, the episode can be used to illustrate his weakness as a politician; however good his speech on 13 January (and it was not one he chose to publish, although he praises its effectiveness when writing to Spinther (*ad fam.* 1. 2. 1)), it did not convince the consuls, who supervised the filibusters; and Cicero himself admits that his influence in the matter is diminished by his obligation to Spinther (*ad fam.* 1. 1. 4). Cicero could not command a sufficiently broad consensus of senatorial opinion, one might argue. But, it is important to note that *no one* could, and in the end the Senate voted to do nothing. Indeed, one could argue that in this affair the Senate was pursuing the most sensible line of action available; by welcoming so enthusiastically the opportunity to kick the whole issue into touch which the Sibylline oracle provided, and then refusing to countenance the possibility of interference even without military force, it had blocked the possibility of any one commander gaining substantial and destabilizing military glory. The problem remained of how to put senatorial decisions into practice in the field; but what is interesting is the extent to which the Senate was successful. Spinther was deterred from action (despite an encouraging letter from Cicero, arguing that, provided he was successful, he would get away with action in Egypt (*ad fam.* 1. 7. 4–6)) and Gabinius, who did take on the task with notable efficiency in 55, had to encourage him a letter from his patron Pompeius, by then consul, as well as the prospect of 10,000 talents from a grateful Ptolemy to urge him on. Moreover, Gabinius was prosecuted on his return to Rome, and when the charge of *maiestas* failed to stick he was eventually condemned for extortion.

Gabinius' trials bring us to Cicero's other role, which is as a defence advocate. On four occasions he defended men involved in the affair. In the spring of 56 he defended first Asicius and Caelius, who were accused of involvement in the murder of a member of the embassy which had come from Alexandria to argue against the restoration of Ptolemy (though in Caelius' case a number of other charges were also involved); and late in 54 he very reluctantly defended Gabinius on *repetundae* charges, and later Rabirius Postumus in a related case. The defence of Gabinius was particularly humiliating for Cicero, since he had only just been dissuaded from *prosecuting* Gabinius at his *maiestas* trial, and had given evidence against him; it would have been clear to everyone that he had crumbled in the face of pressure from Pompeius: the fact that Gabinius was condemned only made matters worse. The defence of Rabirius, a protégé of Caesar, was also an indication of Cicero's dependence on the two; and while his defence of Caelius can be explained simply by the friendship between the two men (not to mention the opportunity to attack Clodius), the most probable explanation for his defence of Asicius is that Pompeius asked him to undertake it.

The forensic aspect demonstrates how oratory was not always under Cicero's command, but instead came to control him: in three of the four cases, Cicero is acting under pressure from Pompeius, and, so far from being opportunities to augment his reputation, could seriously weaken it. Even if he were successful—and both Asicius and Rabirius Postumus were acquitted—the fact of his speaking was a demonstration that he was not entirely free, and the Gabinius trial was clearly a disaster.[3] Cicero's forensic brilliance made him a valuable tool: it is noticeable that, although he is not very active in the Senate after the consulship of Pompeius and Crassus in 55, he is extremely busy in the courts defending the friends and allies of Pompeius and Caesar.[4]

The discussion may seem to be moving rather far from

[3] The protestations at *Rab. Post.* 32–3 are revealing, and see also C. Klodt, *Ciceros Rede pro Rabirio Postumo: Einleitung und Kommentar* (Stuttgart: Teubner, 1992), ad loc.

[4] In addition to the trials of Gabinius and Rabirius, Cicero defended Balbus, L. Caninius Gallus, C. Messius, and P. Vatinius: all were connected either with Pompeius or with Caesar.

Cicero's rhetoric of empire, but his involvement in the Ptolemy affair is not, I would argue, without relevance for this study. At the basic level, it demonstrates how important it was for senior politicians to participate in imperial matters. Cicero's summary of the senatorial debate for Spinther (*ad fam.* 1. 1. 3) systematically lists the position of every consular; and while there was more freedom whether or not to speak in the courts or before the people, it was generally the case that Cicero, as a rising and then as an established political figure, needed, if he was to maintain his authority, to contribute and be seen to contribute to the ongoing debate about the nature of power, both of the state and of its magistrates. In relation to the Ptolemy affair, Cicero was unable to persuade the Senate to follow his advice (and this failure may explain why he did not publish a version of what he said on 13 January) but none the less he had to take some sort of stance. The distinction that I set up earlier in this book between *what* Cicero says and the *identity* he assumes to say it—that is, between Chapters 1–3 and Chapter 4—is in fact to be treated with caution: it may be a useful method of approaching the speeches, but ultimately Cicero's authority derived not only from his self-presentation and skill in speaking but from the content of his speeches too. This statement might seem painfully obvious: but if this is the case, then what he said is central to how he operated as a politician.

A second point which the Ptolemy affair brings out is Cicero's weakness. He was unable in this case to get things done, that is to secure Spinther's position as restorer of Ptolemy, and his involvement in the various trials highlight his loss of independence after May of 56, the point at which he was forced to accept the ascendency of Pompeius and Caesar. Oratory, quite clearly, was not enough, even when combined with the authority of a senior consular; and indeed becomes a symbol of his failure, when Pompeius persistently demanded his services as an advocate. But the response should not be to dismiss oratory. The question, rather, is to determine what could be accomplished by oratory in the late Republic: how good was Cicero in exploiting this medium, and how did it relate to the many other ways of getting things done?

These two observations—the need to participate, and the limits of oratory—can be applied to the whole range of Cicero's oratory, not simply that concerned with imperial problems. I want to conclude with a final pointer provided by the Ptolemy affair, which does relate more closely to the subject of this study. Cicero's response to the problem—his support for Spinther—indicates that he regarded it as perfectly legitimate to use the empire to forward individual ambitions, provided, of course, that they belonged to the right people. That in this case the ambition is that of someone generally regarded as an optimate should not obscure the point; and it is interesting to speculate what line Cicero would have followed had he not been under an obligation to Spinther. Of course individual ambition was the motor of Rome's imperial expansion, and Spinther's aspirations were supported by precedent; and he acknowledged senatorial authority, and did not intervene in Egypt. But although Cicero's stance in this case had no effects, it is the same attitude as the one which colluded in the efforts of Caesar and Pompeius to entrench their positions. However, rather than simply condemn Cicero for his failure to see new dangers in traditional patterns of behaviour, it is more interesting to ask *why* he pursued lines of action that were eventually so destructive; and I hope that even if this book has not suggested fully satisfactory answers it has at least demonstrated that any answer must take Cicero's oratory seriously.

Bibliography

A few works which are mentioned only once in the text are not included here.

ACHARD, G., *Pratique rhétorique et idéologie politique dans les discours 'optimates' de Cicéron* (Leiden: *Mnemosyne* suppl. 68, 1981).

ADAMIETZ, J., M. *Tullius Cicero Pro Murena* (Darmstadt: Wissenschaftliche Buchgesellschaft, 1989).

ALBERT, S., *Bellum Iustum* (Kallmünz: Lassleben, 1980).

ALCOCK, S. E., *Graecia Capta: The Landscapes of Roman Greece* (Cambridge: Cambridge University Press, 1993).

ALEXANDER, M. C., *Trials in the Late Roman Republic, 149 BC to 50 BC* (Toronto: University of Toronto Press, 1990).

ALFÖLDI, A., *Oktavians Aufstieg zur Macht* (Bonn: Habelt, 1976).

ANGELINI, V., 'Riflessioni sull'orazione pro L. Cornelio Balbo', *Athenaeum*, 68 (1980), 360–70.

ASTIN, A. E., *Cato the Censor* (Oxford: Oxford University Press, 1978).

BADIAN, E., 'P. Decius P.f. Subulo' *JRS* 46 (1956), 91–6.

——*Foreign Clientelae* (Oxford: Oxford University Press, 1958).

——'The Early Career of A. Gabinius (cos. 58 B.C.)', *Philologus*, 103 (1959), 87–99.

——'Waiting for Sulla', *JRS* 52 (1962), 47–61.

——'M. Porcius Cato and the Annexation and Early Administration of Cyprus', *JRS* 55 (1965), 110–21.

——*Publicans and Sinners* (Oxford: Blackwell, 1972).

——'Marius' Villas: The Testimony of the Slave and the Knave', *JRS* 63 (1973), 121–32.

BALSDON, J. P. V. D., 'Sulla Felix', *JRS* 41 (1951), 1–10.

——*Romans and Aliens* (London: Duckworth, 1979).

BEARD, M., 'The Roman and the Foreign: The Cult of the "Great Mother" in Imperial Rome', in N. Thomas and C. Humphrey (eds.), *Shamanism, History and the State* (Ann Arbor: University of Michigan Press, 1994), 164–90.

——NORTH, J., and PRICE, S., *Religions of Rome*, vol. 1 (Cambridge: Cambridge University Press, 1998).

BELL, A. J. E., 'Cicero and the Spectacle of Power', *JRS* 87 (1997), 1–22.

BERGER, D., *Cicero als Erzähler: forensische und literarische Strategien in den Gerichtsreden* (Frankfurt: Lang, 1978).

BERRY, D. H., *Cicero, Pro P. Sulla oratio* (Cambridge: Cambridge University Press 1996).

BRAUND, D. C., 'Gabinius, Caesar, and the *publicani* of Judaea', *Klio*, 65 (1983), 241–4.

—— *Rome and the Friendly King* (London: Croom Helm, 1984).

—— 'The Politics of Catullus 10: Memmius, Caesar and the Bithynians', *Hermathena*, 160 (1996), 45–57.

—— '*Cohors*: The Governor and his Entourage in the Self-Image of the Roman Republic', in R. Laurence and J. Berry (eds.), *Cultural Identity in the Roman Empire* (London: Routledge, 1998), 10–24.

BRUNT, P. A., *Italian Manpower* (Oxford: Oxford University Press, 1971).

—— 'The Romanization of the Local Ruling Classes in the Roman Empire', in D. M. Pippidi (ed.), *Assimilation et résistance à la culture gréco-romaine dans le monde ancien* (Bucharest: Editura Academiei, 1976), 161–73; repr. in Brunt, *Roman Imperial Themes* (Oxford: Oxford University Press, 1990), 267–81.

—— '*Laus Imperii*', in P. D. A. Garnsey and C. R. Whittaker (eds.), *Imperialism in the Ancient World* (Cambridge: Cambridge University Press, 1978), 159–91; repr. in Brunt, *Roman Imperial Themes* (Oxford: Oxford University Press, 1990), 288–323.

—— 'The Legal Essue in Cicero *pro Balbo*', *CQ* 32 (1982), 136–47.

—— '*Nobilitas* and *Novitas*', *JRS* 72 (1982), 1–17.

—— 'The Fall of the Roman Republic', in Brunt, *The Fall of the Roman Republic and Related Essays* (Oxford: Oxford University Press, 1988), 1–92.

—— 'Italian Aims at the Time of the Social War', ibid. 93–143.

BUCHHEIT, V., 'Chrysogonus als Tyrann in Ciceros Rede für Roscius aus Ameria', *Chiron*, 5 (1975), 193–211.

BURCKHARDT, L., 'The Political Elite of the Roman Republic: Comments on Recent Discussion of the Concepts *nobilitas* and *homo novus*', *Historia*, 39 (1990), 77–99.

BUTLER, H. E., and CARY, M., *De prouinciis consularibus* (Oxford: Oxford University Press, 1924).

CERUTTI, S. M., *Cicero's Accretive Style: Rhetorical Strategies in the Exordia of the Judicial Speeches* (Lanham: University Press of America, 1996).

CHAMPEAUX, J., *Fortuna: Recherches sur le culte de la Fortune à Rome et dans le monde romain des origines à la mort de César*, vol. 2 (Rome and Paris: Collection de l'École française de Rome 64, 1987).

CLARKE, K., *Between Geography and History: Hellenistic Constructions of the Roman World* (Oxford: Oxford University Press, 1999).

CLASSEN, C. J., 'Ciceros Kunst der Ueberredung', in W. Ludwig (ed.), *Rhétorique et éloquence chez Cicéron* (Geneva: Entretiens Hardt 28, 1982), 149–84.

——— *Recht – Rhetorik – Politik: Untersuchungen zu Ciceros rhetorischer Strategie* (Darmstadt: Wissenschaftliche Buchgesellschaft, 1985).

CLOUD, D., 'The Constitution and Public Criminal Law', *CAH* 9, 2nd edn. (1994), 491–530.

COARELLI, F., 'Architettura sacra e architettura privata nella tarda Repubblica', in *Architecture et société* (Paris and Rome: Collection de l'École française de Rome 66, 1983).

COLLARD, C., CROPP, M. J., and LEE, K. H., *Euripides: Selected Fragmentary Plays*, vol. 1 (Warminster: Aris and Phillips, 1995).

COMBÈS, R., *Imperator: Recherches sur l'emploi et la signification du titre d'imperator dans la Rome républicaine* (Paris: Presses universitaires de France, 1966).

CONNORS, C., 'Field and Forum: Culture and Agriculture in Roman Rhetoric', in W. J. Dominik (ed.), *Roman Eloquence: Rhetoric in Society and Literature* (London: Routledge, 1997), 71–89.

CORBEILL, A., *Controlling Laughter: Political Humour in the Late Republic* (Princeton: Princeton University Press, 1996).

CRAIG, C. P., 'Cato's Stoicism and the Understanding of Cicero's Speech for Murena', *TAPhA* 116 (1986), 229–39.

——— *Form as Argument in Cicero's Speeches: A Study of Dilemma* (Atlanta: Scholars Press, 1993).

CRAWFORD, J. W., *M. Tullius Cicero: The Fragmentary Orations* (Atlanta: Scholars Press, 1994).

CRAWFORD, M. H., 'Italy and Rome from Sulla to Augustus', *CAH* 10, 2nd edn. (1996), 414–33.

CROOK, J. A., *Law and Life of Rome* (London: Thames and Hudson, 1967).

DAMON, C., *The Mask of the Parasite: A Pathology of Roman Patronage* (Ann Arbor: University of Michigan Press, 1997).

DAVID, J.-M., *Le Patronat judiciaire au dernier siècle de la République romaine* (Rome: BEFAR 277, 1992).

DENNISTON, J. D., *Orationes Philippicae prima et secunda* (Oxford: Oxford University Press, 1926).

DE SOUZA, P., *Piracy in the Graeco-Roman World* (Cambridge: Cambridge University Press, 1999).

DÖBLER, C., *Politische Agitation und Öffentlichkeit in der späten Republik* (Frankfurt am Main: Lang, 1999).

DU MESNIL, A., *Ciceros Rede für Flaccus* (Leipzig, 1883).

DYCK, A. R., *A Commentary on Cicero, De Officiis* (Ann Arbor:

University of Michigan Press, 1996).

EDWARDS, C., *The Politics of Immorality in Ancient Rome* (Cambridge: Cambridge University Press, 1993).

EISENBERGER, H., 'Die Funktion des zweiten Hauptteils von Ciceros Rede für den Dichter Archias', *WS* 92, NS 13 (1979), 88–98.

EPSTEIN, D. F., *Personal Enmity in Roman Politics, 218–43 B.C.* (London: Croom Helm, 1987).

ERICSSON, H., 'Sulla Felix: Eine Wortstudie', *Eranos*, 41 (1943), 77–89.

ERSKINE, A., 'Money-Loving Romans', *Papers of the Leeds International Latin Seminar*, 9 (1996), 1–11.

FANTHAM, E., 'The Contexts and Occasions of Roman Public Rhetoric', in W. J. Dominik (ed.), *Roman Eloquence: Rhetoric in Society and Literature* (London: Routledge, 1997), 111–28.

FEAR, A. T., *Rome and Baetica: Urbanization in Southern Spain c.50 B.C.–A.D. 150* (Oxford: Oxford University Press, 1996).

FECHNER, D., *Untersuchungen zu Cassius Dios Sicht der Römischen Republik* (Hildesheim: Olms, 1986).

FEENEY, D. C., ' "Stat magni nominis umbra." Lucan on the greatness of Pompeius Magnus', *CQ* 36 (1986), 239–43.

——*Literature and Religion at Rome* (Cambridge: Cambridge University Press, 1998).

FEHRLE, R., *Cato Uticensis* (Darmstadt: Wissenschaftliche Buchgesellschaft, 1983).

FERRARY, J.-L., *Philhellénisme et impérialisme* (Rome: *BEFAR* 271, 1988).

FITZGERALD, W., *Slavery and the Roman Literary Imagination* (Cambridge: Cambridge University Press, 2000).

FUHRMANN, M., *Cicero and the Roman Republic*, trans. W. E. Yuill (Oxford: Blackwell, 1992).

GABBA, E., *Republican Rome, the Army and the Allies*, trans. P. J. Cuff (Oxford: Blackwell, 1976).

——*Aspetti culturali dell'imperialismo Romano* (Florence: Sansoni, 1993).

GALSTERER, H., *Herrschaft und Verwaltung im republikanischen Italien* (Munich: Beck, 1976).

GARNSEY, P., *Famine and Food Supply in the Graeco-Roman World* (Cambridge: Cambridge University Press, 1988).

GELZER, M., *Die Nobilität der römischen Republik* (Leipzig: Teubner, 1912).

——*Pompeius* (Munich: Bruckmann, 1949).

——'Cato Uticensis', in *Kleine Schriften*, vol. 2 (Wiesbaden: Steiner, 1963).

——*Caesar*, trans. P. Needham (Oxford: Blackwell, 1968).

GOLD, B. K., *Literary Patronage in Greece and Rome* (Chapel Hill: University of North Carolina Press, 1987).

GOTOFF, H. C., *Cicero's Elegant Style: An Analysis of the pro Archia* (Urbana: University of Illinois Press, 1979).

GOW, A. S. F., and PAGE, D. L., *The Greek Anthology: The Garland of Philip, and Some Contemporary Epigrams*, vol. 2 (Cambridge: Cambridge University Press, 1968).

GREEN, P., 'Caesar and Alexander: Aemulatio, Imitatio, Comparatio', *AJAH* 3 (1978), 1–26.

GRIFFIN, J., *Latin Poets and Roman Life* (London: Duckworth, 1985).

GRIFFIN, M. T., and ATKINS, E. M., *Cicero on Duties* (Cambridge: Cambridge University Press, 1991).

GRUBER, J., 'Cicero und das hellenistische Herrscherideal. Überlegungen zur Rede "De imperio Cn. Pompei"', *WS* 101, NS 22 (1988), 243–58.

GRUEN, E. S., 'The Trial of C. Antonius', *Latomus*, 32 (1973), 301–10.

——— *The Last Generation of the Roman Republic* (Berkeley: University of California Press, 1974).

——— *The Hellenistic World and the Coming of Rome*, 2 vols. (Berkeley: University of California Press, 1984).

——— *Culture and National Identity in Republican Rome* (Ithaca: Cornell University Press, 1992).

HABINEK, T. N., 'Ideology for an Empire in the Prefaces to Cicero's Dialogues', *Ramus*, 23 (1994), 55–67.

HALEY, S. P., 'Archias, Theophanes and Cicero: The Politics of the *Pro Archia*', *CB* 59 (1983), 1–4.

HALL, E. M., *Inventing the Barbarian* (Oxford: Oxford University Press, 1989).

HANDLEY, E. W., and REA, J., 'The Telephus of Euripides' (London: *BICS* suppl. 5, 1957).

HARRIS, W. V., *War and Imperialism in Republican Rome* (Oxford: Oxford University Press, 1979).

HAURY, A., *L'Ironie et l'humour chez Cicéron* (Leiden: E. J. Brill, 1955).

HEINZE, R., 'Auctoritas', *Hermes*, 60 (1925), 348–66; repr. in Heinze, *Vom Geist des Römertums*, ed. E. Burck (Leipzig: Teubner, 1938).

HELLEGOUARC'H, J., *Le Vocabulaire latin des relations et des partis politiques sous la république* (Paris: Les Belles Lettres, 1963).

HENDERSON, J. G. W., *Fighting for Rome: Poets and Caesars, History and Civil War* (Cambridge: Cambridge University Press, 1998).

HILLMAN, T. P., 'The Alleged *Inimicitiae* of Pompeius and Lucullus: 78–74', *CPh* 86 (1991), 315–18.

HOPKINS, K., and BURTON, G., 'Political Success in the Late

Republic', in Hopkins, *Death and Renewal* (Cambridge: Cambridge University Press, 1983), 31–119.

HUTCHINSON, G. O., *Cicero's Correspondence: A Literary Study* (Oxford: Oxford University Press, 1998).

JASHEMSKI, W. F., *The Origins and History of the Proconsular and Propraetorian Imperium to 27 B.C.* (Chicago: University of Chicago Press, 1950).

JEX-BLAKE, K., and SELLERS, E., *The Elder Pliny's Chapters on the History of Art* (London: Macmillan, 1896).

JONKERS, E. J., *Social and Economic Commentary on Cicero's De Imperio Cn. Pompei* (Leiden: Brill, 1959).

KALLET-MARX, R. M., *Hegemony to Empire: The Development of the Roman Imperium in the East from 148 to 62 B.C.* (Berkeley: University of California Press, 1995).

KLODT, C., *Ciceros Rede pro Rabirio Postumo: Einleitung und Kommentar* (Stuttgart: Teubner, 1992).

KNOX, P. E., *Ovid's Metamorphoses and the Traditions of Augustan Poetry* (Cambridge: PCPhS suppl. 11, 1986).

KRENKEL, W. A., '*Fellatio* and *Irrumatio*', *Wissenschaftliche Zeitschrift der Wilhelm-Pieck-Universität Rostock*, 29 (1980), 77–88.

KÜNZL, E., *Der Römische Triumph: Siegesfeiern im antiken Rom* (Munich: Beck, 1988).

LACEY, W. K., *Cicero and the End of the Roman Republic* (London: Hodder and Stoughton, 1978).

LASER, G., *Populo et scaenae serviendum est: Die Bedeutung der stadtischen Masse in der späten Römischen Republik* (Trier: Wissenschaftlicher Verlag Trier, 1997).

LAURENCE, R., and BERRY, J. (eds.), *Cultural Identity in the Roman Empire* (London: Routledge, 1998).

LEEMAN, A. D., 'The Technique of Persuasion in Cicero's *Pro Murena*', in W. Ludwig (ed.), *Rhétorique et éloquence chez Cicéron* (Geneva: Entretiens Hardt 28, 1982), 193–228.

LEVICK, B., 'Morals, Politics, and the Fall of the Roman Republic', *G&R* 29 (1982), 53–62.

LINTOTT, A. W., 'Imperial Expansion and Moral Decline in the Roman Republic', *Historia*, 21 (1972), 626–38.

—— 'The *Leges de Repetundis* and Associate Measures under the Republic', *ZRG* 98 (1981), 162–212.

—— *Imperium Romanum: Politics and Administration* (London: Routledge, 1993).

—— 'Dio and the History of the Late Republic', *ANRW* 2. 34. 3 (1997), 2497–523.

LONG, A. A., 'Cicero's Politics in *De officiis*', in A. Laks and M. Schofield (eds.), *Justice and Generosity: Studies in Hellenistic Social and Political Theory* (Cambridge: Cambridge University Press, 1995), 213–40.

LOUTSCH, C., *L'Exorde dans les discours de Cicéron* (Brussels: Collection Latomus 224, 1994).

LURIE, A., *The Language of Clothes*, 2nd edn. (London: Bloomsbury, 1992).

MACDOWELL, D. M., *Andokides: On the Mysteries* (Oxford: Oxford University Press, 1962).

MAGIE, D., *Roman Rule in Asia Minor*, 2 vols. (Princeton: Princeton University Press, 1950).

MANUWALD, B., *Cassius Dio und Augustus* (Wiesbaden: Steiner, 1979).

MARCONE, A., 'Il nuovo stile dell'uomo politico: Pompeo "princeps civilis" ', *Athenaeum* 78 (1990), 475–81.

MARSHALL, A. J., 'Romans under Chian Law', *GRBS* 10 (1969), 254–71.

MATTINGLY, D. J. (ed.), *Dialogues in Roman Imperialism* (*JRA* suppl. ser. 23, 1997).

MAY, J., *Trials of Character: The Eloquence of Ciceronian Ethos* (Chapel Hill: University of North Carolina Press, 1988).

MEIER, C., *Res publica amissa*, 2nd edn. (Frankfurt: Suhrkamp, 1980); 1st edn. (Wiesbaden: Steiner, 1966).

MICHEL, D., *Alexander als Vorbild für Pompeius, Caesar und Marcus Antonius: Archäologische Untersuchungen* (Brussels: Latomus, 1967).

MILLAR, F. G. B., 'Some Speeches in Cassius Dio', *MH* 18 (1961), 11–22.

—— *A Study of Cassius Dio* (Oxford: Oxford University Press, 1964).

—— 'The Political Character of the Classical Roman Republic, 200–151 B.C.', *JRS* 74 (1984), 1–19.

—— 'Politics, Persuasion and the People before the Social War (150–90 B.C.)', *JRS* 76 (1986), 1–11.

—— *The Crowd in Rome in the Late Republic* (Ann Arbor: University of Michigan Press, 1998).

MITCHELL, S., *Anatolia: Land, Men and Gods in Asia Minor*, 2 vols. (Oxford: Oxford University Press, 1993).

—— 'The Administration of Roman Asia from 133 BC to AD 250', in W. Eck, *Lokale Autonomie und römische Ordnungsmacht in den kaiserzeitlichen Provinzen vom 1. bis 3. Jahrhundert* (Munich: Oldenbourg, 1999), 17–46.

MITCHELL, T. N., *Cicero: The Ascending Years* (New Haven: Yale University Press, 1979).

—— *Cicero: The Senior Statesman* (New Haven: Yale University Press, 1991).

MOURITSEN, H., *Italian Unification* (London: *BICS* suppl. 70, 1998).

MURRAY, O., '*Peri Basileias:* Studies in the Justification of Monarchic Power' (D.Phil., Oxford University, 1970).

NARDUCCI, E., *Cicerone e l'eloquenza romana* (Rome and Bari: Laterza, 1997).

NICOLET, C., ' "Consul togatus": Remarques sur le vocabulaire politique de Cicéron et de Tite-Live', *REL* 38 (1960), 236–63.

——*L'Ordre Équestre à l'époque républicaine*, vol. 1: *Définitions juridiques et structures sociales* (Paris: *BEFAR* 207, 1966).

——(1974), *L'Ordre Équestre à l'époque républicaine*, vol. 2: *Prosopographie des chevaliers romains* (Paris: *BEFAR* 207, 1974).

——*The World of the Citizen in Republican Rome*, trans. P. S. Falla (London: Batsford, 1980).

NISBET, R. G. M., *In Pisonem* (Oxford: Oxford University Press, 1961).

——'The Orator and the Reader: Manipulation and Response in Cicero's *Fifth Verrine*', in T. Woodman and J. G. F. Powell (eds.), *Author and Audience in Latin Literature* (Cambridge: Cambridge University Press, 1992), 1–17; repr. in Nisbet, *Collected Papers on Latin Literature*, ed. S. J. Harrison (Oxford: Oxford University Press, 1995), 362–80.

——and HUBBARD, M., *A Commentary on Horace Odes, Book 2* (Oxford: Oxford University Press, 1978).

NOÈ, E., '*Cedat forum castris*: esercito e ascesa politica nella riflessione ciceroniana', *Athenaeum*, 83 (1995), 67–82.

NORTH, J. A., 'The Development of Roman Imperialism', *JRS* 71 (1981), 1–9.

OBER, J., *Mass and Elite in Democratic Athens* (Princeton: Princeton University Press, 1989).

OOST, S. I., 'Cato Uticensis and the Annexation of Cyprus', *CPh* 50 (1955), 98–109.

OOTEGHEM, J. VAN, *Pompée le Grand: Bâtisseur d'Empire* (Brussels: Académie Royale de Belgique, Mémoires 49, 1954).

ORMEROD, H. A., *Piracy in the Ancient World* (Liverpool: University Press of Liverpool, 1924).

PERELLI, L., *Il pensiero politico di Cicerone: tra filosofia greca e ideologica aristocratica romana* (Florence: La Nuova Italia, 1990).

PERNOT, L., *La Rhétorique de l'éloge dans le monde Gréco-Romain* (Paris: Institut d'Études Augustiniennes, 1993).

PETROCHILOS, N., *Roman Attitudes to the Greeks* (Athens: Ethnikon kai Kapodistriakon Panepistemion Athenon, 1974).

PIETILÄ-CASTRÉN, L., *Magnificentia Publica: The Victory Monuments of the Roman Generals in the Era of the Punic Wars* (Helsinki: Societas Scientiarum Fennica, 1987).

PINA POLO, F., *Contra Arma Verbis: der Redner vor dem Volk in der später römischen Republik*, trans E. Liess (Stuttgart: F. Steiner, 1996).

POHL, H., *Die römische Politik und die Piraterie im östlichen Mittelmeer vom 3. bis zum 1. Jh. v. Chr.* (Berlin: de Gruyter, 1993).

PORTER, W. M., 'Cicero's *Pro Archia* and the Responsibilities of Reading', *Rhetorica*, 8 (1990), 137–52.

POWELL, J. G. F., *Cicero: Cato Maior de senectute* (Cambridge: Cambridge University Press, 1988).

PURCELL, N., 'The City of Rome and the *plebs urbana* in the Late Republic', *CAH* 9, 2nd edn. (1994), 644–88.

RAWSON, E. D., 'Lucius Crassus and Cicero: The Formation of a Statesman', *PCPhS*, NS 17 (1971), 75–88; repr. in Rawson, *Roman Culture and Society: Collected Papers* (Oxford: Oxford University Press, 1991), 16–33.

—— *Cicero: A Portrait* (London: Allen Lane, 1975).

—— 'The Introduction of Logical Organization in Roman Prose Literature', *PBSR* 46 (1978), 12–34; repr. in Rawson, *Roman Culture and Society: Collected Papers* (Oxford: Oxford University Press, 1991), 324–51.

—— *Intellectual Life in the Late Roman Republic* (London: Duckworth, 1985).

REINHOLD, M., *History of Purple as a Status Symbol in Antiquity* (Brussels: Latomus, 1970).

REYNOLDS, J., 'Cities', in D. C. Braund (ed.), *The Administration of the Roman Empire* (Exeter: University of Exeter, 1988), 15–51.

RICH, J. W., 'Fear, Greed and Glory: The Causes of Roman War-Making in the Middle Republic', in J. W. Rich and G. Shipley (eds.), *War and Society in the Roman World* (London: Routledge, 1993).

RICHARDSON, J. S., *Hispaniae: Spain and the Development of Roman Imperialism* (Cambridge: Cambridge University Press, 1986).

—— '*Imperium Romanum*: Empire and the Language of Power', *JRS* 81 (1991), 1–9.

—— 'The Administration of the Empire', *CAH* 9, 2nd edn. (1994), 564–98.

RICKMAN, G., *The Corn Supply of Ancient Rome* (Oxford: Oxford University Press, 1980).

RIDLEY, R. T., 'The Extraordinary Commands of the Late Republic', *Historia*, 30 (1981), 280–97.

RIGGSBY, A. M., *Crime and Community in Ciceronian Rome* (Austin: University of Texas Press, 1999).

ROSE, P. W., 'Cicero and the Rhetoric of Imperialism: Putting the Politics back into Political Rhetoric', *Rhetorica*, 13 (1995), 359–99.

SAID, E. W., *Culture and Imperialism* (London: Chatto and Windus, 1993).

SCHNEIDER, W. C., *Vom Handeln der Römer* (Zurich and New York: Olms, 1998).

SCHUBART, W., 'Das hellenistische Königsideal nach Inschriften und Papyri', *Archiv für Papyrusforschung und verwandte Gebiete*, 12 (1937), 1–26; repr. in H. Kloft (ed.), *Ideologie und Herrschaft in der Antike* (Darmstadt: Wissenschaftliche Buchgesellschaft, 1979).

SEAGER, R., *Pompey: A Political Biography* (Oxford: Blackwell, 1979).

—— 'The Rise of Pompey', *CAH* 9, 2nd edn. (1994), 208–28.

SEBESTA, J. L., '*Tunica Ralla, Tunica Spissa*: The Colors and Textiles of Roman Costume', in J. L. Sebesta and L. Bonfante (eds.), *The World of Roman Costume* (Madison: University of Wisconsin Press, 1994), 65–76.

SEGAL, C., *Orpheus: The Myth of the Poet* (Baltimore: Johns Hopkins University Press, 1989).

SHACKLETON BAILEY, D. R., *Cicero's Letters to Atticus*, vol. 1 (Cambridge: Cambridge University Press, 1965).

—— *Cicero's Letters to Atticus*, vol. 3 (Cambridge: Cambridge University Press, 1968).

—— *Cicero* (London: Duckworth, 1971).

—— *Cicero: Epistulae ad Familiares*, vol. 1 (Cambridge: Cambridge University Press, 1977).

—— *Cicero: Epistulae ad Quintum Fratrem et M. Brutum* (Cambridge: Cambridge University Press, 1980).

SHATZMAN, I., *Senatorial Wealth and Roman Politics* (Brussels: Latomus, 1975).

SHERWIN-WHITE, A. N., *The Roman Citizenship*, 2nd edn. (Oxford: Oxford University Press, 1973).

—— *Roman Foreign Policy in the East, 168 B.C. to A.D. 1* (London: Duckworth, 1984).

SPIELVOGEL, J., *Amicitia und res publica* (Stuttgart: Franz Steiner Verlag, 1993).

STEINBY, E. M. (ed.), *Lexicon topographicum urbis Romae* (Rome: Quasar, 1993–).

STOCKTON, D. L., 'Cicero and the *Ager Campanus*', *TAPhA* 93 (1962), 471–89.

—— *Cicero: A Political Biography* (Oxford: Oxford University Press, 1971).

STROH, W., *Taxis und Taktik: Die advokatische Dispositionskunst in Ciceros Gerichtsreden* (Stuttgart: Teubner, 1975).

SWAIN, S., *Hellenism and Empire: Language, Classicism, and Power in the Greek World, AD 50–250* (Oxford: Oxford University Press, 1996).

SYME, R., *The Roman Revolution* (Oxford: Oxford University Press, 1939).

TATUM, W. J., *The Patrician Tribune: Publius Clodius Pulcher* (Chapel Hill: University of North Carolina Press, 1999).

TAYLOR, J. H., 'Political Motives in Cicero's Defense of Archias', *AJPh* 73 (1952), 62–70.

TREGGIARI, S., *Roman Freedmen during the Late Republic* (Oxford: Oxford University Press, 1969).

VANDERBROECK, P. J. J., *Popular Leadership and Collective Behaviour in the Late Roman Republic* (Amsterdam: Gieben, 1987).

VASALY, A., *Representations: Images of the World in Ciceronian Oratory* (Berkeley: University of California Press, 1993).

VERSNEL, H. S., *Triumphus: An Inquiry into the Origin, Development and Meaning of the Roman Triumph* (Leiden: Brill, 1970)

VON ALBRECHT, M., 'Das Prooemium von Ciceros Rede pro Archia poeta und das Problem der Zweckmässigkeit der *argumentatio extra causam*', *Gymnasium*, 76 (1969), 419–29.

VRETSKA, H., and VRETSKA, K., *Marcus Tullius Cicero: Pro Archia Poeta: Ein Zeugnis für den Kampf des Geistes um seine Anerkennung* (Darmstadt: Wissenschaftliche Buchgesellschaft, 1979).

WALBANK, F. W., *A Historical Commentary on Polybius*, vol. I (Oxford: Oxford University Press, 1957).

WATKINS, O. D., 'Caesar solus? Senatorial Support for the *lex Gabinia*', *Historia*, 36 (1987), 120–1.

WEBSTER, T. B. L., *Pro Flacco* (Oxford: Oxford University Press, 1931).

WEIPPERT, O., *Alexander-Imitatio und Römische Politik in Republikanischer Zeit* (Inaug. diss. Würzburg: Augsburg, 1972).

WELCH, K., and POWELL, A. (eds.), *Julius Caesar as Artful Reporter: The War Commentaries as Political Instruments* (London: Duckworth/Classical Press of Wales, 1998).

WILLIAMS, R. S., '*Rei publicae causa*: Gabinius' Defense of his Restoration of Ptolemy Auletes', *CJ* 81 (1985), 25–38.

WISEMAN, T. P., 'The Ambitions of Quintus Cicero', *JRS* 56 (1966), 108–15.

—— *New Men in the Roman Senate 139 B.C.–A.D. 14* (Oxford: Oxford University Press, 1971).

—— '*Pete nobiles amicos*: Poets and Patrons in Late Republican Rome', in B. K. Gold (ed.), *Literary and Artistic Patronage in Ancient Rome* (Austin: University of Texas Press, 1982), 28–34.

—— 'Caesar, Pompey and Rome, 59–50 B.C.', *CAH* 9, 2nd edn. (1994), 358–423.

WISSE, J., *Ethos and Pathos from Aristotle to Cicero* (Amsterdam: Hakkert, 1989).

WISTRAND, E., *Felicitas Imperatoria* (Göteborg: Acta Universitatis Gothoburgensis, 1987).

WOOD, N., *Cicero's Social and Political Thought* (Berkeley: University of California Press, 1988).

WOOLF, G., *Becoming Roman: The Origins of Provincial Civilisation in Gaul* (Cambridge: Cambridge University Press, 1998).

YAVETZ, Z., *Julius Caesar and his Public Image* (London: Thames and Hudson, 1983).

INDEX OF PASSAGES DISCUSSED

GENERAL INDEX

Roman citizens are listed under their *nomen*.

Segesta 34–5
Semiramis 50–1
C. Sempronius Gracchus 26
  n. 14, 129, 176
senatorial commissions 215–16
Senate, Roman 157–60, 216,
  223, 229–32
C. Sergius Catilina 53–4, 68,
  139, 168
  supporters 89
Q. Sertorius 100
P. Servilius Vatia Isauricus
  35–6, 230
Sibylline oracles 229–30
Sicily 145, 151
  see also Verres
Social War 7, 76, 155, 163–4,
  208–9
Spain 183, 219, 222
Sparta 54
Spartacus 24
Stoicism 101 n. 78, 170
Ser. Sulpicius Rufus 135, 170,
  172
Syracuse 26
Syria 181–3, 206, 221
  confused with Assyria 50
  organization as a Roman
    province 101, 215, 217
  Roman prejudice against
    inhabitants 51

taxation 129
tax-collectors 51–2, 130, 196–9,
  205, 227–8
Telephus 64–5
temperantia 133
M. Terentius Varro Lucullus
  80–1, 229
Tigranes 152–3, 215
Tigris 126
Timarchides 37–9, 40–3
trade 63

treasury, Roman 202–3
triumphs 207
M. Tullius Cicero, *passim*
  aedileship 28–9, 163–4
  auctoritas 110
  and brother Quintus 195
  and Caesar 187–8
  and *Catilinarians* 168–70
  Catilinarian conspiracy,
    opposition to 89–91
  in Cilicia 2–3, 197–202, 221
  consulship 171 –3
  and *de imperio Cn. Pompei*
    101, 173–81, 226–7
  and *de inuentione* 165–6
  de officiis 192–3
  and *de prou. cons.* 157, 181–9
  disinclination to leave Rome
    2–3, 163–5
  exile 2, 183
  interests in Greek culture
    46–7, 65–6
  and poetry 87–9
  praetorship 174–5
  and *pro Balbo* 109–10
  and *pro Murena* 136–9,
    170–3
  and *pro Roscio Amerino* 166
  quaestorship 2
  and restoration of Ptolemy
    Auletes 229–33
  self–presentation as an orator
    162–89
  and trial of Verres 22–3
Q. Tullius Cicero 184, 195–7
tyranny 34–5, 51

uirtus 132–3, 136, 144–5, 156,
  159
L. Valerius Flaccus 53–4
Valerius Maximus 147
C. Valerius Triarius 126
P. Vatinius 114